Elgar the
Music Maker

Elgar the
Music Maker

Diana McVeagh

THE BOYDELL PRESS

First published 2007
The Boydell Press, Woodbridge

ISBN 978–1–84383–295–9

The Boydell Press is an imprint of Boydell & Brewer Ltd
PO Box 9, Woodbridge, Suffolk IP12 3DF, UK
and of Boydell & Brewer Inc.
668 Mt Hope Avenue, Rochester, NY 14620, USA
website: www.boydellandbrewer.com

A CIP record for this book is available
from the British Library

This publication is printed on acid-free paper

Printed in Great Britain by
Antony Rowe Ltd, Chippenham, Wiltshire

Contents

Illustrations

'As to the phases of pride, despair, anger, peace & the thousand & one things that occur between the first page & the last, I prefer the listener to draw what he can from the sound he hears.'

Edward Elgar

To the memory of

Eric Blom (1888–1959)
who commissioned my first book on Elgar

and Frank Howes (1891–1974)
who encouraged it

Preface and Acknowledgements

A hundred and fifty years after Elgar's birth, the flood of fresh material about him ever rises. Jerrold Northrop Moore, tireless author of the monumental study Edward Elgar: A Creative Life (1984) and editor of four volumes of his letters, has led the way. To him, and to Percy Young, Michael Kennedy, and Robert Anderson, I gratefully owe a very great deal. Books and articles about Elgar pour out, not only in this country. His music is increasingly getting the scholarly attention it deserves. The Elgar Society promotes lectures, concerts and recordings, publishes books, a newsletter, and a quarterly journal, and maintains a website on www.elgar.org. Elgar's birthplace cottage at Broadheath near Worcester has become not only a place of pilgrimage but also a centre for exhibitions and research. In the foreseeable future all Elgar's music will be in print, in the handsome Collected Edition. All his recordings conducting his own music have been reissued on CD.

His life and music have come to inspire composers, novelists, and playwrights. Jonathan Harvey admits the influence of *Gerontius* on his opera *In Quest of Love*. Thomas Adès pays tribute to 'Nimrod' in his *Arcadiana*. James Hamilton-Paterson's novel *Gerontius* depicts Elgar in old age, as he journeyed up the Amazon. David Pownall in his play *Elgar's Rondo* considers the crisis implicit in the Second Symphony. Since Ken Russell's famous television programme in 1962, radio and television documentaries on Elgar abound.

When I wrote my *Edward Elgar: His Life and Music* (1955), I had never heard the pre-*Gerontius* cantatas. Recording has changed everything. I have continued to write about Elgar here and there, and this anniversary year seems the right moment for harvest. In this book I concentrate on the music, covering his complete output, but Elgar the man keeps elbowing his way in. I am grateful for permission to reprint material from

Elgar Studies edited by Raymond Monk (Scolar Press, 1900), *Edward Elgar: Music and Literature* edited by Raymond Monk (Scolar Press, 1903), *Words on Music: Essays in Honor of Andrew Porter* edited by David Rosen and Claire Brook (Pendragon Press, 2003), *The Cambridge Companion to Elgar* edited by Daniel Grimley and Julian Rushton (Cambridge, 2005), *The New Grove Dictionary of Music and Musicians* (2001), and from programme notes for the BBC.

The photographs come from Arthur Reynolds's Archive. I thank him, John Norris, and the Broadheath Museum most warmly for their help.

I thank Andrew Porter and Bruce Phillips for their enthusiasm and constructive criticism, and the team at Boydell, for being the most sympathetic and efficient of publishers.

CHAPTER ONE

The Making of an Enigma
1857–1899

Elgar never received a composition lesson in his life. The fact that his father kept a music shop has often been seen as a social disadvantage: being born into trade certainly contributed to the chip on his shoulder. But should not the emphasis be on *music* shop, for what better environment could the penurious young composer have had than the music, scores, books, and instruments all around him? The shop formed his private library, his laboratory, and familiarized him with the ways of publishers. He learnt by listening and doing.

Edward William Elgar was born in 1857 in a cottage at the village of Lower Broadheath, in sight of the Malvern Hills, the fourth child of William Henry Elgar and Ann Greening. He was baptized at St George's Roman Catholic Church, Worcester. When he was two, the family moved into the city, where three more children were born.

His earliest notated tune is *Humoreske*, which he dated 1867. He would have been ten. It is a single line in the bass clef. Already present are two abiding elements of his style: loping compound rhythm, and sequences. In the answering phrase the first sequential repeat is modified by an accidental, A sharp in G major (Ex. 1.1a). In 1919 Elgar completed his Cello Concerto. The main theme is a single line of three two-bar sequences played by the violas; in the soloist's answering phrase the second repeat is modified by an accidental, C sharp in E minor (Ex. 1.1b). The distance between the ten-year-old and the sixty-two-year-old composer at that moment seems touchingly short.

Ex. 1.1

He attended local schools, and for a year was apprenticed to a solicitor. Worcester offered good opportunities for a young musician, since every three years, in rotation with Gloucester and Hereford, the Three Choirs Festival based on the Cathedral is held there. After taking a few lessons, in 1876 Elgar began teaching the violin, and in March 1877 he composed his first surviving violin piece, the fluent but undistinguished *Reminiscences* (strange but prophetic title for a twenty-year-old to choose). That year he had a brief course of lessons in London from Adolf Pollitzer (1832–1900), who as a boy had played Mendelssohn's Concerto in the presence of its composer. One result was the fiendishly difficult five *Études caractéristiques* (1878) for solo violin, almost certainly prompted by Paganini's *Caprices* (not to be confused with Elgar's *Six Very Easy Melodious Exercises* of 1892). Modern violinists reckon that the *Études* were too difficult for Elgar himself to play, though he was competent enough to perform all Beethoven's Violin Sonatas in lecture-recitals at the Worcester Girls' High School in 1892. (A sixth study was published in 1920 in the *Daily Telegraph* account of the nineteen-year-old Heifetz's visit to Elgar; he called it a 'trifle which interested a great teacher of the past and a very great artist of the present'.) Measuring himself against the great Wilhelmj (1845–1908), who gave a recital in Worcester, Elgar in his own time reached the conclusion that he would never be a first-class violinist, and that his way was to compose. Technical exercises the *Études* may have been, but composing them expanded Elgar's range. His violin and piano *Romance* of 1878 slightly foreshadows the mysterious Introduction of *King Olaf*, its melody tensed or suppled by the appoggiaturas that

became so significant a part of his expressive style; and the
fioritura looks forward to the Violin Concerto. A *Pastourelle* (1884)
again looks forward to *King Olaf*, to the lilting Thyri music.
Gavotte (1885) is a showy compendium of double stopping,
glissandi, harmonics, *spiccato*. The Allegretto on GEDGE (1885) is
based, Schumann-like, on the musical letters of Elgar's pupils,
the Gedge sisters. That does not limit this accomplished piece,
in which violin and piano interchange conversationally.

As a boy Elgar was renowned for his improvisations.
Although he composed little piano music when he was mature
– no great sonata, no completed concerto – his early pieces
show sympathy with the instrument. *Chantant* (1872) is his
most substantial piano piece until the *Concert Allegro* of 1901.
It is more dance than song, for it begins in mazurka-style
(as do two of Schumann's *Kinderscenen*). What sounds like an
extended final cadence turns out to begin a solemn chant-
like central section with running counterpoints (like No. 41
of Schumann's *Album für die Jugend*). In the brief airy *Griffinesque*
(1884) every bar has the same rhythmic pattern – again Schu-
mannesque, but also like Elgar's later *Skizze*. Two waltzes, *Enina*
(1886) and *Laura* (1887), are lightly teasing.

Elgar composed the song 'The Language of Flowers' (1872)
when he was not quite fifteen. The verses are by the American
poet and botanist, James Gates Percival (1795–1856). To 'tell
the wish of the heart in flowers' (so runs the last line) was
a favourite conceit of the period, prettily illustrated in many
books. Elgar's setting is conventional too, with stock accompanying figures, but not just strophic: both piano and voice parts
are slightly varied. 'A Soldier's Song' (1884, C. Flavell Hayward,
1863–1906) is beefy, the chorus-refrains ('Glory or death')
bolstered by repeated triplet chords. It was reissued as 'A War
Song' in 1903. In 'Through the long days' (1885, by another
American, John Hay, 1838–1905) Elgar's treatment of the two-
bar phrases is subtle: he keeps the melodic pattern, but shifts it
up and down the scale. 'Is she not passing fair' of 1886 (translated by L. S. Costello, 1799–1870, from Charles d'Orléans)
is more extrovert. 'Queen Mary's Song' (1887, Tennyson) is
poignant when Elgar turns in the third verse to the major for
'we fade and are forsaken', and is made pathetic with spread

'lute' chords. 'As I laye a-thynkyng' (1887) is a romance about
a noble Knyghte by 'Thomas Ingoldsby' (R. H. Barham, 1788–
1845). Though the material is uninteresting, the song is an
extended piece, almost a mini-cantata. Elgar described it as
being 'japed together'. 'A Song of Autumn' (?1887, Lindsay
Gordon, 1833–70) brings no harvest, only last leaves, sere and
yellow boughs. Elgar's numb repeated chords might suggest
Schubert, were his chromatic inflections less sentimental; but
the curving phrase at 'falling of the year' looks ahead to *The
Spirit of England*.

Elgar's father belonged to the Worcester Glee Club, which
performed instrumental as well as vocal music. Young Elgar
became the accompanist, then violinist, composer, arranger,
and, in 1879, the conductor. In 1878 he composed an Introductory Overture (lost) for a Christy Minstrel concert in
Worcester Music Hall, and he also arranged songs for them.
When the Amateur Instrumental Society was formed in 1877,
he became its leader and coach, and in 1882 its conductor. In
1878 he joined the Three Choirs Festival orchestra, playing in
among things Mozart's G minor symphony No. 40. As a disci-
pline he began a movement modelled on it, no doubt realizing
that composing freely on such a broad scale demanded more
musical stamina than he could yet command.

◈

In 1879 Elgar moved from his parents at 10 High Street to
lodge first with his married sister Polly Grafton at Chestnut
Walk, then in 1883 to 4 Field Terrace to his other married
sister, Lucy Pipe. A Paris holiday with her husband Charles Pipe
in 1880 led to his giving French titles to some quadrilles.

◈

He had taught himself the bassoon, and among his friends he
had two competent flutes and an oboe, and a weak clarinet.
He formed a wind quintet. For such an unorthodox combination there was no repertory, so he provided it. The Intermezzos
(1879), which he later affectionately called 'mine own children', are high-spirited epigrammatic vignettes. The Dances
and Promenades (1878 onwards), which sometimes have

piquant inner parts, are shortish, usually in ternary form. The 'Evesham' Variations – strikingly unlike the later 'Enigma' – are purely decorative, not motivic.

In what Elgar called the Harmony Music (after the German *Harmoniemusik* wind ensembles) he began to teach himself how to extend his material. There are movements of ten to twelve minutes that demand organization. In these he explores the basic elements of classical design, of key structure, of strong simple modulations, of development and recapitulation. Lessons from Mozart had been well learnt. Harmony Music No. 2 and No. 4, both lasting over ten minutes with their repeats, are resourceful full-scale sonata movements. Harmony Music No. 5 is in four movements, lasting altogether twenty minutes. Never less than engaging, these wind pieces sound more like Haydn than Elgar, except perhaps in their airy instrumentation. The final bars of Promenade No. 4 and Variation IV of the 'Evesham' Andante (1878) are not so very far in texture from the first nine bars of 'R. B. T.' (Variation III) in the 'Enigma' Variations or the six bars after cue 13 in 'W. M. B.' (Variation IV). For the most part the wind music is classically orthodox and diatonic but with some wit. Its emotional transparency and directness, contrasted with his symphonies of 1908 and 1911, show how long and arduous was Elgar's journey of self-discovery.

Between 1879 and 1884 Elgar was director of the Powick Asylum Band. This consisted at most of a piano, some strings, two cornets, euphonium, piccolo, flute, and clarinet – did he think of the awkward combination with a chuckle when he composed Falstaff's 'scarecrow' march? For this scratch band he wrote quadrilles in the traditional five sections (no odder this than Fauré's quadrilles on themes by Wagner), polkas, and lancers. Some are based on popular tunes, all are formulaic, but most are catchy and fun to dance to. In later life he used this early unpublished music as a quarry. Ideas from the wind quintets (the Menuetto from Harmony Music No. 5, and the Promenade No. 5) went into the *Severn Suite* of 1930. The Andante Arioso in Harmony No. 6 of 1879 became the *Cantique* of 1912. All the time he was composing chamber music for strings, too, some incomplete, some absorbed by the wind music. An Intermezzo for a D minor quartet of c. 1888 became No. 3 of the organ Vesper Voluntaries. In old age he intended using an early Sarabande in his projected opera *The Spanish Lady*. Part of an 1881 piano trio was recast as *Douce pensée* for solo piano in 1882, and in 1915 it became *Rosemary* for small orchestra. Elgar's 1929 recording of this, with seductive *portamento*, is a perfect period piece.

All Elgar's 'liftings' show the transforming power of his orchestration. The fifth section of the quadrille *L'assom[m]oir*, already borrowed from a proposed children's play, later became 'The Wild Bears' in the second *Wand of Youth* suite. In 1879 the bears are heavily grounded by a booming pedal bass; in 1907 the 'pedal' is given to mid-register wind, while the lower strings' light *staccato* allows a dancing presto. Seven chords from the polka 'Helcia' open 'Sabbath Morning at Sea', the third of the *Sea Pictures*: jolly 'Helcia', given a pedal point, with wind backed by divided low register strings, added horns, and a timpani roll at the climax, gains a 'solemn face' and contributes to the song's elevated ending. Such quotations have no emotional significance; they merely show a prudent creator using up old ideas.

From the age of fifteen Elgar deputized for his father as organist of St George's Roman Catholic Church. This Jesuit foundation was dedicated in 1830, one year after Catholic Emancipation. Music played a large part in the services, which included Mozart, Haydn, Beethoven, and Weber. Singers from touring opera companies visiting Worcester sometimes joined the choir; the great Sims Reeves had sung there, and the church could gather an orchestra for High Mass, even before Elgar's father was appointed in 1846.

In 1885 Elgar succeeded his father. He had already composed music for the choir. His early settings of parts of the Ordinary of the Mass are exercises in the Viennese tradition. A Gloria in F and a Credo in A, both for chorus, soloists, and organ date from the 1870s, his mid-teens. The lively Gloria is based on Mozart's violin and piano sonata K.547. Elgar maintains the structure, slightly amends the piano part for organ, and composes new vocal parts in place of the violin. For the Credo he linked Beethoven's themes from the second movement of the Seventh Symphony, the Adagio ('Et incarnatus est') of the Ninth, and the first movement of the Fifth ('et resurrexit') but he shaped his own form.

Among many original pieces, some incomplete, there is a lively *Tantum ergo* of 1876 ('Therefore we before Him bending'), which has a striking Adagio interpolation and an expanded cadence; it was performed at the fiftieth anniversary of the church. A ambitious Credo in E minor begins quietly, moves to three-four for 'Et incarnatus est', to a ff 'Crucifixus' taking the sopranos from top G to low B, to unison for 'one Church' and an Amen that dies away to nothing. Early biographers record that Elgar composed many Masses, but none has survived. There are half-a-dozen settings of the Benediction hymn *O salutaris hostia*, of which two were published, the F major having some very Elgarian overlapping part-writing. Some of his hymn tunes he raided in later life.

His best-known motets, from 1887, were slightly revised and published as his Op. 2. The expressive cadence of the *Ave verum* was added in 1902. In *Ave maris stella* the two-and-three bar phrases are nicely varied, and the *Ave Maria* has a charming lullaby lilt. They are more polished, if less adventurous, than his earlier pieces. Elgar's part-writing is sweet and euphonious. The notes may look simple, even boring on paper; but when sung, the sound is seductive. His 'intercession' style in *Gerontius*, the semi-chorus, the magical hushed Kyrie, the haunting litany, has its source in this early music for St George's.

So it was a hands-on apprenticeship. His compositions were tailor-made for his resources. He learned what would sound good, not because any teacher, but because his own ear, told him. He knew what worked on the fiddle because he played it and taught it. He knew what came off in an orchestra. He was promoted to the first violins in the Three Choirs orchestra in 1881, and he played in William Stockley's orchestra at Birmingham from 1882 to 1889. This is not to decry academic training; few would-be composers working on their own are as industrious, receptive, and discriminating as Elgar. When he was Master of the King's Musick, he drew up on his official writing paper a bill for his complete education: it came to £56 10s.

൙

Among Elgar's earliest friends were the Leicester family. Hubert
Leicester (1855–1939), two years Edward's senior, was the son
of a Worcester printer who lived only a few doors from Elgar
Bros. The family was Catholic, Hubert's parents were Elgar's
godparents, and Hubert became choirmaster at St George's. He
was one of the flautists in the wind quintet. Charles William
Buck (1851–1932) was a Yorkshire GP and keen amateur musician who befriended Elgar when he attended the Worcester
meeting of the British Medical Association in 1882.

So far Elgar's compositions were for domestic and local use.
Then in 1882 he spent three weeks on holiday in Leipzig,
attending concerts of Brahms and Schumann (his 'ideal'),
whose influences can be heard in the broad melodies of the
violin and piano *Virelai* and *Idylle* (both 1884). He attended
performances of Wagner's *Tannhäuser* and *Lohengrin*, and heard
the Prelude to *Parsifal* (some months before its first complete
performance). He was ready for Wagner: in his early St
George's days he had played the overture to *Tannhäuser* on the
organ, telling Hubert Leicester 'it was by a man who is not
yet understood. You will hear more of him one day.' Home
from Leipzig, he composed his own *Intermezzo moresque* (later
called *Sérénade mauresque*). The following year (1883) he went to
London for the Wagner memorial concert at the Crystal Palace,
hearing the *Siegfried Idyll* and excerpts from *Tristan* and *Götter-
dämmerung*. Perhaps that exposure spurred him to compose the
substantial orchestral piece *Sevillana* (1884, rescored in 1889),
rumbustious, but with an enchanting middle section worthy
of *The Sanguine Fan* and *The Starlight Express*. *Sevillana* and the *Sérénade
mauresque* are the earliest examples of Elgar's 'Spanish' idioms,
found later in *The Black Knight* and the Piano Quintet. August
Manns (1825–1907) conducted *Sevillana* at the Crystal Palace on
12 May 1884; it was London's first hearing of Elgar's music.

The *Sérénade* and a *Mazurka* (later to become the Suite in D)
of the same period foretell important characteristics. In both,
Elgar enriches the repeats with embellishments or counter-
tunes, so fertile is his imagination. This he had already done in

the wind quintet piece *Mrs Winslow's Soothing Syrup* (1878), and it was to become a feature of the 'Enigma' Variations. (In a school ensemble class he added 'impromptu counterpoints', and as late as 1897 he wrote 'little experimental counterpoints' to standard works and to his own for the Worcester Philharmonic Society to try out.[1]) In the *Sérénade* the wistful middle section is comparable with a passage (cue 10) of *In the South*, and at one bar after L a timpani roll under strings muted and *tremolo* adds to the mystery much as in the 'Romanza' in 'Enigma'.

∽❈∾

In 1883 Elgar became engaged to Helen Weaver, whose family shop was near the Elgars', but the following year the engagement was broken off. In 1884 Dvořák visited the Worcester Festival, and Elgar played his D major symphony under him. That year he also heard Hans Richter (1843–1916) give the first British performance of Brahms's Third. Elgar's Op. 1, *Romance*, was published by Schotts in 1885, and in 1888 his Suite in D was performed by Stockley in Birmingham. In 1886 Caroline Alice Roberts (b. 1848) became his piano pupil, and in September 1888 they were engaged. She was living with her widowed mother at Hazeldine House, Redmarley d'Abitot, south of the Malvern Hills.

∽❈∾

In 1888 Elgar composed *Salut d'amour*, one of his most popular pieces, and also *Mot d'amour*, both for violin and piano. Both – aptly for tender declarations of love – show the withdrawal into private territory, often by a single chord, that became so vital a part of his musical personality. *Mot d'amour* begins shyly, not reaching a settled tonic of D major till the tenth bar, but attains a sweeping *Largamente*, which unexpectedly withdraws on to a first inversion dominant of F sharp. Such 'out-of-key' chords are always *pianissimo*, usually under a fermata. They are more than a harmonic resource, more of an emotional confession. Possibly Elgar gave a clue to the meaning this held

---

[1]   R. Burley and C. F. Carruthers, *Edward Elgar: The Record of a Friendship* (London, 1972), pp. 34, 106.

for him in *For the Fallen*, when in 'we will remember them' (two bars before cue 22) the syllable 'mem' escapes on to a second inversion of an F major chord among the prevailing sharps (see p. 168). Pieces such as *Salut* and *Mot d'amour* invite a melting rubato. The violin and piano *La Capricieuse* (1891), beloved of Kreisler and Heifetz, would lose most of its charm without rubato, appropriately for such a teasing title. Many of Elgar's early pieces are hard to date precisely and exist in several arrangements made to suit their publishers, who found that foreign titles sold best.

'The Wind at Dawn' of 1888 was Elgar's first collaboration with his fiancée Alice Roberts, whose poem it was. The wind rises with impetuous cascades in the piano, and after minor chords for the grey skies, the wan moon, the sun brings back the cascades as the wind 'in his strength unseen, in triumph upborne' rides out (twice, *grandioso*) 'to meet with the dawn'. Particularly in its 1912 scoring, the song brims with confidence. During the summer after his marriage he composed a virtuoso piano piece called *Presto*, which shares the exuberant style of 'The Wind at Dawn'. He dedicated it to the daughter of the Fitton family with whom he played chamber music. She (later 'Ysobel' of 'Enigma') played the viola, so perhaps the piece was aimed at her pianist mother. He composed the Sonatina (1899) for his eight-year-old niece May Grafton, and revised it in 1930.

1888 Ecce sacerdos magnus ('Behold a great priest')

In 1888 the Roman Catholic bishop of Birmingham visited St George's, so music was needed for the gradual from the Mass for a Confessor Bishop, *Ecce sacerdos magnus*. Elgar set it for chorus and organ, possibly basing the opening bars on the 'Benedictus' from Haydn's *Harmoniemesse*. He dedicated it to Hubert Leicester, in gratitude for his blowing the organ when Edward explored Wagner's music. This processional piece is one of Elgar's earliest to have an instrumental accompaniment with a motivic character of its own. It is also a jubilant early example of his ceremonial style – a broad melody over a regular bass – at its most popular in 'Land of Hope and Glory', at its most sublime in 'Go forth in the Name' from *Gerontius*. The choral writing is a judicious balance between sturdy octaves and gentler imitations. The anthem was accepted by the Catholic publishers Alphonse Cary (and Elgar orchestrated it in 1893).

∼✣∽

On Elgar's marriage to Alice Roberts on 8 May 1889, his wife's small income spurred them to adventure to London. He hoped to make his name and fortune. He made neither, so the year is often looked on as a failure. But those months gave him the chance to hear all the up-to-date music the capital could offer, and could be regarded as his university year, his professors being Weber, Brahms, Liszt, and Wagner. The Elgars lived first at 3 Marloes Road, West Kensington, then spent the summer in Malvern at Alice's rented house 'Saetermo'. During the winter of 1889–90 they were lent a house by her cousin in Upper Norwood, near the Crystal Palace, and day after day Elgar attended the concerts where August Manns – the Henry Wood or the William Glock of his day – was performing a wide repertory of the most recent continental as well as British music, with a mainly permanent orchestra and fine soloists. Elgar had made exhausting day visits from Worcester to the Crystal Palace ever since Pollitzer had introduced him to Manns in 1878, but now he had a season ticket and sometimes attended three events a day. *Salut d'amour* was performed there on 11 November 1889, and his Suite in D on 20 February 1890.

In 1890 the Elgars moved to 51 Avonmore Road, West Kensington, where their daughter Carice was born. During their time in London they heard Richter conduct Schubert's Great and Brahms's Third symphonies. They went regularly to St James's Hall. They went also to Covent Garden, hearing *Otello*, Meyerbeer's *Le prophète*, and three performances (cut, and in Italian) of *Die Meistersinger*. In his early thirties, Elgar was young enough to be impressionable, old enough not to be artistically swamped. His time in the capital was immensely valuable. But he gained no London footing, so in 1891 the Elgars retreated to the provinces, not back to Worcester but to Malvern Link, renting a house in Alexandra Road they called 'Forli'. Elgar resumed his playing and teaching jobs.

In 1891 he met Rosa Burley, then aged twenty-five, the owner and headmistress of the Mount School, Malvern, where he taught the violin. Her memoirs[2] are significant because she was the only professional woman, earning her own living, in the Elgars' circle.

Partsongs, 1889–94

One thing Elgar learnt in the wider sound-world of London was the importance of texture. All through his life he composed partsongs, some with light accompaniment, some *a cappella*. From the start his touch was sure. His wife was some-times his poet, for before their marriage Alice Roberts had published two novels, *Isabel Trevithoe* (1879) in blank verse, and *Marchcroft Manor* (1882). Elgar's 'O Happy Eyes' (1889, revised 1893), to stanzas she wrote before their engagement, shows his resourcefulness. The sound is delicate and precise, with sustained against moving voices, and a nicely varied third stanza of the four, with an enviable tenor part. For the atmos-pheric 'My Love dwelt in a Northern land' (1889) Alice wrote substitute words when it seemed that the poet Andrew Lang (1844–1912) would not grant permission to use his, though he then relented. The song was Elgar's first music published by Novello. No wonder they accepted it: the forlorn opening in octaves hints at the final disclosure, that the lover lies under the grass, his heart colder than clay. In the central stanza the men are *divisi*, sopranos and first tenors in octaves, second basses holding a pedal, the others making a rhythmic accompani-ment, as in sad ghostly memory the lovers watch the great white moon. The *Spanish Serenade*, 'Stars of the Summer Night' (1892), might be heard as a trial run for *The Black Knight*, as its words are by Longfellow from *The Spanish Student*. Elgar's ravishing song has the thrum of guitars in the light accompa-niment and a sensuous refrain for 'my lady sleeps'. 'The Snow'

[2]   R. Burley and C. F. Carruthers, *Edward Elgar: The Record of a Friendship* (London, 1972).

and 'Fly, Singing Bird' for women's voices with piano and two violins (1894, orchestrated in 1903), both to Alice's words of 1878, are fluent and charming, though they do not quite avoid clichés.

1890 Froissart, Concert Overture, Op. 19

At the beginning of 1890 Elgar, then living in London, was invited to compose an orchestral piece for the secular concert during the coming Three Choirs Festival in his home town of Worcester. He wrote ahead to introduce himself to Joseph Bennett, the music critic of the *Daily Telegraph*, stressing his local connection. He worked on the overture between April and July 1890. The title is the name of the fourteenth-century Jean Froissart, chronicler of the chivalric exploits of English and French nobles. Elgar acknowledged a specific source in Walter Scott's *Old Mortality*, in which John Claverhouse asks Henry Morton 'did you ever read Froissart?', and praises his description of a knight's 'loyalty to his king, pure faith to his religion, hardihood towards the enemy, and fidelity to his lady-love'. Elgar prefixed the score with the quotation 'When Chivalry/ Lifted up her lance on high', from Keats's poem beginning 'Hads't thou lived in days of old'.

At about twelve minutes, *Froissart* is his longest orchestral movement till then (earlier overtures to be called 'Lakes' and 'Scottish' remained only fragments). Its panache and confidence are clear from the opening resolute attack: high strings dashing away in octaves – chivalry's lance lifted indeed! The romantic atmosphere is that of Weber and Dvořák, though many of its themes, in their combined curve and rhythm, suggest Wagner. A three-note cell, possibly derived from the opening of Walther's Prize Song in *Die Meistersinger* (E, B, C: a drop of a fourth followed by a semitone rise), becomes part of Elgar's melodic vocabulary.

Wagner's influence at this point is purely melodic. The overture's development might owe more to Mendelssohn's *Hebrides*: rhythmic wind and melodic string figures call in dialogue through sustained texture, evoking distance and space (in Mendelssohn between cues C and D, in Elgar between cues L

and N). Elgar heard the Mendelssohn in 1881, and on a Scottish holiday in 1884 he visited Staffa and pencilled into his
guidebook two of the Hebrides themes. However, Froissart sounds
like no-one but Elgar, particularly in his own lively recording
of 1933. The influences are simply an acceptance of his inher-
itance. What is totally Elgarian is the abundance of melody:
there are at least five well-defined ideas in the exposition,
each worth and each getting musical discussion. It is remarkable how well formed and individual his personality is, how
phrase after phrase can be matched in a later work, and how
familiar are the melodic features – sequence, crotchet-quaver
rhythm, upward-thrusting arpeggios, and leaps of sixths and
sevenths. The orchestration is assured, though it is not yet his
subtle best. In 1891 he thought Froissart too long, but in 1900
he considered it 'not quite what I'd write now but it's good,
healthy stuff'.[3]

He conducted the first performance in the Public Hall on 10
September 1890. Ivor Atkins, then assistant organist of Hereford Cathedral, watched his 'shy entry on to the platform'.
In the artists' room afterwards each man was too nervous to
speak, but, Elgar recalled, 'we both knew that a real friendship
had begun'.[4]

1892 Serenade for String Orchestra in E minor, Op. 20

I Allegro Piacevole II Larghetto III Allegretto

Elgar probably based the Serenade on his three earlier pieces
(Spring Song, Elegy, and Finale) played in Worcester in 1888, about
which he told his Yorkshire friend Dr Buck 'I like 'em. (The first
thing I ever did).'[5] Maybe the promise early in 1892 of a visit
to Bayreuth prompted him to rework them as Edward's Idyll,
as it were (he first heard the Siegfried Idyll in 1883). On the
arrangement for piano duet he wrote 'Braut helped a great deal
to make these little tunes'. (He used the German for his wife,

[3]   To Jaeger, 20 March 1900.
[4]   E. Wulstan Atkins, The Elgar–Atkins Friendship (London, 1984), pp. 25–6.
[5]   8 July 1888.

as earlier he had for Helen Weaver.) 'Really stringy in effect',[6] he called the Serenade, and always held this early work dear.

As in the *Spanish Serenade*, the texture is beguiling. Often in the opening five-strand Allegro Piacevole Elgar thins the sound to three strands, aerates it with rests, or thickens it with *divisi*, enjoying the effect of the differing registers, in sophisticated sonic shading. The delicate first movement is typical of his lyrical, pastoral music. Here he first uses the term *piacevole*, possibly learnt from the last movement of Beethoven's violin sonata in A, Op. 12 No. 2 – he performed all the sonatas that year. The movement is bound together by the opening dotted figure for violas alone. Then the pensive main theme sweeps up first to a seventh, then to an octave, then in the reprise up to a ninth, with the climax (cue H) formed by a three-fold sequence.

After the airy Allegro, the half-jubilant, half-elegiac Larghetto is rich and full. Framed by serious, questioning imitations, a strongly sculptured melody again grows by expanding intervals of a seventh, an octave, then a ninth (see Ex. 3.2b). At the reprise (cue L) the first cellos reinforce the melody at the fourth bar *crescendo*, then slip away back into accompanying during the *diminuendo* (another Elgar characteristic, of scoring). The triplets pulsing away in the middle strings send the big tune soaring. The fluent Allegretto makes as if to return to the opening of the first movement, but slides instead into its *second* subject; and after one joyous *crescendo* fades away in reminiscence. Even so, the last movement is not quite independent enough to match the strong Larghetto.

Elgar rehearsed the Serenade with his Ladies' Orchestral Class; he was 'always writing these things and trying them out on us'.[7] Maybe that is where he learnt to give such detailed expression marks. He marks his salon music no less scrupulously. Novello turned the Serenade down, but Breitkopf accepted it.

[6] To Jaeger, 11 November 1898.
[7] R. Burley and C. F. Carruthers, *Edward Elgar: The Record of a Friendship* (London, 1972), p. 31.

᠗ᴔᴥ

In 1892 Alice's friend Mary Frances Baker took the Elgars to
Bayreuth where they saw *Tristan und Isolde* and *Parsifal* for the
first time. They then went holidaying on and reached Heidel-
berg. They went back to Bavaria in August 1893 on their own
resources, joined by Rosa Burley, going this time to Garmisch
and Munich (the *Ring*). The Elgars returned to Bavaria on
holiday in 1894 for seven weeks, and again in 1895.

In 1895 Miss Baker married the widower rector of Wolver-
hampton, the Revd Alfred Penny, whose daughter Dora in
1899 became 'keeper of the Elgar archives', to assist Alice.
Elgar called her Dorabella, after Mozart's *Così fan tutte*.

ᴥᴖᴔᴥ

1893 The Black Knight, Op. 25

Elgar now turned to extended texts and to cantatas. He knew
that such works were 'much in request', as he pointed out to
Novello in September 1892, for the best opening an aspiring
British composer could find was at one of the many choral
societies and festivals. Elgar's main works of the 1890s are the
substantial choral and orchestral *The Black Knight*, *The Light of Life*,
King Olaf, and *Caractacus*. His reading was wide and deep, as well
as quirky, but here he chose texts that are sometimes muddled
dramatically and commonplace in style. It seems that he could
ignore these liabilities if he found the emotional challenge
he needed. A personal element may be significant: in each
story there is an outsider. *The Black Knight* attacks the established
court and castle, *King Olaf* takes Christianity to a pagan land,
and the Blind Man (*Light of Life*) and the Bard (*Caractacus*) are
cast out by their companions when they gain vision. Possibly
without realizing it Elgar, rejected by the metropolis, identified
with these situations. That may not make the cantatas better or
worse, but it does make their strengths and weaknesses more
easily understood.

Elgar was already thirty-six when *The Black Knight* was
produced in 1893. But he had it in mind as early as the year
of his marriage, for sketches are dated 1889, signed touch-

ingly 'C. Alice & Edward Elgar'. The opening theme can even
be found, with no designation, in a sketchbook of 1879. 'How
strange', Elgar later wrote over it, pondering at the way the
subconscious can retrieve early memories. The pretty opening
of the third scene came from an incomplete violin and piano
sonata of 1887. He did not complete the work till 1892 when
Hugh Blair, the assistant organist of Worcester Cathedral and
its festival choral conductor, heard him play it through. 'If you
will finish it,' he said, 'I will produce it at Worcester.' Elgar
headed his new draft 'The Black Knight / (proposed!) ... / music
by Edward Elgar /if he can'. Indeed he could, and he composed
it between 18 April and 30 September 1892, and scored it
between 31 December 1892 and 25 January 1893. Gratefully,
he dedicated it to Blair, and conducted the first performance
in Worcester's Public Hall on 18 April 1893.

As in Froissart, the subject is romantic and medieval, but while
the earlier work emphasized the chivalrous side of knightly
life, this is gruesome. Johann Ludwig Uhland's verse has been
set by many of his compatriots, for example by Schumann in
his choral ballad Des Sängers Fluch ('The Minstrel's Curse'). But
Elgar came to Uhland's Der schwarze Ritter through the translation
in Hyperion; A Romance (1839) by Longfellow, a poet his mother
had introduced him to, and to whom he turned many times.

A king and his court celebrate Pentecost. His son wins all
jousts, till in the second scene he is challenged and defeated
by a 'sable knight'; as they fight the sky darkens and the castle
rocks. In Scene 3 the festivities are interrupted by the strange
knight, who asks for the hand of the king's daughter and
dances with her, blighting her 'fair flowerets'. Scene 4 is a
banquet, but the king's children look sick and pale until the
grim guest gives them a healing drink – which kills them. The
king cries out piteously, begging to be taken too, but the black
guest replies 'roses in the spring I gather'. Death spares the old
man, the Gerontius, but snatches the young in their flowering
prime. There appears to be no moral cause for the evil, which
seems gratuitous and random.

Elgar intended, he said, to compose a 'symphony for chorus
and orchestra' in four movements, though Novello called it a
cantata. The opening scene is broad and shapely, commodious

enough for pastoral and martial elements before a full reprise.
There are no soloists, so the chorus describes the setting,
narrates the action, and sings the words given to the crowd, to
the anonymous stranger 'of mighty sway', to the old king, and
to his son and daughter. Fortunately the music does not allow
close scrutiny of Longfellow's words. What the ballad does
provide is strong situations that Elgar grasps whole-heartedly:
for example, the sudden silence, creepy unisons, and stutter
from the march (Ex. 1.2), before the knight's first monotone
words, his sinister scuttle away at the close of Scene 2, and the
expressive violin solo as the children die.

Ex. 1.2

The idea of a symphony is made explicit at 'when he rode
into the lists', where the words are treated instrumentally
(Elgar adjusted the underlay for the reprint in 1898). He knew
what he was doing: 'Where a "picture" is suggested, the words
are repeated; at the dramatic points, the action is correspond-
ingly rapid.' He scores charmingly for chorus alone at 'pipe
and viol', the basses singing the tune, the other voices the
light accompaniment. There is languid and tango-ish music
with flattened supertonic and cymbal for the 'weird and dark'
dance. There is a sumptuous banquet tune in the last scene,
and a passionate outcry for the father as he too longs for death.
When his children give courteous thanks for the 'cooling'
drink, the orchestra with dramatic irony plays the motif of
the stricken prince over that of the Black Knight (Ex. 1.3).

At 'roses in the Spring' in the final scene Elgar hints at the
gracious Pentecost theme, which allows him to recapitulate
the bourgeoning opening music – dramatically incongruous
but musically satisfying – though the Black Knight has the last
word, pianissimo.

Ex. 1.3

There are Wagnerian echoes. The Black Knight's own motif is Klingsorish. In Scene 2 the King's castle rocks to a series of chromatic chords over bass tritones (the four bars before K, repeated before cue M) markedly like the version of 'magic sleep' as Valhalla burns in the final orchestral bars of *Götterdäm-merung*. But there are also pre-echoes of mature Elgar, of *Pomp and Circumstance* in the neat little march in Scene 2, and even of the Priest's 'Proficiscere' from *Gerontius* in the solemn chords before the children die in Scene 4 at cue N.

The weaknesses of *The Black Knight* include the sometimes senseless word-setting ('son and daughter; and their faces [gap] Colourless grow utterly'), and the automatic sequences, hitched up by step, expedient rather than structural. But the cantata is compact, and the balance between the lyrical and the dramatic is just right. A work so fresh, direct, and unselfconscious is still appealing.

1894 Sursum corda (Lift up your hearts), Op. 11

Early in 1894 Hugh Blair invited Elgar to compose a piece for the visit of the future George V, then Duke of York, to Worcester Cathedral on 8 April. So the organist of the Catholic church down the High Street made his first contribution to the great Anglican cathedrals, and to royal occasions. He found a sketch of 1887 for a violin sonata, which he had begun to recast as an Andante Religioso. He hurriedly completed it, and scored it for strings, brass, timpani, and organ, making a rich satu-rated Wagnerian sound (he was at the same time arranging the Good Friday Music from *Parsifal* for the Worcester High School). *Sursum corda* runs along lines similar to those of the

Larghetto of the Serenade: an introduction repeated to close
the piece, a big *cantabile* tune, a section of dialogue, then the
cantabile tune again, now grandly in octaves. Particular to *Sursum
corda* is the three-note brass call heard eight times – down an
octave, up a fourth – which creates a solemn sense of awe. The
devotional, aspiring tune is a model for such pieces as Walford
Davies's *Solemn Melody*, but it lacks the harmonic tension that
braces Elgar's later such themes. He took the rehearsal, but was
forbidden by his doctor (he regularly suffered from nervous
complaints) to conduct the performance, so Blair conducted
it for him.

Solo Songs, 1892–99

In 1892 Elgar turned to the poem 'Like to the Damask Rose'
by Simon Wastell (1560–1635). Its theme ran through much
poetry of that time. 'E'en such is man whose thread is cut',
say Wastell and Elgar. 'My thread is cut, and yet it is not spun',
says Chidiock Tichborne; 'Even such is time … with age and
dust', says Walter Raleigh; '… and come to dust', says Shakespeare, all born within eight years of Wastell. Elgar's music
for the first two verses is urgent and fruity, but each sad
simile slows his pace; as life shortens, so his phrases lengthen,
becoming more heedful. The merry 'Shepherd's Song' (Barry
Pain, 1864–1928) has a Schubertian accompaniment and a
sudden spurt of feeling for 'in the dreamtime answer, answer
me'. The dramatics of 'The Poet's Life' – that suffering enno-
bles the artist, 'one sobbing note reached the world's heart'
– provoke an over-blown reaction from Elgar. He responded
more sensitively to a finer related idea in *The Music Makers*. (The
poet is 'Ellen Burroughs', 1861–1909.) For Froissart's 'Rondel',
translated by the now familiar Longfellow, Elgar found a neat
baroque-style. In 'After' (P. B. Marston, 1850–87) each verse
begins 'A little time …', for a love ended by desertion or
death. The song could easily have become maudlin, but Elgar
keeps it touchingly simple; when a change from three-four
to four-four threatens to provoke inflation ('long, long years
to weep in') his restraint is moving. The god in 'The Pipes of
Pan' (Adrian Ross [Arthur Ropes]) turns out to be tame and

Victorian, even in the panic of war, and Elgar obliges with a skittish arch piece, more suitable for elves than for satyrs. 'Dry those fair, those crystal eyes' (Henry King, 1592–1669) was composed for a charity volume in aid of the Charing Cross Hospital. It is a simple strophic song over chordal accompaniment.

1895 From the Bavarian Highlands, Op. 27

The Elgars enjoyed their holidays in Bavaria. There, in a country predominantly of his own Catholic faith and away from Malvern social constraints, Elgar was at his most relaxed. Twice they stayed at a pension owned by an English couple, and watched Tyrolese dancers in the Schuhplättl, Bavarian country dances. Home again, Alice wrote six poems during March 1895, each based on a happy memory and subtitled with the place they had visited. The words fitted the rhythms her husband suggested, and could be adapted in any way he wanted.

The music for chorus and piano (later orchestra) is slight but enchanting, along the lines of Brahms's *Liebeslieder* waltzes and Dvořák's dances (five of the six *Bavarians* are in triple time). The merry 'Dance (Sonnenbichl)' has the speed and swing of the coming *King Olaf* ballads. 'False Love (Wamberg)', though cruel eyes mock, is sweetly anodyne, with even a limpid piano descant over 'false art thou'. The setting has something of the simple directness of the solo song 'After'. In 'Lullaby (Hammersbach)' the vocal lines are soothingly *cantabile*, but the delicate piano part has one of Elgar's airy skipping rhythms (Ex. 1.4), to become familiar in *Caractacus* and the *Pomp and Circumstance* marches. It was this 'Lullaby' that Dorabella found so irresistible that she had to dance to it.

Ex. 1.4

In 'Aspiration (St Anton)' Alice imagined a pilgrims' chapel in winter. A crystal-clear two-part passage serenely depicts God's mercies falling like silent snow. In 'On the Alm' (a mountain pasture) the men mimic the 'mellow bell' and the women, as the 'maiden dear', pick up the accompaniment figure to a roulade 'ah!' 'The Marksmen' is fast and vigorous; the no-nonsense hunters, 'manly in mind and heart', stick close to monotones, leaving the tunefulness to the piano. There comes an early example of Elgar's lingering sunsets, then a mock-academic *fugato* leads to the triumphant homeward march with the prizes.

Elgar had composed the vocal score by 9 April 1895 and the first performance was on 21 April 1896 by the Worcester Choral Society. During February and March 1896 he scored 'Dance', 'Lullaby', and 'The Marksmen' for orchestra only as the *Bavarian Dances*, and Manns performed them at the Crystal Palace on 23 October 1897.

1889 Vesper Voluntaries, Op. 14
1895 Organ Sonata, Op. 28

It seems inevitable that Elgar should have composed an organ sonata, since he more or less grew up in the organ loft of St George's. He also absorbed as much music as he could in the Cathedral down the road. On his bachelor trip to Paris he heard Saint-Saëns on the Madeleine organ. In 1885 he succeeded his father. Not that he much enjoyed it: 'I am a full fledged organist now,' he wrote to Dr Buck, '& – *hate* it. I expect another three months will end it; the choir is awful, & no good to be done with them.'[8]

His first composition after his temporary move to London had been the Eleven Vesper Voluntaries Op. 14, for the chamber organ installed in the house he and his wife were lent in Upper Norwood. He composed them between October and December 1889 using earlier sketches, and he dedicated them to the owner of the house, Mrs Raikes. There are eight voluntaries framed by an Introduction and a Coda with a central Inter-

---

[8]   8 January 1886.

mezzo, the three sharing a pair of themes, their order reversed in the Intermezzo and Coda. They are all agreeable pieces, if not distinctive (except perhaps in the favourite Elgarian direction *piacevole* and the unusual *pensoso*). Overall they suffer from automatic sequences and too many short phrases.

Back in Worcester, Elgar wrote to Buck: 'Blair (of the Cathedral) & I are pulling together & making things lively here.'[9] Blair was appointed chief organist in 1895. It was he who had encouraged *The Black Knight* and had asked for the *Sursum corda*, in which the organ has a major part. In July that year the American Organists' Convention visited Worcester on a tour of English cathedrals famed for their choral services. Blair invited his friend to compose a voluntary for the occasion. He may have been pleasantly startled when Elgar provided an ambitious four-movement sonata lasting some twenty-five minutes.

On the autograph Elgar noted that the Sonata was 'one week's work'. In fact, he had sketched the Intermezzo second movement in April that year, and the melody of the Andante dates from 1887. The putting-together of the work was indeed a last-week affair, with Blair going over to Malvern almost every day. In the end poor Blair had only a few days to learn what is by no means an easy work, demanding an athletic performer with a large stretch. He included the sonata in a recital after Matins in the Cathedral on 8 July 1895, on the Hill organ in the south transept. That had been installed in 1874: 'a great event', Elgar recalled, 'which brought many organists to play there at various times. I went to hear them all.'[10]

The Organ Sonata is his longest abstract instrumental work before the First Symphony and it brims with confidence and brio. The opening theme (with a characteristic third beat triplet) is almost that of *The Black Knight* (a tribute, conscious or unconscious, to Blair, the *Knight's* dedicatee and the Sonata's performer?). It lengthens in leaping sequences to form a grand paragraph, which includes a forceful group of block chords. A flowing transition tune over repeated chords, and a compound-time second subject, suggest the easy-going

---

[9]   20 January 1891.
[10] R. de Cordova, 'Elgar at "Craeg Lea"', *Strand Magazine*, May 1904, p. 538.

Vesper Voluntaries. But in the development Elgar shows a new contrapuntal resource. He combines the opening of the first subject in the treble, the flowing transition tune in the bass, and between them a decorative strand, new but with the triplet (Ex. 1.5).

Ex. 1.5

He then inverts the two top lines. Next he changes the character of two of the themes: the flowing tune comes in the block chords in dialogue, then the outline of the initial block chords becomes a ruminative meditation over fragments of the flowing tune. Such dramatic character changes are new in Elgar's music. As well as being tuneful, vigorous, and dashing, the Allegro Maestoso shows his growing interest in transforming and combining themes.

After the massive first movement, the tracery of the Schumann-esque Allegretto sounds delicate, with elegant trio writing, the theme in the tenor. A rather awful three-chord 'organist's modulation' introduces the long, rhythmically varied melody of the Andante. The final Presto is more high-spirited than distinguished. The opening dactylic figure is propulsive, the second theme jaunty. But Elgar brings back the Andante's big tune underpinned by the dactyls, and the second bar of the jaunty tune turns surprisingly serious, as it augments itself into a modulating progression, foreshadowing the 'O Ye Priests' chorus in *The Kingdom*. Finally with a *fortissimo* full organ Elgar recalls the Andante, now in the arresting style of the first movement, before a bravura ending.

Elgar recognized that the Sonata is thematically integrated. He refused to let Novello publish it in separate movements, and sent it to Breitkopf and Härtel, who accepted it as a whole. It has come to be seen as a forerunner of his two symphonies (particularly in the orchestration of 1946 by Gordon Jacob).

1896 Scenes from the Saga of King Olaf, Op. 30

On 15 July 1894 Alice Elgar noted in her diary 'E. wrote Sagas all day'. Later that year he borrowed books of sagas from Rosa Burley. Then Charles Swinnerton Heap, the newly appointed chorus-master of the Birmingham Festival Society, decided to perform *The Black Knight*, and offered to produce the next choral work Elgar might compose at the 1986 North Stafford-shire Festival. (In gratitude Elgar dedicated the Organ Sonata to him.) So in January 1895 Elgar turned again to Longfellow, to his *Tales of a Wayside Inn* based on Nordic sagas, and began shaping a libretto. A neighbour, the retired civil servant H. A. Acworth, offered to help him. Together they cut and reordered Longfellow's sections, and Acworth wrote new scenes and provided linking recitatives. In November 1895 Elgar settled down, completing the vocal score in February 1896, and the scoring between June and September. Alice guaranteed £100 towards Novello's publication.

The Norwegian King Olaf, after long exile, returns to his homeland to avenge his slain father and to convert the heathen followers of the god Thor, led by Ironbeard, to Christianity. Elgar and Acworth tamed both the real-life Olaf Tryggvessön (c. 950–1000) and Longfellow's Olaf, to make him more saint than pirate. A new scene by Acworth gives Ironbeard a defiant dying speech, and Olaf a conversion achieved more by persuasion than by force. The final scene, of Olaf's mother the Abbess in her convent, is Longfellow. As in *The Black Knight*, the performers are anonymous, a company of Skalds, or Bards, who narrate the story. The tenor is Olaf, one soprano sings in turn the three women, the bass takes both Ironbeard and the recitatives of the narrator.

   King Olaf at once shows an acute new feeling for atmosphere (it was Elgar's first major work after hearing the complete *Ring* at Bayreuth in 1893). The brooding G minor opening is the essence of 'wondrous' and 'ancient': a falling melody with interlocking rising violas (Ex. 1.6). Many of Elgar's best themes are more than a single line.

Ex. 1.6

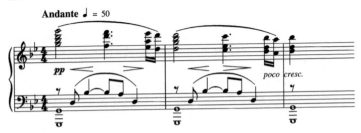

The heroic 'Legends' theme in the Introduction modulates by sequence (no longer stepwise) to reach a blazing E flat major at the critical word 'begin'. The menacing 'Challenge of Thor' chorus (No. 2) nearly bursts with suppressed energy. Beethoven's *Egmont* rhythm is hammered out over an *ostinato* that leaps excitingly into the treble at 'Jove is my brother'. The awestruck pagans admit, *pianissimo* over shivery drum rolls, that 'Thou art a God, too, O Galilean'. Then the tenor narrates Olaf's past in a long solo (No. 3), moving fluently through tempos and ideas in a golden stream of melody. The vocal line has a Verdian thrust and scope (Elgar had played in the *Requiem* in 1887). This is not so far from Gerontius's 'Firmly I believe and truly'. Example 1.7a from *Olaf*, and 1.7b from *Gerontius*, show the same lyricism, the second phrase generously expanding the first.

   Olaf sails into Dronheim fiord to a flexible three-four 'sailing' motif. That, squared into four-four, becomes the bass for Olaf's memory of his flight by sea and his baptism in the Scillies; and in the next scene, back in three-four, it becomes

Ex. 1.7

the bass for the chorus as he lands at Nidaros. This plastic use of themes begins to show symphonic development. As he mentions his dreams, the music takes on that special quality that 'dream' always invoked in Elgar (Ex. 1. 8.)

Ex. 1.8

In a fierce confrontation (No. 5) between Olaf and the pagan Ironbeard, Olaf shatters Thor's image, and Ironbeard is struck by an arrow. Dying, he nobly affirms his faith, as with intense triplet chromatics and suspensions he fearlessly faces Valhalla. Miraculously the Cross of Christ appears and converts his followers, though musically Ironbeard's death would seem to be far more persuasive. The transition from fight to prayer is well done, and the following chorus, 'King Olaf's axe was lowered', is mesmerizing, with ground-swelling *crescendos* and an oboe twining chromatically round the chords as 'the golden censers' swing. The atmosphere is as strong as the end of Part I of *Gerontius*. In a chorale affirming their new faith the people sing of water to 'lave' their brows of blood, over the 'sailing' motif – again musically satisfying, but perhaps rather salty.

Things go less well when Olaf entangles himself with three women. First he thinks to redeem his murder of Ironbeard by marrying his daughter Gudrun (No. 7). Not surprisingly, she attempts to stab her husband on their wedding night, then flees. The stilted exchange between them is feeble. Then Olaf courts the haughty Sigrid (No. 11). Their conversation begins well with music of charming mock-courtesy (*grazioso molto*) and silky modulations, but when she refuses to be converted he taunts her: 'Thou has not beauty, thou hast not youth, shall I buy thy land at the cost of truth?' (no diplomat, he). Her scornful rejection – 'Sigrid yet shall be Olaf's death' – spans an octave and a half in genuine passionate revenge. Next Olaf biga-mously weds Thyri the Dane (No. 14), whose pretty six-eight suggests rather a tepid lady. His gift of a fragrant bouquet of 'angelicas uprooted' is not enough to stop her hankering after her lost lands, despite a yearning orchestral suggestion that Olaf finds her 'sweet and fair'. Their lilting love-duet is dainty rather than fervent, for all their show of unity in octaves.

Between Olaf's amorous adventures come two splendid choral ballads. 'The Wraith of Odin', in which Odin's ghost appears to the carousing Skalds, is fast, furious, and sinister (No. 9). The monotone refrain 'Dead rides Sir Morten of Vogelsang' is taken from Robert Buchanan's *Scandinavian Ballads*, and the orchestra sets it differently each time with mounting horror. As the guest tells tales of old, the 'sagas' and 'legends' themes roll out majestically. (The watchdogs' bark will turn up again in 'Enigma' for Dan.) In 1924 Elgar declared 'If I had to set K. O. again I shd. do it just in the same way, – the atmosphere is "right" & the technique – I have never done anything like "Dead rides".'[11] The gossips' rumour ballad (No. 13) – 'A little bird in the air' – might come from the *Bavarian Scenes* except that the construction is satisfyingly more complex

[11] To Troyte Griffith, 25 April 1924.

as it waltzes joyously through keys as far apart from its home
G major as D flat and B major.

The menfolk of Olaf's slighted women take their revenge in
a sea battle (No. 16), 'King Olaf's dragons take the sea', graphic
with clangs and thumps. (Elgar subsumed one of his earlier
Mill-wheel songs here.) Motifs crowd back: the 'wild wind
wailing' from Olaf's first solo, the sailing motif, and Olaf's
bugle. Chromatically overwhelmed, Olaf sinks and drowns,
and up through the waves triumphantly rises Sigrid's venge-
ance motif. The sea calms. A tolling bell leads to the Epilogue
in a convent where Olaf's mother, Astrid the Abbess, hears a
mystic voice introduced by chords (cue B) that foreshadow
the great Judgment climax in *Gerontius* (cue 118). In a final
reversal unmotivated except by piety, Christianity's champion
Olaf having been defeated and drowned, Thor's brutal rhythm
is smoothed for 'It is accepted' and melodically transformed
for the famous unaccompanied 'As torrents in summer'. The
weak lapse into the sugary 'Stronger than steel is the sword of
the spirit' is mercifully followed by a return to the opening of
the whole work. Gradually the tale recedes into the mysterious
distance from which it emerged.

Novello thought *King Olaf* too long. Elgar cut several recitatives, a solo, and abbreviated other numbers, shortening
the work by thirty pages. It still lasts an hour and a half. He
conducted the first performance on 30 October 1896 at Hanley,
North Staffordshire. The audience, when 'The Challenge of
Thor' burst upon them, 'knew that they were on the verge of
a new age in music – that this young man who had fiddled
among them had now found his true vocation'.[12] Mackenzie
wrote that Stanford 'enthusiastically drew my attention to the
almost unknown newcomer's splendid gifts'.[13] With hindsight,
the breakthrough in Elgar's career looks like 'Enigma'. But Elgar
himself dated the beginning of his national acclaim to *King Olaf*,
and in old age he looked back on it in these words: 'I shall be

---

12 Reginald Nettel, *Music in the Five Towns, 1840–1914* (Oxford, 1944), p. 41.
13 A. Mackenzie. *A Musician's Narrative* (London, 1927), p. 205.

thrilled by *King Olaf* after thirty-six years. It does sound well.'
'It always sweeps me off my feet.'[14]

There are memorable orchestral effects: flutes icily picking
out the tops of the chords following Ironbeard's death; the
shimmering sea-foam in 'Olaf's Return'; the three cellos
introducing Gudrun, intimate but evil; the crashing entry
of the organ in the sea battle. Elgar had now fully learnt the
emotive power of chromaticism. He had also learnt how to
use sequences as harmonic propulsion, not just as a lazy way
of lengthening melodic phrases. No longer does Wagner's
influence show itself in passages patched into Elgar's earlier
style: the difference is between imitation and of absorbing the
principles. Elgar has assimilated Wagner's methods, has learnt,
partly by using open-ended phrases to avoid perfect cadences,
how to achieve continuity and length. His leitmotifs are now
not just referential but structural, in linear and contrapuntal
combinations. For the first time melody, harmony, and orchestration are integrated at the service of drama. His admiration
for *Die Meistersinger* must have encouraged his arching melodies
with their triplets tied over strong beats, their appoggiaturas,
and sinuous inner parts.

1896 The Light of Life, Op. 29

The two big works so far produced in Worcester, *Froissart* and *The
Black Knight*, had been secular. At the suggestion of the Festival
secretary, Elgar set his mind on offering an oratorio for the
Three Choirs Festival. He approached Edward Capel Cure, an
Anglican clergyman he played chamber music with. From the
three subjects he suggested, Elgar chose the healing of the man
blind from birth (Elgar himself suffered from intermittent eye
problems, which may have been psychosomatic). Capel Cure
produced a libretto from John ix, 1–38, adding verses of his
own (though Elgar cut some of these), and the offer of *Lux
Christi* was accepted for the Festival. He composed the vocal
score, using some previous sketches, between February and
April 1896, and scored it during May and June. Novello asked

14   To Ivor Atkins, 30 December 1922.

for an English rather than the Latin title, and a guarantee of £40, which Alice promised from her own income. The first performance was on 8 October in Worcester Cathedral so, with *King Olaf* at Hanley on 30 October, Elgar had two big premières within eight weeks, and he was still teaching during term time. He dedicated *The Light of Life* to Swinnerton Heap (his second dedication) in recognition of his encouragement of *Olaf.*

The opening orchestral 'Meditation' aspires to something more profound than the Romantic and picturesque earlier choral works. The first theme is rounded and supple, the last the soaring 'Light' melody, at once four-square and suave, that Elgar uses, modified, throughout the work and was to use again in *The Apostles* (Ex. 1.9).

Ex. 1.9

In between, in triple time, come the beseeching themes of the Blind Man; their syncopated sinuous chromatics, with inner parts in octaves, are tenderly sentimental. Overlapping the final chord the unison male voices steal in, singing of night – 'the seven stars and Orion' – a thrilling, poetic moment. The chorus and the Blind Man (tenor) alternate in this all-male opening. Many of the sixteen numbers follow continuously, linked by the contralto narrator. The Blind Man's mother (soprano) sings a self-searching aria, 'Be not extreme' (No. 4), rather unpleasantly questioning whether her son's blindness is 'sin's own signature'. (Exception was taken to her words 'Hads't Thou a son, O Lord', which were changed when Elgar revised the solo parts for the 1899 edition.) The baritone Christ declares that her son is no sinner, but is blind so 'that the works of God should be made manifest in him'. Example 1.9 scrambled in diminution heralds a chorus 'Light out of darkness' (No. 6). It has some perfunctory writing, but also two mystic episodes for sopranos in thirds over *tremolo* strings as the words describe

Jesus' Passion, prophetic of 'What are these wounds in Thy hands' in the finale of *The Apostles*.

The narrative of the miracle now begins. Jesus anoints the blind man (No. 7) and directs him to wash in the pool of Siloam. At that critical moment Capel Cure interrupts the action for a duet, 'Doubt not thy father's care', with the bathetic comment 'life has missed its mark'. Much of the duet is conventional, but it is just redeemed by a repeated swaying figure inspired by the 'starry night'. The crucial moment of gaining sight is baldly recounted in a recitative. The people question the 'blind' man's identity, and it is dramatically otiose – through it follows the Gospel –to have him recount Jesus' instructions. The crowd accepts that a miracle has taken place, and dismiss their so-called wise men in a pedantic *fugato*. This culminates in a visionary eight-part unaccompanied passage, which gloriously opens up in contrary motion from G major to E major as 'the eyes of the blind shall see'. It closes down again to lead into 'As a spirit', in which the healed man longs to meet his healer. This floating flowing aria (No. 10) lifts the work above the level of one man's physical blindness to that of spiritual blindness. These pages are the finest in the oratorio.

The male Pharisees with stubborn octave monotones now object to Jesus performing a miracle on the Sabbath, but the women more flexibly interject 'He is of God'. The contralto defends Him in a fulsome chromatic aria (No. 12), which ends with moving directness 'So make a silence in my soul' over the simple diatonic opening. The tenor boldly asserts that whoever healed him, now he can see. Still the Jews doubt and cast him out. The women lament, in metaphors of shepherds and sheep (No. 14). Jesus confronts the 'blind' man, who declares 'Lord, I believe'. Over the orchestral phrase beginning three bars after C in No. 15 (Ex. 1.10), Elgar wrote the unsung words 'And he worshipped Him' (as he was to write 'Eli, Eli, lama sabachtani' unsung over the crucifixion in *The Apostles*). The phrase is then movingly interwoven with Jesus' prayer to His Father (cue F). It is a *Tristan*-esque phrase loaded with emotional significance for Elgar. It symbolizes 'inspiration' in *The Music Makers* (cue 39) and occurs at the crux of the Cello Concerto (cue 69). A rather

Ex. 1.10

chirpy final chorus in three-four closes the work in which poetic and pedestrian passages lie too close for comfort.

As a believing Catholic, Elgar must have felt some weight of responsibility composing his first oratorio. *The Light of Life* is less spontaneous than the fiery *King Olaf*. While he was correcting the proofs, he was interviewed at 'Forli' by R. J. Buckley, the music critic of *The Birmingham Gazette*, who became Elgar's first biographer.[15] He recorded Elgar as saying 'I thought a fugue would be expected of me. The British public would hardly tolerate oratorio without fugue ... There's a bit of canon, too, and in short, I hope there's enough counterpoint to give the real British religious respectability!' Buckley rightly felt this was badinage; and Elgar went on to talk seriously of his veneration for Bach. It would be understandable if he had felt some constraints of propriety, and his earnest desire to compose up to his own religious ideals and that of the great Cathedral may have inhibited him.

Music for Queen and Country, 1897–99

There were no such inhibitions over his next works. By 1897 Victoria would have reigned for sixty years. According to the *St James's Gazette*, the Queen-Empress held sway over 'one continent, a hundred peninsulas, five hundred promontories, a thousand lakes, two thousand rivers, ten thousand islands'. It was the most extensive empire in history. So, with the diamond jubilee in their sights, Novello thought to bring together the Empire, St George, and Elgar. They sent him a libretto – the only one he did not choose for himself – by a Bristol writer, 'Shapcott

15 Robert J. Buckley, *Sir Edward Elgar* (London and New York, 1905), p. 31.

Wensley' [H. S. Bunce], and he composed *The Banner of St George*, Op. 33.

Novello were prescient in also commissioning an *Imperial March* from Elgar, foreseeing where his popular talent lay. Marches were a recognized way of paying homage to rulers – Mattheson considered that they should convey 'grandeur and fearlessness' (1717). Many were derived from operas: Handel, Mozart, Meyerbeer, Wagner; Schubert's military marches were for piano duet. But in earlier times ceremonial was largely confined to royal courts. Far from being long established, the splendid coronations, public parades, public pageantry, were comparatively new in Elgar's day. Queen Victoria's coronation was a shabby affair and most of her time in widowhood seclusion offered nothing to celebrate. But her sheer longevity, together with her position as matriarch of Europe and the Empire, brought her veneration. During her final years, royal occasions became imperial occasions. As the effective power of the monarchy declined, so its symbolism became a unifying force. Descriptions of London celebrations could reach a wide public through the new popular press. The flowering of English ceremonial happened to coincide with Elgar's maturity. Had he been born fifty years earlier, there would have been no stimulus or outlet for his marches.

Elgar sent a sketch for the march on 7 December 1896, saying confidently that it would have a 'great, broad, brilliant effect with orchestra'. (How right he was; the piano reduction is dull by comparison.) Already he could say 'I am *sure* of my orchl. effects'.[16] Novello replied criticizing it for having so many short phrases of two bars or even one. Elgar agreed to amend it (making it 'now concise and effective'). On 6 February he sent the full score and suggested asking Sir Walter Parratt, Master of the Queen's Musick, if he might dedicate it to the Queen. Parratt (1841–1924) had been organist to the Earl of Dudley at Witley Court near Worcester, where Elgar senior had tuned the pianos.

Elgar's *Imperial March* Op. 32 was his first detached ceremonial piece, composed the same year as Kipling's *Recessional* and

16 To A. Littleton, 14 January 1897.

Sousa's *Stars and Stripes*. He cast it in traditional ternary form, opening it with crackling rhythms, a *strepitoso* four semi-quaver group, the last quaver silent, so making the rat-tat-tat familiar from *The Black Knight* march (the last beat of Ex. 1.2, p. 18). The more melodious central section has also the skipping rhythm familiar from the *Bavarian Scenes* (Ex. 1.4, p. 21). Reed recalled that Elgar confessed to 'a great liking for the *Coronation March* by Meyerbeer'. His eyes used to shine with excitement when they 'hummed the strong rhythmic tune: the strength of that triplet on the first beat of the bar gripped him'.[17] Elgar's *Imperial March* is for symphony orchestra, though the first performance under Manns at the Crystal Palace on 19 April was in the version for massed bands. It was then played at the Queen's Hall, at a royal garden party, and a state concert. Later Elgar composed better marches, but it was his *Imperial March* that first carried his name throughout the land.

The plot of *The Banner of St George*, Op. 33, is simple. A dragon demands a daily ration of maidens; the king's daughter offers herself as lunch; St George arrives in the nick of time, slays the dragon, and rides off to oppose new tyrants, leaving the chorus to hymn the 'blood-red cross', the banner of England (St George, patron of Elgar's local church, was 'adopted' for England by Edward III). The story was known, even to the name of the princess, Sabra, and took place at Silene, Libya.

Elgar submitted sketches to Novello to a draft libretto on 30 November 1896, and completed the orchestration the following March. The ballad for chorus (the princess is an optional solo) was first performed on 18 May 1897 by the St Cuthbert's Hall Choral Society in Earl's Court, London, and for a time it was taken up by the smaller choral societies. It then seems to have died a natural death until Elgar conducted a rumbustious recording of the Epilogue, 'It comes from the misty ages', in 1928.

It is splendid stuff, full of every possible verbal and musical cliché, just about redeemed by its tunefulness. Most of it swings along in a cheerful three-four. The sinister and confrontational idioms of *The Black Knight* and the coming *Caractacus* are reduced

[17] William H. Reed, *Elgar as I Knew Him* (London, 1936), p. 86.

to basic formulas. There is a plodding theme with a ponderous second-beat accent expressing danger, but the poor dragon, even when *triple forte* and *con fuoco*, is hardly worthy even of a pantomime. Elgar manipulates his leading themes appropriately. Hope and righteousness swell out over throbbing repeated triplets, leading to the concluding march in which the percussion has a high old time, and the moral tale ends by hymning England, Empire, and the blood-red cross on white. Luckily Novello paid Elgar well for it.

For the Queen's eightieth birthday in 1899 Parratt commissioned choral songs by various writers and composers to be published in her honour. Some, including Elgar's, were given by two hundred and fifty Windsor and Eton singers beneath the room in which the Queen breakfasted at Windsor Castle on 24 May 1899. Even Elgar's patriotism must have been stretched by the words Parratt sent him, by Frederic W. H. Myers, in which the English 'Outsoar the Caesar's eagle flight, Outrun the Macedonian reign', and reach from 'flamy Northern night' to 'the Austral main'. He composed what he called a 'partrigal', a dutiful rather rambling partsong, 'To her beneath whose stedfast [sic] star'. He was present at the performance so he saw the Queen at her window and heard her voice her thanks.

≈❧≈

In 1896 Novello handed Elgar's affairs over to August Johannnes Jaeger (1860–1909). Born in Düsseldorf but long settled in England, Jaeger had joined Novello in 1890. His official job was as publishing manager, but he was also valued as a musical adviser. He became Elgar's fervent supporter and confidant, at times his creative partner, and from Elgar's first letter to him on 4 August 1897 their correspondence is not only entertaining but revealing of Elgar's music and character.

By 1897 Elgar, restless and wanting to spread his wings, was hinting at a move to London, possibly encouraged by a performance of *King Olaf* at the Crystal Palace on 3 April. As an incentive to keep him, local musicians founded the Worcestershire Philharmonic. He conducted from the first concert on 7 May 1898 until he was succeeded by Granville Bantock in 1904. Winifred Norbury ('W. N.' of 'Enigma') was an honorary secretary. The orchestra numbered about fifty, the choir over a hundred. Elgar described it as – 'a sort of toy I suppose for a petulant child'.[18] Another 'Enigma' friend made at this time was Arthur Troyte Griffith (1864–1942), a Malvern architect. His office was in the Priory Gateway, and he designed All Saints' Church, Malvern Wells.

On his Bavarian holiday in 1897 Elgar heard Strauss conduct *Tristan* and *Don Giovanni*. The Elgars were still living at 'Forli', but in spring 1898 they took a lease of Birchwood Lodge, a remote and simple cottage in the woods north of the Malvern Hills. It became his summer composing retreat.

1897 Te Deum and Benedictus, Op. 34

In 1897 came another Three Choirs invitation, this time from Hereford, so even more welcome than from his home city. It was for two morning service canticles, the *Te Deum and Benedictus*. Elgar worked on the vocal score between 28 May and 15 June, but on 5 June took his sketch to play to G. R. Sinclair, the Hereford Cathedral organist, for his approval. Also listening was Sinclair's eighteen-year-old assistant Percy Hull, who remembered Elgar being 'as nervous as a kitten'. Sinclair found the work 'very very modern',[19] which says more about him than about Elgar, for the music is conservative. It was for the opening service of the Festival on 12 September, a grand occasion with full chorus, orchestra, and soloists, and a congregation of dignitaries, so – with the organ sonata behind him (the *Te Deum* would more often be performed with organ than orchestra) – Elgar launched boldly into an impressive twenty instrumental bars before the chorus enters, the right scale for a work that lasts twenty minutes. The music's design is spacious and the texture well laid out. But the opening theme, which acts as a *ritornello*, becomes rhythmically over-insistent and relies much on sequences – though that is appropriate enough for 'world without end'. Passages of praise are

18   To Joseph Bennett, 15 November 1897.
19   Percy Hull, 'Elgar at Hereford', *RAM Magazine*, 1960, p. 6.

strongly and full-heartedly scored, and the petitions ('help thy
servants') are submissively unaccompanied. There are inward
moments: an *andante* interlude of swaying thirds in tied triplets
at cue J recurs in the lyrical *Benedictus* and looks forward to the
oratorios. The *Te Deum* music is recapitulated after it. As early
as 1905 Buckley singled out the passages at the eleventh bar
and the Example 1.11 as 'so Elgaresque that they sound like
"soul-transcriptions"'.

Ex. 1.11

The performance presented much exposure for the ambitious but insecure Elgar, and at the end of his orchestral score
he wrote 'Inter spem et metum' (between hope and fear).
Jaeger travelled to Hereford to hear it, and wrote to tell the
composer it was 'your finest, most spontaneous & most deeply
felt & most effective work'.

◈

Nicholas Kilburn (1843–1923) was an iron merchant and
pump manufacturer who lived at Bishop Auckland, County
Durham. He was also the founder-director of three musical
societies. He had already conducted *King Olaf* when he met Elgar
at the 1897 Three Choirs, and he went on to conduct each new
choral work. Elgar dedicated *The Music Makers* to him.

Lady Mary Lygon (1869–1927), sister of Earl Beauchamp,
lived at Madresfield Court, where in 1896 she started a music
competition festival with which Elgar became involved. She
was on the committee of the Worcestershire Philharmonic
Society. From 1895 she was a Woman of the Bedchamber to

the future Queen Alexandra. On her marriage she became Lady Mary Trefusis and lived in Cornwall.

Short Instrumental Pieces, 1897–99

It was probably in 1897 that Elgar composed the piano Minuet Op. 21 for Nicholas Kilburn's son Paul. He composed little music for a child and, interestingly, this Minuet is among his least nostalgic pieces. It also suggests that Paul was quite an accomplished musician. Elgar liked it enough to score it for light orchestra. He conducted it at one of Granville Bantock's New Brighton concerts on 16 July 1899, and recorded it in 1929. At the same concert he conducted the first perform- ance of his Three Characteristic Pieces. Novello had suggested he produce something like Edward German's Dances from Henry VIII. He looked out his unpublished Suite in D, performed in Birmingham in 1888. The last movement had been an even earlier piece, Pas redoublé March. He revised the other three as his Op. 10, and dedicated the Suite to Lady Mary Lygon.

Chanson de nuit, Op. 15, No. 1, originally for violin and piano, is dark and intense, opening richly on the violin's G string below the piano's supporting chords. The piano picks up the violin's rhythm as if in conversation, and chromatic moves lead to a recapitulation at the wrong pitch, which then subtly slips back into the home G major. Chanson de matin, Op. 15, No. 2, is lighter, with the charm of the morning Severnside music of Caractacus. Elgar quoted the climax in the Piacevole move- ment of his Quartet of 1918. He orchestrated both Chansons, and Henry Wood conducted them at the Queen's Hall on 14 September 1901.

1898 Caractacus, Op. 35

Elgar now considered composing a work for the Leeds Triennial Festival, next to be held in 1898. This, a secular festival with international status, its chorus the finest in the country, was considered more prestigious than the Three Choirs. Sullivan was its conductor-director, though already failing in health. Elgar had in mind to offer an orchestral suite, but Leeds made

it clear they wanted a cantata. He mulled over the flight into
Egypt as a subject (he had recently performed L'enfance du Christ
with the Worcestershire Philharmonic) and also St Augustine
(a theme Tippett later took up). Then on 4 August 1897 he
visited his mother who was staying at Colwall, on the west
side of the Malvern Hills. Looking along their silhouette, she
suggested he should compose something based on the 'lovely
old Hill', the Herefordshire Beacon crowned by the earthworks
of British Camp. 'Can't we write some tale about it? ... so much
historical interest.' Locals believe it was the last stronghold of
the British king Caractacus, who stood out but lost against
the Roman invaders, as described by Tacitus. Elgar's interest
caught, he turned again to Acworth for a libretto. The historical
Caractacus had a daughter; Acworth called her Eigen and gave
her a young lover, Orbin, a 'member of a half-priestly order of
minstrels'. Caractacus was taken prisoner to Rome in AD 51,
where his noble bearing so impressed the emperor Claudius
that he was pardoned and released. Elgar worked on the vocal
score during February to June 1898, and scored it during June
to August.

He and Acworth devised six scenes. Caractacus and his
troops enter the British Camp at night to a muttered march
(sordamente), alert the watchmen to danger (the 'Watchmen,
alert!' motif acts as a refrain), and exhort each other to defiance. Caractacus, apart under the stars, sings of nature's sweetness, showing himself to be poet as well as soldier. Eigen (in
twelve-eight against the four-square soldiery), accompanied
by Orbin, recounts her meeting with a prophesying Druid girl.
All are introduced by their characteristic motifs. But Elgar's
references look further ahead. Throughout the scene there
are snatches of coming leitmotifs. For instance, the chorus's
second sentence is sung over 'Romans' (Ex. 1.12a), which will
come into its own in the Triumphal March in the last scene.
'Britons', heard here in diminution, comes full out at cue 16,
and is inflated in Scene 2 at cue 23 (Ex. 1.12b).

Between cues 29 and 30, as Caractacus senses the sad end to
the heroic story, a downward chromatic outpouring foretells
the captives embarking in Scene 5. Orbin's motif is entwined
with Eigen's even before he sings. Eigen's mention of mistletoe

Ex. 1.12

at cue 41 brings a bar of the mystic dance from Scene 2, cue 3. And so on. All is intricately, skilfully done and yields more at each hearing. The downside is that the whole work needs to be known for the motifs to make their point when they first appear. In spite of this, Elgar's control of this extended span is strong.

The scene changes (is this cantata, opera, masque?) to a sacred oak grove with Druids treading a 'mystic circle'. The trouble here is the discrepancy between the poor invention and the sophisticated orchestration. Some of the themes are almost frivolous, the Druid maidens ('Tread the measure') might belong to Bunthorne (1881). The Invocation to the pagan god Taranis (the chorus boldly in octaves) is portentous rather than impressive. Elgar wrote to Jaeger on 1 March, probably about this passage, 'Caractacus frightens me in places'. Yet Elgar's orchestration is so atmospheric (eerie solo divided violas, for instance) that he nearly gets away with it. More serious are the dramatic complications. Orbin attempts to read the omens but can see only shadows, suggesting disaster. The Arch-Druid falsifies Orbin's warnings and, when Caractacus enters, advises him 'Go forth O King to conquer'. The motivation for this, the crux of the action, is unclear. Presumably it was so as not to discourage Caractacus, but the Arch-Druid overreaches himself and usurps authority. Elgar missed the chance of a great aria here, when the Arch-Druid night have struggled with his conscience. Falsely spurred on, Caractacus sings a spirited three-stanza Sword Song. Orbin has two attempts (one too many) to convince the Britons of their impending defeat. (Moreover, in the following Scene 3, he relates the previous night's happenings.) His warning ignored, Orbin throws off his bardic robes and joins the British army. The combination of Druids cursing Orbin and soldiery cheering Caractacus makes an energetic and fiery final chorus to the scene.

For Scene 3, morning near the Severn, Elgar went back to 1887 sketches for the dewy-fresh opening. Over two lovely bars, he wrote to Jaeger, 'the trees are singing my music or have I sung theirs', and indeed over this Eigen later sings 'O'er-arch'd by leaves ...'. There is a decorous chorus for garland-weavers. Then Eigen, in Elgar's maidenly twelve-eight, sings as she waits for Orbin. (Elgar's ladies lean toward compound time, Thyri in six-eight, Gudrun and Sigrid in nine-eight.) The love-duet is pleasant and flowing, and becomes momentarily passionate with twining chromatic triplets ('thine in death ...'), but it ends tranquilly over the 'morning' music in some future 'far-off land'. Elgar could not equal Strauss for love-music.

In Scene 4, a 'rumour' chorus for women, like the ballad in *King Olaf* but darker and more agitated, tells of the British defeat. Eigen recounts another meeting with the tiresome Druid prophetess. The tattered army describes the lost battle, 'dying with the day', in an expertly paced scherzo, in effect a long *diminuendo*. This leads into Caractacus' tragic lament for his dead warriors. The seven-four pulse gives it heaviness and dignity but also suppleness, and Elgar's pervasive triplet, usually perky, is smoothly integrated into the melody. This great piece is as eloquent as anything in Elgar's output, and for the first time in *Caractacus* the listener's emotions are fully engaged. Scene 5, the captives boarding the Roman galleys, is equally expressive, and the transition from the mournful 'captive Britons' theme to the triumphal march in Rome (triplet once more snappy) is grand Elgar.

The British, expecting execution, are brought before Claudius, at whose command Caractacus pleads his case, not for himself but for his people. He and the young lovers recall the music of their sweet native land. Claudius grants them life but in exile, and they sing together of his grace, their lost freedom, and of the 'golden' (sustained top C for Eigen) chain. Then the chorus – Romans or Britains? – sings enthusiastically, in music from the opening scene, of the decline of the Roman Empire, and hymns the praise of Britain. Very odd, until it is remembered that Queen Victoria's diamond jubilee had been celebrated the previous year. Elgar was granted permission to dedicate the work to her. He admitted to Jaeger that he had suggested 'we should dabble in patriotism in the Finale' but that his librettist instead of merely 'paddling' 'goes & gets naked & wallows in it'.[20] But the next month he wrote: 'I knew you wd. laugh at my librettist's patriotism (& mine) never mind: England for the English is all I say – hand's off! there's nothing apologetic about me.'[21] Indeed no apology is needed for the 'gift of freedom', of 'equal law to all men'. Even 'for ever your dominion From age to age shall grow' is less aggressive than the second verse of the National Anthem. The chorus shows a strand, a genuine celebration of patriotism, that was to make Elgar the nation's troubadour, leading to the five *Pomp and Circumstance* marches and the official compositions for great state occasions.

When *Caractacus* was to be revived at the 1970 Cheltenham Festival after years of neglect, there was unease at the political incorrectness of that final chorus. The words, deemed vainglorious, were suppressed, and new anodyne United Nations words supplied. It made little odds: no-one heard any words at all. None came through. The original grand, celebratory sentiments did – in the music! In such a case it is best not to be lily-livered, but to perform the original with as much gusto as possible, mentally placing it in its historical context.

Caractacus deserves admiration. It is soundly constructed, ambitious, and inventive. It is the most substantial and elaborate of Elgar's 'early' works. It should be the most personal, set as it is on the hills he so loved, striding along their crest from end to end. He composed much of it at Birchwood, surrounded by trees. But it is a less engaging work than *King Olaf*, and it is hard to care about any of the characters, save at moments for Caractacus himself. The first performance, conducted by Elgar, was on 5 October 1898. Parry, Stanford, and Cowen were in the audience, also Gabriel Fauré from France. Many of Elgar's friends travelled to Leeds to support him.

After Elgar's death for a long time his 1890s works were rarely played, and it came to seem that the 'Enigma' Variations

[20]   21 June 1898.
[21]   12 July 1898.

had sprung from him fully formed, Minerva-like. Since then, the revival of his earlier works has shown his steady progression, through the opportunities available to him in the provincial festivals. Mastery of 'Enigma' did not materialize from nowhere. At first hearing Elgar's skill in orchestration seems unaccountable. His only compositions for orchestra before the Variations were *Froissart* and some slight pieces. But his development can be traced in the full scores of the cantatas.

In all four choral works Elgar used leitmotifs. He claimed to have learnt the technique from Mendelssohn's *Elijah*, but he had gone out of his way to hear Wagner's operas. He knew the difference between the reminiscence motif and (as he wrote in 1898) Wagner's way of 'illustrating character and ideas … in poetic and suggestive touches'. There are passages in Elgar's 1890s works of real 'Wagner sound', and he was consistently expanding his harmonic resources by chromatic and augmented progressions. There are other influences, as wide apart as Gounod and Schumann, and though Elgar's personality is strong enough not to be subdued, in sum the works are uneven. At times the mood turns mawkish or aggressive, and then the interaction of melody, harmony and rhythm seems too easily come by. There is some dull invention (mostly in *The Light of Life*), and some trivial (for example, the choric measure in *Caractacus*). But the best of *The Black Knight* is direct, the best of *The Light of Life* intense. The whole of the first five scenes of *King Olaf* is memorable, with a young man's athletic vigour, and wide-ranging in mood with grand, rolling passages anticipating the symphonies. *Caractacus*, though more ambitious, is stiffer, but the control of pace over certain spans – the long *diminuendo* of hope dying into the Lament, for instance – is characteristic of Elgar at his best. All four choral works of the 1890s can still be heard with enjoyment, not simply as a foretaste of things to come. If the inspiration in them is fitful, their energy, zest, and eloquent melodies are irresistible.

CHAPTER TWO

To the Greater Glory of God, 1899–1909

1899 Variations on an Original Theme ('Enigma'), Op. 36

I[1] 'C. A. E.' Caroline Alice Elgar, 'a romantic and delicate inspiration'.

II 'H. D. S.-P.' Hew David Steuart-Powell, an amateur pianist, 'humorously travestied' in the semi-quavers.

III 'R. B. T.' Richard Baxter Townshend, 'low voice flying off occasionally into "soprano" timbre'.

IV 'W. M. B.' William Meath Baker, hurriedly leaving with 'an inadvertent bang of the door'.

V 'R. P. A.' Richard P. Arnold, 'serious conversation … broken up by whimsical and witty remarks'.

VI 'Ysobel.' Isabel Fitton, an amateur viola player, an 'exercise for crossing the strings'.

VII 'Troyte.' Arthur Troyte Griffith, the 'boisterous mood is mere banter'.

VIII 'W. N.' Winifred Norbury, 'a characteristic laugh'.

IX 'Nimrod.' A. J. Jaeger, the record of a talk when he 'discoursed eloquently' on Beethoven.

X 'Dorabella.' Dora Penny, 'a dance-like lightness'.

XI 'G. R. S.' George Robertson Sinclair, organist, and Bulldog Dan, 'paddling up' the river Wye, and barking.

XII 'B. G. N.' Basil G. Nevinson, amateur cellist, 'serious and devoted friend'.

XIII '* * *'. Lady Mary Lygon, 'the name of a lady … on a sea voyage'.

XIV 'E. D. U.' Elgar, to show what the composer intended to do.

---

[1] Extracted from *My Friends Pictured Within* (Novello, 1949), and Elgar's notes for the pianola rolls in 1929.

The Variations were the first of Elgar's great orchestral works. He was at the time 'possessed' by the idea of composing a symphony to commemorate General Gordon of Khartoum. He proposed it for the 1899 Three Choirs Festival, and it was announced in the press. But even after the success of *Caractacus* earlier that month he was not certain enough of himself to embark on a symphony. The grand theme he sketched for it on 20 October 1898 became the Committal in *The Dream of Gerontius*. The same day he wrote dismally to Jaeger, 'I have to earn money somehow & it's *no good* trying this sort of thing.' On 21 October he had a hard day's violin teaching. Tired and depressed, he improvised that evening on the piano. His wife interrupted him, saying 'Edward, that's a good tune', and the theme for the Variations was born. With Alice's encouragement, he went on to play it in the manner of various friends; and memories, thoughts, idiosyncrasies, and associations came gathering round it. The work, he said, was begun 'in a spirit of humour & continued in deep seriousness'.[2]

So the Variations, which were to bring Elgar international acclaim, were not commissioned, but composed spontaneously. Each is complete in itself, with its own identity. One of the strengths of this self-taught composer is how well he was guided by his intuition to fill his needs. Until then he had composed mostly for the market, knowing what would sell or working to commission. During the 1890s he had taught himself to achieve continuity, by depending on texts. He was not yet ready for the challenge of an abstract symphony. A set of variations, each brief but all derived from the same idea, was not only within his powers but was a perfect exercise in extending them. Possibly he might have been encouraged by the considerable success of Parry's *Symphonic Variations* of 1897. Later in life he admitted to admiring William Hurlstone's Variations on an Original Theme of 1896. He had just heard the Brahms–Haydn Variations at the Gloucester Festival.

In every sense, his are character variations. No listener can be unaware of how he felt about 'C. A. E.', 'Nimrod', 'Dorabella', and 'B. G. N'. Some variations relate to a mannerism (the trilly

[2]   Elgar's programme note for an Italian performance in 1911.

laugh of 'W. N.'), or an episode ('if I were a policeman,' wrote
Donald Tovey, 'I think I should ask Mr G. R. S. of variation XI
to produce his dog-licence').[3] Each variation was a living character, and all the 'variationees' had been part of the Elgars' life
during those autumn months. In the end none of these exter-
nals matter. They are 'amusing to those behind the scenes', as
Elgar wrote to Jaeger, '& won't affect the hearer who "nose
nuffin"'.[4]

Elgar's theme was original and compelling. All his finger-
prints are there, his falling thirds and sevenths, his chains of
thirds. At first hearing it appears to be a simple ternary ABA[2].
There are two contrasted strains, of unequal lengths. In the
first (A) in G minor, each of the six bars begins with a silent
beat in the melody, and the paired quaver-crotchet rhythm
(rest, two quavers, two crotchets) is teasingly reversed in the
following bar (rest, two crotchets, two quavers). The blank first
beats in the melody suggest something unfulfilled, waiting for
completion. Elgar described the theme as 'Nothing – but something might be made of it.'[5] In sum, the theme is eloquent,
romantic, and melancholy. In his *Music Makers* (1912), Elgar
introduced it under the words 'sitting by desolate streams'
because at the time the Variations were written, he said, 'it
expressed ... my sense of the loneliness of the artist ... and
it still embodies that sense'.[6] The second strain (B) is in G
major, with smooth sustained sequences and regular rhythm.
It consists of four bars of a rising repeated figure in thirds
beginning in turn on B, D, F sharp, and back to B. Over it, for
flute and oboe, are four scale notes descending from F sharp,
sounding like surface harmonic filling-in. That is deceptive, for
those four notes are thematic material, much used in the variations (they permeate the finale, for instance). Then the first
strain (A[2]) is repeated, more fully scored. Though the melody
is identical, it sounds radically different, for it is enriched with
sixths and octaves and the bass is sustained. And in its third

[3]   D. F. Tovey, *Essays in Musical Analysis*, Vol. IV (London, 1937), p. 150
[4]   24 October 1898.
[5]   Basil Maine, *Elgar: The Works* (London, 1944), p. 101.
[6]   14 August 1912 to Ernest Newman, notes on *The Music Makers*.

bar the lower strings surge in with a heart-stopping counter-
melody, an eloquent synthesis of A and B. Its first two notes are
from the second bar of A; the next two are the last two of A's
bar three, rising instead of falling; the next four are in shape
the 'insignificant' descending notes of B (Ex. 2.1). This tenor
counter-melody is then repeated, the intervals stretching even
higher, as if to 'essay much'.

Ex. 2.1

So the repeat is itself a variation, and the 'enigma' theme is
multi-layered and fertile, perfect material from which to draw
variations. Adding counter-melodies is a trait that goes back
to Elgar's early wind music. There it was decorative; here,
and even more in the symphonies, it fortifies or adds new
emotional weight to the music.

In earlier Baroque and Classical variation sets more often
than not the composer decorated a discrete melody, leaving the
harmonic structure intact. Brahms, and particularly Schumann,
were adept at taking a motif from the theme and transforming
it; the melody of the theme as a whole need not appear in
the variation, though the ground-plan was usually maintained.
Elgar does not even retain the ground-plan of his theme. Some
variations are longer ('Nimrod' lasts four minutes), some
shorter ('W. M. B.' only thirty seconds). His relationships with
the theme are usually melodic, but flexible, and the cohesion is
poetic and allusive rather than structural. In 'C. A. E.', properly
closest to the original, Elgar gives his wife a two-bar link from
the theme, an extra bar to move the second strain warmly into

E flat, and a four-bar coda that brings together both B and A. Hers is the only variation in which the two strains overlap at the centre. B cadences on to E flat major instead of G minor, and rises *largamente* to passionate heights, under which A enters on brass. The first statement is threaded through with Elgar's home-coming 'whistle' (triplets on oboes and bassoons). No wife can have received a more loving tribute.

In 'Troyte', strain A is reduced to a *presto* tonic and dominant cross-rhythm *ostinato*, and for the rhapsodic cellos of 'B. G. N.' it is luxuriously expanded with passing notes. It becomes a bass *cantus fermus* for the finger exercises of 'H. D. S.-P.', it is compressed into two bars for Sinclair's paddling bulldog, and in 'Ysobel' it is relegated to an accompanying figure in thirds. In 'R. B. T.' and 'W. M. B.' the melody is retained, but in 'R. B. T.' it is turned into a capricious waltz, and it is emphatically joined-up without rests in 'W. M. B.' (who has an extra few bars of A in canon at cue 13). In 'R. P. A.' strain A becomes the bass of a sonorous new melody, the two being inverted at the reprise.

As sequences are a natural part of Elgar's style, they figure largely in fashioning extensions. In 'Nimrod' the six-bar strain A is extended to eight bars, then under emotional pressure of the falling sevenths it stretches out to eleven bars. The final statement surges rhetorically to a soaring *fortissimo*, but instead of a triumphal end it recedes in sudden humility to a *pianissimo*. That is true spiritual grandeur.

The theme ends in the major, so successive minor variations sound fresh. Variation II is all in the minor, variation III all in the major. Variations V–VII form a central block with C as the tonic, showing that Elgar organized the fourteen variations overall. The most famous key-change comes between variations VIII and IX: the one-note link, a tonic G, from the delicate 'W. N.' becomes the mediant, and the key drops solemnly to E flat for the heart-felt 'Nimrod'. A distant harmonic point is reached in '* * *', aptly since its associations are with lands across the seas. It moves from the G major opening to a mysterious A flat for its quotation from Mendelssohn's *Calm Sea and Prosperous Voyage*. Only the rhythm of strain A is maintained, rocking wave-like on violas over a single chord. Repeated in F minor, heavily scored, with sombre trombones and covering a top-to-bottom register, the quotation becomes almost threatening, laden with so much emotion.

It is tempting to describe the variations as Elgar's own salon pieces raised to their highest plane. But that does them less than justice. Take 'W. N.'. Bars 1–4 are melodically derived from A, but with the sequence extending upwards, not falling back (suggesting B), and with each rhythmic pattern reversing the one before (as in A). Bars 5–8 repeat bars 1–4, but are chromatically inflected and the rhythmic pattern is doubly reversed. Bars 9 and 10 are derived from B, but with a chuckling pendant. Bar 15 is bar 11 of the variation but a semitone higher, with the sequence extended by two bars. Bars 23 and 24 repeat bars 5 and 6, but are enriched with the trills and the even semiquavers from bars 9 and 10. That sweetest, sunniest Allegretto would charm the birds off the trees if standing on its own, with no relationship to the theme. But compared with, say, the open melody, regular sequences, and light chordal accompaniment of *Chanson de matin*, blithe though that piece is, the variation is compressed, ingenious, and superbly integrated. It is Elgar wittily at play.

In contrast to such delicacy, 'G. R. S.' is a tempestuous blunt juxtaposition of the two strains. After a helter-skelter bar of descending strings (sliding down the river bank?), strain A is reduced to two rapid even-quaver bars (paddling upstream?). Strain B has one bar before a victorious bark. A brisk three-bar rerun leads to strain A brilliant on brass (full organ?). Ten bars of strain A, its rhythm in *ostinato* below a mock *fugato*, lead to a reprise. Strain A now fits over its own descending sevenths in sequence. The strings rush helter-skelter down over an excited Strain B (stick retrieved and a good shake?). The Variation is amusing enough for the dog and scholarly enough for his organist master.

The Finale, according to Elgar, was to show his *intentions*. So the 'bold and vigorous' march-like introduction, the final 'triumphant, broad' presentation of the theme, were not the Elgar of 1899, but the composer he was willing himself to become. His resolution is staggering! The two strains of the 'enigma' theme are extended, combined, modified, counter-

pointed, with recollections of 'C. A. E' and 'Nimrod'. Elgar
transforms the duple metre of the 'enigma' theme into
augmented three-beat measures. Eloquent and flowing, the
music sounds symphonic and ends, more prophetically than
he could have realized, with the outline of the opening of his
First Symphony.

There are three extra-musical puzzles: the 'enigma', the identity of ' * * *', and the 'Tasso' quotation. Elgar dedicated the
Variations to 'my Friends pictured within', so at first there was
the human interest of identifying them. ('There are portraits we
cannot recognize, there is an enigma we cannot solve, there is
a theme (the principal theme!) we cannot hear.'[7]) 'Dorabella' was
the only 'Friend' to write about the composer, and in her book
she describes and prints photographs of her co-variationees.
They seem to have been chosen for their idiosyncrasies. If their
closeness as friends was Elgar's criterion, why were not Hubert
Leicester, Charles Buck, or Nicholas Kilburn among them?
Parry and Sullivan were allegedly considered but rejected, as
including them would have meant parodying their musical
styles. An incipit headed I[vor] A[tkins] was given in the end
to 'R. B. T.'. 'Dorabella' was possibly derived from an 1880s
theme. In 'Nimrod' Elgar omitted Jaeger's 'outside manner' and
portrayed his 'good, lovable honest SOUL'.[8] (Jaeger, German
for hunter, became Nimrod, the biblical mighty hunter, in
Elgar's allusive mind.) The Variation's elegiac associations came
later, perhaps when it was played at Jaeger's memorial concert,
certainly after it became part of the Cenotaph ritual. When
Elgar composed it, it was simply an ardent tribute from the
composer to his friend who, by citing Beethoven's example,
talked him out of a deep depression.

A week-by-week chart can be drawn up of the Variations'
progress from their conception to the publication of the
printed score in January 1900, and to a change of metro-
nome mark from crotchet 72 to crotchet 52 for 'Nimrod' in
1903. Elgar scored the Variations between 5 and 19 February
1899, fast work even for him. At that point, there had been

[7]   F. Sparshott, *Portraits in Music* (London, 1933), p. 238.
[8]   To Jaeger, 13 March 1899.

no mention of any 'enigma'. On 21 February, encouraged by Jaeger and Parry, he sent the full score to Hans Richter's concert manager, Nathaniel Vert. Vert forwarded it to Richter in Vienna, with news of the success of *Caractacus*. In late March Richter agreed to produce the Variations. Elgar made a piano arrangement (which would sell well) and proofs of that were sent to C. A. Barry, Richter's programme note writer. In a letter to Elgar of 10 April 1899 Barry referred to 'Enigma', which was seemingly its first mention. Elgar would not explain: 'Its "dark saying" must be left unguessed ... through and over the whole set another and larger theme "goes", but is not played.' On the autograph of the piano reduction, now at Stanford University, there is no mention of 'Enigma'. It first appeared over the theme itself, written in Jaeger's hand in pencil on the autograph full score. Only when Novello received that back from Richter on 8 April would Jaeger have had the chance to write it. Elgar was in London between 17 and 22 March, when Jaeger had seen the piano score. Was it possibly some comment by Richter in a letter, or by Jaeger, that gave rise to the 'enigma'? News about it got around before the first performance. It has even been suggested that the whole thing was a publicity ploy.

So the 'enigma' was not born with the theme or the variations, which makes it unlikely that Elgar had some musical counterpoint in mind when he was extemporizing. Dozens of solutions have been proposed, summarised up to September 1994 in the *Elgar Society Journal* of that date, and considered in 1999 by Julian Rushton and Patrick Turner.[9] It has generally come to be accepted that Elgar meant the theme to represent himself, using it, for instance, in place of a signature in a letter to Dorabella.

As to '* * *', Elgar's letter of 16 February 1899 to F. G. Edwards, editor of *The Musical Times*, shows that he recognized the 'ill-luck attaching to the number'. He placed Lady Mary Lygon's initials, LML, over a sketch, but doubts were raised

---

[9] Julian Rushton, *Elgar: 'Enigma' Variations* (Cambridge, 1999); Patrick Turner, *Elgar's 'Enigma' Variations* (London, 1999).

when he remarked that he could not seek her permission as the lady was on a sea voyage. But Lady Mary took tea with the Elgars on the day he finished the full score, when he could have asked her. Ernest Newman suggested in 1956 that the depth of feeling in Variation XIII revealed a parting which had 'torn the very heart out of' Elgar, and did not accord with a social relationship. (Newman did not discern this in 1906.[10]) Wulstan Atkins, Ivor's son, then revealed[11] the significance of Elgar's early love for Helen Weaver, who had emigrated to New Zealand; some Elgarians are convinced that hers was the sad memory Elgar had in mind.

After the double-bar at the close, Elgar wrote 'Bramo assai, poco spero, nulla chieggio', the famous line of Tasso's *Gerusalemme Liberato* (canto 2, stanza 130), with the poet's third-person verbs altered to first-person. He translated it as 'I essay much, I hope little, I ask nothing'. Elizabeth Barrett Browning (1806–61) had used the Tasso line unaltered as a modest disclaimer in her ambitious *Essay on Mind* (1826). In 1695, the year of Tasso's death, Gervase Markham prefaced his *Most Honourable Tragedy of Sir Richard Grenville* with his first-person rewording of the contemporary poet's line: the rewording that Elgar used. Markham's poem was reprinted in 1871; Tennyson's ballad *The Revenge* followed in 1878; and Stanford's very successful setting thereof in 1886. From the reprint of Markham's poem Elgar may well have found his own 'modest disclaimer'. He repeated it at the close of *The Music Makers*.

The first performance of the Variations was in London, on 19 June 1899, at St James's Hall. Richter, who had given the premières of Wagner (the first complete *Ring*), Brahms, and Dvořák, conducted. He had since 1885 been director of the Birmingham Festival and knew that Elgar had already been invited to compose the principal work for 1900. The Finale was shorter then than it is now. Jaeger, Elgar's champion but also his fiercest, most perceptive critic, wrote telling him that some people found the ending ineffective. Elgar at first resisted,

---

[10] E. Newman, *Elgar* (London, 1906), p. 147.

[11] E. Wulstan Atkins, *The Elgar–Atkins Friendship* (London, 1984), pp. 477–9.

pointing out that he had exhausted the key of G, then he
lengthened the Finale by ninety-six bars, quoting Longfellow
on the autograph: 'Great is the art of beginning, but greater
the art of ending'. The original ending was used for Frederick
Ashton's evocative ballet (1968), in which all the characters
came to life.

The Variations quickly found fame. Parry told Landon
Ronald the next day that it was 'the finest work I have listened
to for years', and wrote to congratulate Elgar on his 'brilliant
success'. In 1901 Julius Buths conducted it in Düsseldorf on
7 February, and Stanford conducted it at the Royal College
of Music on 13 December. George Bernard Shaw, in 1920,
remembered that on first hearing it he'd said simply ' "Whew!"
I knew we had got it at last.'

On 21 March 1899 the Elgars left 'Forli' and moved to a more
commodious house on the hillside at West Malvern. They called
it 'Craeg Lea', an anagram of C[arice], A[lice] and E[dward]
Elgar. Carice was sent as a boarder at Rosa Burley's school, The
Mount, along the road in Great Malvern, lest she disturb Elgar's
composing. In about 1899 Elgar came to know Leo Francis
Howard Schuster (1852–1922), Frank to his friends. He was
a wealthy and discerning patron of the arts, who entertained
elegantly at his Westminster home and at 'The Hut', on the
Thames near Maidenhead.

1899 Sea Pictures, Op. 37

In October 1898 the Norwich Festival asked Elgar for a short
choral work for 1899, but he immediately became involved
in the Variations. Then in January Norwich suggested instead
a *scena* for a soloist. Already engaged was the young contralto
Clara Butt, who in 1892 had achieved success as Gluck's
Orpheus in an RCM production. Elgar, perhaps thinking that
one theme had provided him with a focus for fourteen variations, proposed one subject to bind together five songs (he

had heard Berlioz's *Les nuits d'été* in 1881). Two years previously he had set his wife's poem 'Lute Song'. This inland composer revised it as 'In Haven', and chose four more poems with sea associations to go with it.

In 'Sea Slumber-Song' (Roden Noel, 1834–94) the sea sings a comforting lullaby. The first bar shows freedom in its oblique harmony, reaching the tonic E minor only in its second half, the rising and falling strings like a breaking wave reaching its crest. As often with Elgar, the idea is two-stranded, the alto part falling against the rising strings. The 'mother' sings in E major; the *ostinato* pedal has the drag and pull of deep ocean swells flecked by harps and a sponge-headed gong. There is a nice touch when the violinist composer illustrates the elfin violins with a harp arpeggio. Alice's 'In Haven' was subtitled 'Capri' in memory of a holiday there before she met Edward. His delicate strophic setting, with muted strings and *pizzicato*, clings closely to C major, reflecting the constancy of 'love alone will stand', 'will last', 'will stay'.

The rising chords that introduce 'Sabbath Morning at Sea' by Elizabeth Barrett Browning anticipate something grand and elevating (Elgar first set them down in 1883, see p. 6). The *quasi rit.* of the first verse is repeated a semitone higher for the fourth. 'He shall assist me to look higher', sings Browning, and Elgar obeys, repeating the phrase up a third, bringing back the breaking wave of the first song, and setting the final words to the opening aspiring chords. It is very nearly a great song, anticipating the solemnity of Mahler's 'Um Mitternacht' (Mahler conducted *Sea Pictures* and the Variations in the New York season 1910–11). But in Elgar's song there is something too effortful and self-conscious.

The land 'Where corals lie' (Richard Garnett, 1835–1906) lures the singer away even from the beloved's lips and smile. The open fifths give a touch of exoticism, and the insistence on B minor is obsessive. The final turn to D major, then the B major cadence, suggest fulfilment. In the last song, 'The Swimmer' struggles through rough seas where wrecks abound. Memories of fairer days bring back the happy C major section of the first song. But the rhetorical declamation and the strenuous tune return as the swimmer braves the angry sea to gain the place where 'no light wearies and no love wanes'. Is that a mortal or an immortal shore? Knowing that the poet Lindsay Gordon (1833–70) took his life, and that Elgar talked of suicide, some commentators have heard a death-wish in these songs, a desire to seek oblivion in the ocean. What is without doubt is that the scoring of the set is as delicate and colourful as anything in the 'Enigma' Variations, and that the prettiest, simplest songs are the best.

Clara Butt, then twenty-six and dressed like a mermaid, according to Elgar who conducted, gave the first performance in Norwich on 5 October 1899. She recorded the popular 'Where corals lie' in 1920 under Hamilton Harty.

1900 The Dream of Gerontius, Op. 38

Elgar was forty-one when in November 1898 the Birmingham Triennial Festival Committee, on the strength of *Caractacus*, asked him to compose a sacred choral work for the 1900 meeting. For his subject he considered the teaching of Christ's Church (to become *The Apostles* and *The Kingdom*), but realized he did not have the time to make his own text. He settled on John Henry Newman's poem *The Dream of Gerontius*. His previous choral works, though they might have a private significance, have little outward relevance to his life and times: tales of medieval knights, Norse legends, and ancient Druids. *The Light of Life* dealt with an action, an outward sign of Christ's power, and the text for that was put together for the occasion.

The Dream of Gerontius tells of a man's death, a man old (so the name 'Gerontius' indicates) and sick with fear and fore-boding, who rouses himself for a passionate declaration of his Christian faith before being committed with full ceremonial to the next world. Then, in imagination, but according to the tenets of his Church, he is escorted by his Guardian Angel to his Judgment, hearing on the way the lost souls in hell and the choirs of angels. Finally he is placed in Purgatory. Since no-one can escape death, or – except through faith – know whether it is an end or a beginning, the subject is universal. Part I of *Gerontius* will happen to everyone. Members of Elgar's Church have praised the vision of Part II. To non-believers, the imagery is hardly less powerful. *Gerontius* is one of the great quest stories. The journey is one of discovery, into the unknown or the deep unconscious. Such a subject can leave no-one unmoved.

Cardinal Newman's poem stood for the Church's authority and for the value of revelation in an age in which questioning intellectuals were turning towards free-thinking rationalism. Its beauty and originality were recognized in spite of the fact that in 1891 it was deemed among poems of the nineteenth century 'the least in sympathy with the temper of the present time'.[12] Some people may find its mingling of pain and ecstasy distasteful. But for Elgar to choose it was a decision of moral force, an act of courage: a personal identification. Being born a Roman Catholic in a staunchly Protestant part of England was one of the elements that combined to make him feel an outsider in local society. He confessed on at least one occasion to anxiety and embarrassment in admitting to Catholicism. According to Rosa Burley, he had been passed over – or at any rate felt he had been passed over – for several jobs, because of his faith. Catholicism had cost him dear. His father hated all religions: 'the absurd superstition and playhouse mummery of the Papist; the cold and formal ceremonies of the Church of England; the bigotry and rank hypocrisy of the Weslyan'.[13] Ernest Newman roundly declared that artistic sympathy with *Gerontius* should not 'be affected in any way by one's opinions of the tenets he holds'.[14] Even those whose temperament is alien to the thought and mood of *Gerontius* cannot fail to admit its greatness. In publicly coming to grips with his Catholicism, with a subject of such magnitude, treated from a viewpoint that involved his personal life and forced him to turn into an artistic asset that which had been a social drawback, Elgar created his most intense, most individual score. It was a moment when his will and capacity, his religious and Romantic fervour, were perfectly matched.

Newman (1801–90) wrote the poem in 1865, twenty years after he was received into the Church of Rome. He had

[12] Richard H. Hutton, *Cardinal Newman* (London, 1891), p. 244.
[13] J. N. Moore, *Edward Elgar: A Creative Life* (Oxford, 1984), p. 6.
[14] E. Newman, *Elgar* (London, 1906), p. 57.

been profoundly affected by the death of his fellow Oratorian, John Joseph Gordon. Newman's brother suggested he should write a poem in the manner of Aeschylean drama, undidactic but on a Christian subject. *The Dream of Gerontius* went through many editions, and gained even wider circulation when it became known that it had sustained General Charles 'Chinese' Gordon during the eleven-month siege of Khartoum in the Sudan. Gordon marked passages that gave him particular spiritual comfort. When he and his garrison were slaughtered in 1885, he became a national hero (Strachey's *Eminent Victorians*, which included an iconoclastic chapter on Gordon, was not published till 1918). Gordon's underlinings were printed in several Catholic journals. Elgar copied the markings into his own copy, and in 1887 lent it to his future wife when her mother died. Though he said he 'had the advantage of knowing those portions',[15] it is striking how many of them Elgar the composer omitted, however moved Elgar the man might have been. Possibly the fact that Gordon was an Anglican may have encouraged him to think the poem would have more than just Catholic appeal. On the other hand, William Bennett, who sang in the first performance, remembered that not more than half-a-dozen of the three hundred and fifty choristers (who had single-line choral parts only) had heard of Newman's poem.[16]

The words are not familiar from the Bible, and they are not a Mass, not a *Requiem*, not a *Stabat Mater*. In choosing Newman's poem Elgar was setting religious words that had never previously been set – except by the Revd Bacchus Dykes (1823–76) in his hymn 'Richmond' ('Praise to the Holiest in the height'). Poor Elgar: as he said, 'every ass I meet' hoped he would keep the Ancient and Modern tune. Apart from that, the words were not known through previous compositions. However, the poem had been 'soaking' in Elgar's mind long before he set to work in earnest during January 1990. Many of the phrases

[15] *Musical Times*, October 1900, p. 648.

[16] W. Bennett, 'A Memory from the Choir', *The Monthly Musical Record*, February 1933.

would have recalled the spiritual memories of his childhood
and organist days: the intercessions, the quotations from the
offices, and from the ninetieth psalm. The Recommendation
of a Departing Soul in the *Manual of Prayers* would have been
said at the bedside of a sick or dying man. As the organist,
the young Elgar would not necessarily have been present at
a deathbed, but two of his brothers (Harry and Jo) had died
by the time he was nine, so he may have heard these prayers
said in his own home. Also, Elgar helped Father Knight at St
George's in arranging non-liturgical services. 'One such service
over which Edward took special pains was the Bona Mors,
devotions for a good death.'[17]

Newman follows the Latin words, but in his own translation. 'Job from all his multiform and fell distress' is grander
than 'Job from all his sufferings'; and 'Moses from the land of
bondage and despair' grander than 'Moses from the hands of
Pharaoh, King of the Egyptians'. Newman is selective, giving
the words an even more poetic rhythm, often rhyming them.
He reordered the prayers, to end with 'Go forth in the name',
which the priest would recite at the moment of death. 'Sanctus
fortis, sanctus deus', with which Gerontius begins his expression of faith, is part of the Good Friday service, in the Veneration of the Cross. So the quotations in Newman's poem would
touch Elgar at a deep level. He was, consciously or not, tapping
into tradition, rather as Vaughan Williams later did in *Pilgrim's
Progress* by using Tallis's tune; and as Britten did in *Noye's Fludde*,
when Dykes's hymn 'Eternal Father, strong to save' comes
soaring in at the height of the storm.

Newman's poem is in seven sections, nine hundred lines
long. For his Part I, Gerontius on his deathbed, Elgar cut
Newman's first section only slightly. He condensed the six
further sections drastically, reducing them to three hundred
lines. Even so, he worried that the conversations between the
Angel and the Soul might seem 'wearisome ... I went thro'
the libretto with a priest from the Oratory & we cut out all

[17] J. N. Moore, *Edward Elgar: A Creative Life* (Oxford, 1984), p. 113.

we thought possible', he told Jaeger.[18] Newman's stanzas offer many differing line-lengths and ingenious rhyme schemes. The metre of the poem changes with the thought. The confident assertions of faith have the simplest structures: 'Firmly I believe and truly' and 'Praise to the Holiest' are in four-line verses with predictable rhymes - as if four-square in faith. But the anxious Assistants have a more complicated rhyme scheme. Lines one and seven rhyme ('past' and 'last'), two and eight ('ire' and 'fire'); so do lines three, four, five and six ('dying', 'complying', denying', 'relying'), the double rhymes drooping and pleading in rhythm as well as in meaning.

  Gerontius is through-composed with a break only at the transition between this world and the next. Gone are the old divisions. Elgar knew full well what he was doing. While he was composing *Gerontius*, he wrote: 'The modern methods of writing music destined for the stage are the outcome of the symphony. For instance, the second act of *Tristan* may be viewed in this light as a symphonic movement very much extended, and the tendency nowadays is to seek for continuity in the expression of ideas in place of a patchwork of such accepted "forms" as the duet, aria and so forth.'[19] By 1900 he had made thoroughly his own the free-flowing but detailed system of leitmotifs, which in *Gerontius* refer to abstractions and emotions (Angel and Demons are after all themselves abstractions) and so can effectively pull past and present together. The dramatic Prelude, charged with grandeur, is marked *Lento, mistico*. Elgar is careful not to detract from the main work. He concentrates on motifs from Part I, with no references at this point to the afterlife. The shattering climax when the 'Prayer' theme is thundered out at cue 9 never reappears. The majestic Committal melody, devised for the never-written Gordon Symphony (see p. 46), is more fully developed in the Prelude than when it occurs in the ritual. So both these themes carry added weight and significance in their later context.

  First heard is the 'Judgment' motif, a balanced and self-contained passage. It is a melancholy unison of muted violas,

[18]   7 May 1900.
[19]   For a Worcestershire Philharmonic Society concert on 5 May 1900.

clarinets, and bassoons, remote and impersonal so as to strike awe into any listener. The next motifs are brief. 'Fear' rises gropingly in sequences up four octaves over a bass that slides down eight semitones. 'Prayer' is a sustained serene chant, 'Sleep' is the feverish sleep of a sick man, with uneasy chords tossing over 'Fear' on a pedal bass. The anguished 'Miserere' is again built over 'Fear'. Though each motif has a strong profile, they can be redistributed and their order changed. 'Fear' is followed first by 'Prayer', then is inserted into 'Sleep', then linked to 'Miserere'. 'Sleep' runs into 'Miserere', later into 'Fear'. 'Despair' leads to the violent 'Prayer' climax, then to 'Committal'. The 'Fear' and 'Prayer' motifs, though brief, modulate inside their own length, ending in ways that can move in different harmonic directions. For instance, the twelve bars between cue 2 and cue 4 begin and end in D major. But in between, the 'Fear' and 'Prayer' motifs come to rest on chords of B major, E flat major (first inversion), A flat major, G major, and B major (first inversion), all threaded on to the half-bar sequences of 'Fear'. The fluid tonality of the open-ended motifs allows Elgar to seize the poem's quick-changing feelings. The motifs illumine the text, but are even more important as organic musical structure.

Though the opening 'Judgment' theme seems set apart, its thematic influence is strong. The opening semitone is prominent in the motifs of dread: 'Fear', 'Miserere', 'Despair'. Its five conjunct notes in bars three and four (Ex. 2.2a) shape 'Prayer' (2.2b), and are inverted in 'Committal' (2.2c). 'Committal', the grandest of all Elgar's march tunes, is rhythmically subtle. Its first eight bars are extended to twelve at their repeat, then extended further in a dying fall that ends with an awesome vibrato gong stroke.

For the convenience of publishers and programme planners, *Gerontius* was listed as an oratorio. Elgar never liked that, and the word does not appear on the title-page. Above all, he wanted to avoid 'that dreadful term' sacred cantata. He emphatically did not want the music approached in an affectedly pious attitude. He stressed that Gerontius was 'a man like us and not a priest or a saint, but a sinner, a repentant one of course but still no end of a worldly man in his life, and now brought to

Ex. 2.2

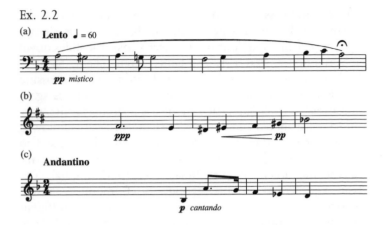

book!'[20] This is the death and resurrection of an Everyman, *l'homme moyen sensuel*, about whose earthly life we learn only what his music implies. The role of Gerontius is both taxing and rewarding to sing, wide-compassed and lyrical, but at times needing a Verdian drive. Ernest Newman (1906) among others commented that the part shows an expressiveness new for Elgar. But the long tenor solo 'And King Olaf heard the cry' in *King Olaf* approaches it. Gerontius's first exhausted entry, 'Jesu, Maria, I am near to death' (cue 22), warms to the confident curve of 'And Thou, Thou art calling me' (Jaeger's 'Christ's Peace'[21]). In 'Sanctus, fortis' Gerontius sings 'Manhood taken by the Son' to the same phrase, which the orchestra repeats and generously expands (see Ex. 1.7b). The sketches show that having the oboe play it a few bars later over 'Manhood crucified' was an afterthought – how it must have pierced him! The phrase also infiltrates the choruses, woven in as part of the fabric. In the 'Be merciful' chorus (from cue 37), it comes first as inner or lower parts, then rises to the sopranos for 'Save him in the day of doom'.

Elgar's diligently refined his ideas. In Gerontius' first solo, Newman set the prayers in brackets ('Jesu, have mercy! Mary, pray for me!') as formal petitions between Gerontius' admis-

---

[20]   28 August 1900.

[21]   A. J. Jaeger, *Analytical & Descriptive Notes* (London, 1900).

sions of fear. Elgar first set all the words over the 'Prayer' theme. In the final composition only the sentences in brackets are sung over the 'Prayer' theme. Writing to Jaeger on 28 August 1900, he said 'I didn't give this "prayer" theme to Gerontius too plainly – solidly – 'cos he wanders: rather[.] If he'd been a priest he wd. have sung or said it as a climax, but as he represents ME when ill he doesn't – he remembers his little Churchy prayey music in little snatches, – See?' And so he decided to reserve the 'Prayer' theme for the bracketed supplications.

In 'Firmly I believe and truly', a versified recital of the Creed, Elgar casts the regular trochaic rhyming verse in triple time, playing the verbal and musical stresses against each other. His early draft for this was surprisingly mild and bland. He composed a stepwise vocal part over the 'Prayer' theme, which would have badly over-worked it. The structure demanded an independent solo here. Finally he set the words as if willing himself to believe them; it as much a straining after faith as a profession of it. In his most desperate cry ('miserere, Judex meus') the harmonies lurch sickeningly down chromatic consecutives. At 'I trust and hope most fully' alien chords strain violently against a plain major triad – ambiguous music for affirmation.

Gerontius is not frightened by physical pain and weakness so much as by a feeling of dissolution –'this strange innermost abandonment', 'that sense of ruin which is worse than pain'. The directions to the singer confirm the emotional drive. In the vocal score can be found: p. 15 *risoluto*, p. 24 *sempre con molto esaltazione*, p. 26 *più agitato*, p. 29 *piangendo*, p. 31 *gemendo*, p. 32 *agitato*, p. 33 *disperato*, p. 37 *plintivo*, p. 38 *mistico*, p. 39 *estinto*. Much of the music had its roots in Elgar's own situation. By temperament he was shy and depressive, needing constant encouragement and support. That made it hard for him to grow into a rounded personality, with the opposing facets of his feelings wholly in touch with each other. His letters show wide swings of mood and defensive cover-ups. As an artist he could make use of his real feelings, applied to deeper concepts, and with a violence that could be formally contained.

How well he understood the spacious acoustics of the great cathedrals, once Roman Catholic, but in his day Anglican. The

first entry of the unaccompanied semi-chorus is wonderfully affecting: Gerontius' friends, around his bed, say a 'Kyrie
eleison' in answer to his anguished 'So pray for me, my friends,
who have not strength to pray'. A *fugato* is apt here because the
words are a chain of intercessions, and each entering voice
calls on a different holy power (Holy Mary, All holy Angels,
etc.). The unity of thought behind the diverse appeals is musically realized. So it is in the litany at cue 64, calling on Noe,
Job, Moses, and David, which so simply conjures up a timeless
ritual. Jaeger states Elgar here 'used an ancient tone'. On Elgar's
sketch for this there is the desperate plea: 'Rescue? my this
Kyrie' (a reference to 'Rescue him ...' at cue 63)'. He identifies
the chant as the 'De profundis', and copied out a Victorian
version of it, barred, and harmonized with a proper perfect
cadence (Ex. 2.3).

Ex. 2.3

On 20 February 1900 he wrote to Hubert Leicester, now
director of the choir at St George's, in Worcester, asking to
borrow 'the old Blue cloth covered book – large 8ve. I think
pubd. by Burns which used to be at the Church: an odd volume
containing some Gregorian things (we did the Te Deum)
& Benediction services.' In the 1880s they could have sung
Example 2.3 at St George's. It might even have been Elgar's
own harmonization. What matters is the use he now made of
it. Below the Amen in his sketch he suggested 'canonette', and
by adding it helped to turn a pleasant Amen into a sublime
one.

'Into Thy hands' sings Gerontius, to an unfinished phrase.
From the lonely death to the universality of priestly trombones,
hieratical Latin, and a chant-like monotone, 'Proficiscere'. The

chorus takes up 'Go forth in the name' then, over pedal points and weaving, crossing strings, spreads as though filling lofty spaces, then thins and fades in a beautiful metaphor of Gerontius' soul rising to heaven.

Gerontius was written down in a smallish house, part of the conventional Malvern society. But much of Elgar's inspiration came in the open air, in the woods, or on the banks of the river he loved so much, the Teme. The bed of the Teme has rocky outcrops, where one can watch a fixed pattern on the water around a rock in the everflowing stream. Some such image may have shaped the Elysian opening of Part II. For strings only, diatonic, shifting between F major and D minor, it perfectly presents refreshment and stillness. For much of the celestial dialogue between the Soul and the Angel Elgar composed the accompaniment first in ink, fitting in the vocal parts after in pencil. Their music has a touch of courtesy that resolves naturally into a duet, the only ensemble for the soloists in the work. Elgar played the entrance of the Angel to the Jaegers at their London home as early as 25 February 1900. Alongside the sketch for this, 'my work is done', he wrote the heartfelt comment 'I wish it were'.

The Demons' Chorus is an audacious intellectual display of the 'mind bold and independent'. It contains a double fugue, the chorus having its own fugal exposition starting two bars after the orchestra. The brutally short lines are tightly packed with invective. Some critics find both Newman's and Elgar's Demons less than convincing in any but a superb performance; it has been suggested that Elgar might have cut the words and composed a diabolical orchestral scherzo. Liszt in his *Faust* Symphony gives Mephistopheles a brilliant *fugato* on a syncopated chromatic subject. Similarly Elgar gives his demons a brilliant *fugato* on a syncopated chromatic subject. In both Liszt and Elgar the effect is sardonic, disruptive: the spirit of negation.

'Praise to the holiest' in Part II is, dynamically, the mirror image of the chorus that ends Part I. It begins with the women's voices gradually swinging down the registers until the whole chorus thrillingly rings out 'Praise' in what Elgar called 'the great Blaze'. His treatment of Newman's words here is compressed and economical. Newman wrote thirty-six stanzas for five 'Choirs of Angelicals'. Elgar floats the opening line as if from on high, treats the next four verses quickly at spoken speed, cuts many of the next, and brings in the full chorus at cue 74 with the stanzas of Newman's Fourth Choir, ending with the final verse of Newman's Third Choir. Elgar's first thought for 'And that a higher gift than grace' was the theme that ended up as 'to the old of the new world's worth' in *The Music Makers*. 'Praise to the Holiest' needed at that point something harmonically stable and neutral, exactly what Elgar's second thoughts, those pages of pedal, point give it (cue 80). The Angel of the Agony's intercession, recalling Christ's own death, reaches the point of extreme dissonance in rhythmic and harmonic dislocations. The ghastly chords that introduce this were originally composed for Judas – Elgar had sent them to Jaeger, begging him not to 'let on'!

In April 1900 Elgar was adamant that 'none of the "action" takes place in the presence of God ... The Soul says "I go before my God" but we don't we stand outside.' By June Jaeger knew the score well enough to chide Elgar for 'shirking' the supreme climax. He begged for a 'few gloriously great and effulgent orchestral chords'. Stung, Elgar at first defended himself, then responded with the mighty sequence, built from the Judgment theme, chords pressing eagerly forward, the bass dragging back in terror, that leads to the crash when 'for one moment' every instrument should exert its fullest force. The impact of the blinding glance of God is the searing force of his reaction: 'Take me away' to the 'Hora novissima est' theme with a top A. An inadvertent result is that the Angel's comment 'for the soul is safe, consumed yet quickened by the glance of God' is strictly speaking out of the sequence of action, because it comes before the great chords. Finally the Angel bids Farewell to the Soul in a compassionate theme, 'aloof from things mundane' as Jaeger said, layered between the austere male chorus and echoes of 'Praise to the Holiest': a serene, fulfilling valediction.

The score is the first in English choral music to raise the orchestra from accompaniment to equal expressive partner with the voices. Much of Elgar's invention came to him fully clothed in orchestral sound, even though he first wrote in short or piano score, and then worked, usually against time, on the orchestration. The awe-inspiring sequence of chords at 'strange innermost abandonment' is there in the sketches as the fifteen-part chords, and alongside Elgar has scribbled each group of strings 'divisi into 3', exactly as it is finally scored.

The first performance, on 3 October 1900 during the Birmingham Festival, was sadly inadequate. Swinnerton Heap, who was training the choir, died suddenly aged only fifty-three on 11 June. The elderly William Stockley (who had been the admirable chorus-master for forty years) was called from retirement and was out of his depth. Elgar had been late in settling his subject, and everyone had underestimated the time needed for copying, engraving, learning and rehearsing so complicated a work. Richter, who had given the first perform-ance of the Variations to general acclaim, received the full score of *Gerontius* the night before the sole London orchestral rehearsal. There was only one combined rehearsal at which Elgar, every nerve stretched, lost his temper. In the perform-ance Plunket Greene (who at sixty-nine made Lieder record-ings of consummate artistry) sang the Angel of the Agony's solo a semitone flat. The choir lost pitch. Richter referred to this in his inscription in Elgar's score: 'Let drop the Chorus, let drop everybody – but let not droop the wings of your Genius.' Vaughan Williams, in the audience, thought Plunket Greene had 'lost his voice' but that the Angel, Marie Brema, 'had none to lose', and that Edward Lloyd, months away from retirement, sang Gerontius like 'a Stainer anthem, in the correct tenor atti-tude with one foot slightly withdrawn'.[22] That performance has gone down in the history of English music as a black day. Richter admitted later: 'I have a gimlet that bores into my fore-head, and that gimlet is Gerontius.'[23]

In spite of it all the quality of the music was recognized by many present. Jaeger had persuaded Julius Buths, the conductor of the Lower Rhine Festival, to attend. He was so impressed that he translated *Gerontius* himself, and put on two performances in

[22] M. Kennedy, *The Works of Ralph Vaughan Williams* (Oxford, 1964), p. 389.
[23] C. Fifield, *True Artist and True Friend: Hans Richter* (Oxford, 1993).

Düsseldorf in December 1901 and May 1902. At the second, Richard Strauss made his famous speech, toasting Elgar as the 'first English progressivist'. There is a tendency to place *Gerontius* as the highest peak of the English choral festival tradition – which of course it was (always remembering *Belshazzar's Feast*, *Hymnus paradisi*, the *War Requiem*, *The Vision of St Augustine*). It is also the meeting point of the English choral and German Romantic movements, to be set alongside Schumann's, Liszt's, Berlioz's and Busoni's Faust music; Wagner's *Parsifal*; Mahler's Resurrection and Eighth symphonies; and Strauss's *Tod und Verklärung*. Had Elgar been born a German, he might well have set passages from Goethe's *Faust*, the poem of the quest for immortality that inspired and challenged so many nineteenth-century artists. Jaeger, in describing the Angel's Farewell, quotes (without giving the source) from the Chorus Mysticus of *Faust* Part II, the 'ever-womanly' that 'draws us onwards'. *Gerontius* and *Parsifal* have much in common. Another comparison might be with the restless chromaticism and augmented harmony of Liszt's *Faust* Symphony, though there is no evidence that Elgar heard it until May 1902. In the opening of *Faust* and at cue 2 in *Gerontius* the actual sound-world is similar: muted rising strings answered by woodwind; the whole repeated. More significant: both string passages contradict their own tonality as they go. The Lizst outlines a series of augmented triads; the Elgar is a series of side-slipping chords over a chromatic bass. Both dissolve the classical major–minor system. Both insinuate destruction. Both give an effect of uncertainty, of the unknown.

The first London performance of *The Dream of Gerontius* was on 6 June 1903, in Westminster Cathedral, the most important Roman Catholic church in England. Designed by the Catholic architect J. F. Bently, it was begun in 1895, and in 1903 was still unconsecrated. Elgar conducted, choosing the North Staffordshire Chorus, and Ludwig Wüllner and Muriel Foster, both of whom had impressed him at the Düsseldorf performances. Gervase Elwes, himself to become a noted Gerontius, thought that Wüllner – who had begun his career as an actor – was over-dramatic and had too strong a German accent, but Elgar admired his intelligence and brains. Frangcon-Davies was the baritone (the following year Elgar wrote the preface to his

Singing of the Future). Stanford, thinking probably of the cathedral's extremely wide, bare nave, had warned Elgar ahead that the acoustics might be bad; but Parry, writing after the performance, found the building 'very imposing indeed and good for sound too'.

At the head of the autograph (now in the Birmingham Oratory) Elgar placed the initials for Ad maiorem Dei gloriam. At the end he quoted from Ruskin's essay 'Of Kings' Treasuries' (in *Sesame and Lilies*): 'This is the best of me; for the rest, I ate, and drank, and slept, loved and hated, like another; my life was as the vapour, and is not; but this I saw and knew: this, if anything of mine, is worth your memory.' In 1886 he had been given five Ruskin volumes, including *Sesame and Lilies* and *The Seven Lamps of Architecture*, by E. W. Whinfield, a Worcester neighbour. 'Of Kings' Treasuries' is in praise of books and reading, and develops into a fierce polemical discussion on the low standards and philistinism of the day. Ruskin distinguishes between books 'of the hour' and books 'of all time'. In the latter the author has 'something to say'; ... 'so far as he knows, no one has yet said it'. More colloquial, no less illuminating, is Elgar's comment in a letter to Jaeger: 'I've written it out of my insidest inside'.[24]

The work's Catholicism only briefly detracted from its success. For the first performance the audience had Jaeger's *Analytical and Descriptive Notes*. Whether or not Jaeger (who described himself as 'rather an Agnostic than anything else'[25]) knew how closely Newman followed the Roman rite, he would not have stressed it for fear of alienating a mainly Protestant audience. It did concern him. He wrote to Elgar in June 1900: 'There is a lot of Joseph & Mary about the work; Very proper for a Roman Catholic lying at death's door to sing about, but likely to frighten some d----d fools of Protestants.' Elgar replied robustly that of course it would 'frighten the low church party ... them as don't like it can be damned in their own way'.[26] 'The poem', he said, 'must on no account be touched.' He did, however,

[24] To Jaeger, 20 June 1900.
[25] K. Allen, *August Jaeger: Portrait of Nimrod* (Aldershot, 2000), p. 5.
[26] J. N. Moore, *Elgar and his Publishers*, Vol. 1 (Oxford, 1987), p. 189.

with the consent of Newman's Trustee, agree to omissions, not alterations, for the 1902 performance in Worcester Cathedral.

Much of this will have no resonance for today's younger Catholics. The *Rituale Romanum*, the Mass, the Prayers, were revised by the Vatican II Council in the 1960s, and are now no longer in Latin but in simple vernacular words for the congregation's active participation. Newman's references will be no longer familiar, whatever they might have meant to Elgar. He told Rosa Burley that he was afraid the insistence on the doctrine of purgatory would prejudice the success of *Gerontius*. On his score he set a quotation from Virgil, 'Quae lucis miseris tam dira cupido?',[27] Aeneas' question, which prompts his father Anchises to describe 'purgatory'. In the thirty-nine articles of the Church of England the twenty-second states that the 'Romish Doctrine of Purgatory ... is a fond thing vainly invented, and grounded upon no warranty of Scripture, but rather repugnant to the Word of God'. Purgatory is not a place of probation, from which the soul may go either to Heaven or Hell. All souls admitted to Purgatory are bound for Heaven sooner or later, and are beyond the reach of sin. So it is purgative rather than penal. That explains the Angel's otherwise puzzling first words to the Soul of Gerontius, spoken before the Soul's judgment: 'my work is done ... for the crown is won ... and saved is he'. It is perhaps strange that the Angel, referred to as He and addressed as My Lord, is sung by a woman. In shortening the poem Elgar omits most references to 'he'. Obviously, he wished to make the Angel sexless, but must also have had in mind the Birmingham committee. Novello's chairman was concerned the work had no part for Madam Albani, the favourite festival soprano of the day. (In the event Elgar cast the Angel as a mezzo, possibly wishing to avoid the suggestion of an operatic love-duet.)

The sketches in the British Library show Elgar shaping the music, trying out this and that, discarding, revising. It is rewarding to observe the creative process if it sharpens an appreciation of the finished work. An early sketch of the Prelude begins with the 'Fear' theme (cue 2) discarded from

[27] Virgil, *The Aeneid*, book vi.

the sketches for *The Light of Life* (1896). The 'Prayer' motif was originally written in April 1898 in G. R. Sinclair's Visitors' Book, to illustrate a mood of his bulldog Dan: 'He muses (on the muzzling order) *piangendo*'. At the climax of the Prelude (cue 9), when the 'Prayer' theme is given out in augmentation, *triple forte*, it was originally in four-four time, and nothing like as effective as the swinging three-four. Elgar's first idea for 'Go forth in the name' became the Nobilmente theme at cue 142 in the finale of the Second Symphony. All through the sketches he was constantly improving the word-setting, sharpening up the final profile as in the first (Ex. 2.4a) and last (2.4b) versions of 'Rouse thee, my fainting soul'.

Ex. 2.4

(a)

(b)

Elgar sent a sketch of the 'Judgment' theme, on which he wrote 'this is the very first idea of the work', to Jaeger in November 1899. Following Elgar, reproductions of this sketch are usually annotated 'first sketch'. But it is in E minor, and there is something scribbled in pencil on the upper stave. In the Prelude the first four bars are a single line in D minor. That sketch is clearly not of the opening. The 'Judgment' theme is in ink, tidy and well-spaced – Elgar's first thoughts never look like that! The sketch is surely Elgar in the process of working out cue 58 in Part II, when the Angel tells of St Francis's reception of the stigmata. The pencil scribbles are of the voice part 'There was a mortal...'. There are further examples in the sketches where Elgar uses the same method: ink for the given, pencil for the variant or the new thought.

It is difficult to discriminate between shades of religion in purely musical terms. Stanford famously said *Gerontius* 'stinks of incense'. Those who find Gerontius too self-lacerating may prefer the serene acceptance of death as part of life's cycle in Janáček's *Cunning Little Vixen*. But Elgar's appalled reaction to the wretched first performance was more that of an artist than of a devout man:

> Providence denies me a decent hearing of my work. I always said God was against art and I still believe it. I have allowed my heart to open once – it is now shut against every religious feeling, of every soft, gentle impulse, for ever.

More significant, perhaps, is the fact that once he stopped being organist of St George's he never composed any more Catholic liturgical music. *Gerontius* was the only major Catholic text he set. Vaughan Williams, an agnostic, composed his fine austere Mass in 1922 for Richard Terry; Britten composed his raw brilliant *Missa brevis* for George Malcolm in 1959, both at Westminster Cathedral. Elgar composed no Mass. But *Gerontius* has a special place and importance, not only in Elgar's output, but in music in England. It is one of the great spiritual adventures of Romantic art. As a sacred music drama, it ranks with Verdi's Requiem, *Parsifal* and the *Symphony of Psalms*.

1901 Cockaigne, Concert Overture (in London Town), Op. 40

In the weeks after the first performance of *Gerontius* Elgar revised *Froissart*, as Novello was at last printing full scores of his earlier works. He also read Langland's *Piers Plowman*, set on his own Malvern Hills. In his last letter of 1900 to Jaeger he called the poem his 'Bible, a marvellous book'. In it the narrator falls asleep and has a fair vision of the Severn valley, seeing in London only the seven deadly sins. Piers arises as the leader to Salvation, but the sleeper wakes to find himself 'meteless and moneyless on Malvern Hills'. That was the quotation Elgar set at the end of his autograph of *Cockaigne*. It echoes his response when a request came in October 1900 from the Philharmonic Society for a new orchestral work. 'What's the good of it?

Nobody else will perform the thing,' he grumbled to Jaeger. He confessed that he was at the end of his 'financial tether … I must earn money somehow – I will not go back to teaching & I think I must try some trade – coal agency or houses.'[28] Yet the new overture is among his most good-humoured works. As he described it to Joseph Bennett, who was to write the programme note: 'It calls up to my mind all the good-humour, jollity and something deeper in the way of English good fellow-ship (as it were) abiding still in our capital.'[29] 'Cockaigne' was the land of plenty, standing for an idealized London.

The Overture opens with the jollity, a *scherzando* pattering theme with the familiar rat-tat-tat rhythm (see Ex. 1.2). Is there another work (other than Beethoven's Fifth Symphony) with a pause in its second bar? No pause, however, interrupts Elgar's full flow when the theme is shortly repeated fff. That leads to a full-hearted tune marked *nobilmente* (his first printed use of the term), which had come to him one day in London's Guildhall, when 'I seemed to hear far away in the dim roof a theme, an echo of some noble melody.'[30] The tune takes a hint from Nuremberg when it is diminished to make a street urchin, though Elgar said he had the idea not from *Die Meisters-inger* but from Delibes' *Sylvia* (he had bought a vocal score on his Paris holiday of 1880). He handles the sequences in the tune ingeniously. He contracts the pattern from its fifth bar onwards so as to alter the fall of the accent. When the tune is diminished, he changes a pair of 'leaning' notes (Ex. 2.5a) into repeated notes (Ex. 2.5b), giving the urchin a stubborn cheeky air. When, *dolcissimo* at cue 11, the theme becomes dreamy and poetic, he repeats the initial two bars at the *same* pitch, then lifts them twice, each time by a third, so suggesting aspira-tion. Even without the differing scoring, accompaniment, and register, the change of character – grand, impertinent, romantic – is remarkable.

The main themes are generously intervalled, with octaves and sevenths. But much is developed from pendant or linking

[28] 26 October 1900.

[29] J. A. Westrup, *Sharps and Flats* (Oxford, 1940), pp. 93–4.

[30] MS at the Elgar Birthplace.

Ex. 2.5

(a)

(b)

ideas. The tranquil episode at cue 23 represents a visit to a peaceful church, and over it in the autograph Elgar wrote 'Braut's part' (meaning that Alice particularly liked it). Its triplet rhythm based on three descending steps seems derived from the bass line three bars after cue 2.

A military band is heralded by a great *crescendo* (cue 16), excited whirling strings, and full percussion, sleigh bells and all. Then the band's tune is blared out on cornets and trombones. Elgar was teaching himself the trombone at this time, and at cue 30 they are directed *glissez fantastico*. (The effect is comparable with the King's approach in *Falstaff*.) The out-of-tune Salvation Army band is humorous – in G flat over a pedal F, then, trying to correct itself, in A flat over a pedal G – but Elgar sets it as if in the distance, scored emptily over a low horn pedal, receding and fading, with just a wistful comment from the violins at each change of key. The effect is poignant as well as funny. (Buckley recounts Elgar's description of an 'unseen band heard at a seaside resort in Italy', the 'peep, peep' of the clarinets, the 'pom, pom' of the trombones, the rush of the trombone's chromatic scale. It would be nice to claim an influence, but alas! the Elgars had not visited Italy by 1901.[31])

Elgar worked at *Cockaigne* during February and March 1901, dedicated it 'to my many friends, the members of British orchestras', and conducted it at the Queen's Hall on 20 June 1901. He described the Overture to Jaeger as 'stout and steaky'.[32]

31   Robert J. Buckley, *Sir Edward Elgar* (London & New York, 1905), p. 39.

32   4 November 1900.

That does it less than justice. It is also impudent and romantic. Even the cheeky urchin has his sad droopy chromatic counter-subject (two bars after cue 7). For all the Overture's pageantry, what lingers in the memory are the endearing moments like that. Teased that the 'lovemaking' was not 'strictly *proper*', Elgar composed a moral coda as one of his 'japes', running Mendelssohn's Wedding March contrapuntally with the lovers' theme.

In 1899 Elgar had come to know Alfred E. Rodewald (1861–1903), a wealthy Liverpool cotton broker, who founded and conducted the Liverpool Orchestral Society. He was Richter's only conducting pupil. He and Elgar had met at the New Brighton concert organized by Granville Bantock (1868–1946). Composer, conductor, educator, Bantock became principal of the Midland Institute School of Music at Birmingham. In November 1900, at Stanford's instigation and on the strength of the Variations, Cambridge University gave Elgar his first honorary doctorate. In 1901 Elgar heard that Herbert Brewer of Gloucester had run out of time to score his oratorio *Emmaus* and was about to withdraw it from the Festival programme, Elgar, out of friendship, scored it for him.

1901–07 *Pomp and Circumstance*, Military Marches
Nos. 1, 2, 3, & 4, Op. 39

In December 1900 Elgar suggested to Sir Walter Parratt that he should set Kipling's poem 'Recessional', written for the Jubilee of 1897: 'Lo, all our pomp of yesterday/ Is one with Nineveh and Tyre'. Parratt encouraged him, but Elgar let the matter drop. Then on 1 January 1901 he sketched a quick march in A minor. Two days later he found the tune that comes 'once in a lifetime'. He wrote to Jaeger on 12 January 1901, 'Gosh! man I've got a tune in my head.' For some time he wondered whether it could be the source of the symphony he so wished to compose. But he decided against that. Then he turned to *Cockaigne*, and perhaps the march in that and the military marches fed into each other. And did Kipling's 'pomp of yesterday' bring to mind Othello's 'Pomp and Circumstance'?

When Dorabella visited the Elgars in early May he told her 'I've got a tune that will knock 'em – knock 'em flat',[33] playing her the March in D with the 'lifetime' tune that was to become 'Land of Hope and Glory'. 'What note does it begin on?' he demanded, and when she replied 'E flat', he responded 'Yah! there's a joke!' The joke is even funnier at the end, when the E flat passage heralds the grand restatement in D of the Trio tune. As in the *Imperial March* (see p. 34), the *Pomp and Circumstance* marches open with sharp jagged peremptory rhythms, then move to smooth melodies with simple direct outlines and harmony. In all of them Elgar cleverly plays on anticipation, the thrilling starts building up to the broad central tunes. The celebrated trio tune in No. 1 is supported throughout its 16 + 16 + 8 bars by a single repeated harmony to each bar, except in bar thirty-two when on the second crotchet an F sharp changes to F natural to swing it round back home. No wonder a tune of such stability has come to represent continuity and tradition! It may be less fine music than Parry's 'Jerusalem', but it has the hallmarks of a great community song: instantly memorable, easy to sing, with enough gravity to suggest ritual.

Elgar saw no reason why a quick march should not be treated on a large scale like the waltz or the polka, and declared that he looked on 'the composer's vocation as the old troubadours or bards did. In those days it was no disgrace to a man to be turned on to step in front of an army and inspire people with a song. … We are a nation of great military proclivities.'[34] In later life he cultivated the look of a military man, growing into his own image, as it were.

His marches, however, celebrate peacetime ceremonial and military pageantry. Even so, the second and third have uneasy undertones. Both are in minor keys. In No. 2 the stealthy

[33] Mrs Richard Powell, *Edward Elgar: Memories of a* Variation (London, 1937) pp 35–36.

[34] *Strand Magazine*, May 1904, pp. 543–4 (only 1 & 2 had been composed).

pattering in A minor is infiltrated by baying horns; their triplets are thematic as well as dramatic, for they forge a link with the major section. The scoring just before that – varied percussion, string harmonics, the rattling side-drum – is hair-raising. No. 3 is in C minor and though it is marked to be played 'with fire', it begins *ppp*. There is nothing blatant or aggressive in this march; rather it is stubborn and ominous, full of anxiety and suppressed emotion. The monotone *crescendo* of unison horns (again) at cues C and M is quite manic, particularly in Elgar's own recording of 1927. The cheerful fourth march is more like the first, with a grand sustained trio tune that invites words (which Alice duly provided).

The title, from Shakespeare's *Othello*, Act 3, Scene iii, smacks of Imperialism. In context, Othello, prompted by Desdemona's supposed adultery, bids farewell to 'the spirit-stirring drum, the ear-piercing fife, The Royal banner and all quality, Pride, Pomp and Circumstance of glorious war! ... Farewell, Othello's occupation's gone!' It seems unlikely that Elgar was thinking of the context, since on the score he also set a verse from 'The March of Glory', beginning 'Like a proud music that draws men on to die/ Madly upon the spears in martial ecstasy.' It is by Lord de Tabley, about whom the *Dictionary of National Biography* wrote: 'He will live as an impassioned writer who chose poetry for his medium, though not inevitably as a poet.'

Elgar dedicated the first March to Rodewald, who conducted the first two with the Liverpool Orchestral Society on 19 October 1901. At the London première three days later, by Henry Wood, 'The people simply rose and yelled ... the one and only time in the history of the Promenade concerts that an orchestral item was accorded a double encore.'[35]

1901 Incidental Music and Funeral March from Grania and Diarmid, Op. 42

The Irish writer George Moore wanted music for his new play *Diarmuid and Grania* [sic]. Maybe through Henry Wood, maybe through having heard Elgar's music at Leeds, Moore wrote to

[35] Henry Wood, *My Life of Music* (London, 1938), p. 154.

Elgar in September 1901 asking for music, particularly for the death of Diarmid: 'A moment comes when words can go no further and then I should like music to take up the emotion and to carry it on.' The play was an uneasy collaboration, 'interrupted by two quarrels, one irritable, the other acrimonious',[36] between George Moore and W. B. Yeats. Yeats recognized Moore's superior stagecraft while remaining adamant that on style he would make no concessions: the final choice of words was to be his. Such problems were sufficiently solved for the play to be produced on 21 October 1901 at the Gaiety Theatre, Dublin. Moore arranged the production with Frank Benson's company, Benson playing Diarmid, his wife playing Grania. It ran for a week, and seems never to have been revived. It had a mixed reception: Grania was found to be 'excessively French in her loves', and there were objections to English actors in Irish theatre. Yeats, who in 1903 described Elgar's music as 'wonderful, in its heroic melancholy', by 1935 could recall only 'Benson's athletic dignity in one scene and the notes of the horn in Elgar's dirge over the dead Diarmuid.'

The characters come from Irish legends about the third-century Finn, warrior and hunter, chief of the Fianna. Finn seeks to marry Grania, the king's daughter, but she elopes with the young, handsome Diarmid. Diarmid's death by a boar is foretold, and in the third act Finn and Diarmid are hunting in the forest. Grania longs for them to make peace. 'Diarmid and I could not be at peace,' replies Finn, and the stage directions tell of a distant hunting horn. Offstage, Diarmid is wounded. Finn supports him on to the stage where he begins swaying his hand as if to music. 'He hears the harp-playing of Aognhus,' says Finn, 'it is by music that he leads the dead.' Diarmid falls back, and dies.

Elgar contributed a song, 'There are seven that pull the thread', to Yeats's words, trumpet and horn calls for Acts I and II, and music for Act III, originally for small orchestra. He then published the Act III music for symphony orchestra, and dedicated it to Henry Wood, who conducted the first concert performance, on 18 January 1902. The song, with a narrow

<hr>

[36] J. C. C. Mays, *Diarmuid and Grania* (Ithaca and London, 2005), p. xxix.

compass and spare accompaniment, is touching, and could well be sung by an actress. Echoing calls for four horns open the published March. Then comes a haunting clarinet phrase – a 'wailing' Moore called it – over harp accompaniment. The March itself begins with one of Elgar's double themes, in Aeolian A minor. The figure of falling octaves, also in the song, accompanied attempts to get water to the wounded Diarmid. The C major trio tune, though characteristic, is not one of Elgar's best, but a vibrating gong stroke marks the death of Diarmid (as it did of Gerontius), and a grand central climax is built from the clarinet melody, again over 'the harp-playing of Aognhus'. Writing to Jaeger, Elgar called the march 'big & weird'. The stage directions read: 'A great man is dead ... all his comrades must mourn him ... see to his burning that it may be worthy of him ... gather the harpers and gather the women that his funeral songs may be well sung ... carry him gently for he was well-beloved when alive.'

Moore felt that 'Elgar must have seen the primeval forest as he wrote, and the tribe moving among the fallen leaves, oak-leaves, hazel-leaves, for the world began with oak and hazel.'[37] He tried to persuade Elgar to develop the music as an opera. (Hamish McCunn's Diarmid had been produced at Covent Garden in 1897.) Even in 1914 Moore wrote, 'I can no longer believe that you were wise from refraining from writing an opera.'

1902 Dream Children, Op. 43

In January 1902 Elgar worked up two old sketches and called them Dream Children, after Charles Lamb's Essay (1823), in which an old bachelor dreams of children round his knee. Elgar headed the pieces with a quotation from the essay:

> And while I stood gazing, both the children gradually grew fainter to my view, receding, and still receding till nothing at last but two mournful features were seen in the uttermost distance, which, without speech, strangely impressed upon me

[37] G. Moore, Hail and Farewell (London, 1911/14).

the effects of speech: 'we are not of Alice, nor of thee, nor are
we children at all ... We are nothing; less than nothing, and
dreams. *We are only what might have been.*'

The quotation prompts strange thoughts: what of the omitted
sentence – 'The children of Alice call Bartrum father'? – and
the fact that the italics are Elgar's, not Lamb's? What did Elgar's
own Alice and twelve-year-old daughter make of it? Elgar's was
a period that idealized childhood: Kenneth Grahame's *Dream
Days* was published in 1898, J. M. Barrie's *Peter Pan* in 1904. In
human terms, it is sad indeed that Elgar should have composed
this piece seemingly ignoring his own little daughter, but
musically the image met a need of his. The sentiment is close
to the first interlude in his *Falstaff*, which in his essay he calls 'a
dream picture', and – again – 'what might have been'.

Dream Children could easily have begun life as piano improvisations, like 'Enigma'. They are almost entirely composed
of sequences, modified just enough to sustain attention. In
the orchestral version the Andante in G minor opens with a
drum roll, forecasting the First Symphony. Clarinets run in
parallel thirds, made tentative by halting syncopation. When
the muted strings take over, they darken the basic E flat with
D flats, and the woodwind gives tiny shudders. So it opens
innocently, then deepens in feeling, becoming richer, more
passionate, and that richer sound-world is sustained over the
reprise. The experience parallels how Elgar's adult life coloured
memories of his childhood. The innocence is shadowed, as it
were, by the subsequent events. That is not confined to these
pieces: these modified recapitulations were an integral part
of his technique. In his symphonic works the repetitions are
weighted emotionally and thematically by what happens as
they are developed. The Allegretto in G major is lighter, though
wistful, with a typical counterpoint at cue H; it is unfinished,
and glances back to the Andante, whose thirds are now warmer
on violas.

The two pieces were first performed at the Queen's Hall on
4 September 1902, conducted by Arthur W. Payne, the orchestra's leader, deputizing for Wood who was on sick leave. Elgar
twice seemed to deny interest and knowledge of *Dream Children*.

When F. G. Edwards asked for information about them in 1907, Elgar replied 'I really can tell you *nothing*.' He knew nothing, he said, of the first performance and had never heard them.[38] In 1926 Ivor Atkins asked for music for the Three Choirs Festival. Elgar turned down *Arthur* and *Sospiri*, and about *Dream Children* he said 'I do not want them or it done.'

1902 Coronation Ode, Op. 44

The old Queen was dead, and Edward VII was to be crowned. Even before the success of the *Pomp and Circumstance* marches, the Covent Garden Syndicate asked Elgar for a celebration work to be performed in the Opera House the evening before the coronation in 1902. The words were to be written by A. C. Benson (1862–1925), son of the Archbishop of Canterbury, and at that time a master at Eton, 'a genuine poet and known to the Royalties', as Sir Walter Parratt put it to Elgar. Benson wrote to Elgar in December 1901 with an outline of his proposal. It is not clear who first had the idea to use the Trio tune from the *Pomp and Circumstance* march in D. Years later Clara Butt remembered that in 1902 she had asked Elgar to write her 'something like' the famous tune, and he had replied 'You shall have that one my dear.'[39] But in 1927 he answered 'King Edward was the first to suggest that the air from the *Pomp and Circumstance* March should be sung and eventually the song as now known was evolved, via the *Coronation Ode*.'[40] There is no evidence that Edward VII heard *Pomp and Circumstance* or met Elgar until 5 February 1902, by which time Elgar had already decided to use the tune. Benson asked him to 'string together a few nonsense words, just to show me how you would wish them to run, I would construct it, following the air closely'.[41]

Elgar's initial idea had been to turn *Caractacus* into an opera for the occasion. The work was to be published by Boosey, but that did not prevent Jaeger from giving Elgar his opinions.

[38] 6 June 1907.
[39] J. N. Moore, *Edward Elgar: A Creative Life* (Oxford, 1984), p. 364.
[40] 21 November 1927.
[41] 3 December 1901.

'Dont cook up *Caractacus* for Covent Garden. It will never do ...
You cant alter a Cantata into an opera, no one can ... Write a
new work.'[42] He also tried to dissuade Elgar from fitting words
to the March in D. 'You must write a new tune to the words &
not fit the words to the tune.'[43]

Elgar opens the Ode grandly, opulently, so as to 'Crown the
King' with life, with might, then more gently with peace, love,
and faith. Benson's tone becomes commanding: 'God shall
save the King ...' and Elgar builds towards a great climax. He
moves in a few bars from E flat through D major, C major, to
a *crescendo* on an expectant dominant seventh, but in a master-
stroke of humility, ushers in the great tune *pp, dolce, semplice*, on
the clarinet. The voices, ignoring both hope and glory, enter
with 'all that hearts can pray'. That is Elgar at his finest.

The following chorus, 'Daughter of Ancient Kings' for the
Danish Alexandra, is modest and hymn-like (it was replaced for
1911 by 'True Queen of British homes' for Mary). In 'Britain,
ask of thyself' Elgar reverts to the bluff and hearty idiom of
Caractacus. Again comes *Caractacus* in 'Hark upon the hallowed
air', much of it in pretty twelve-eight Eigen mode, but as
Benson hymns the arts Elgar turns inward, and the quartet
'Only let the heart be pure' reveals the opera composer he
might have been.

'Might have been' is perhaps the key: 'As the golden days
increase,' hopes Benson, but Elgar's music for that is nostalgic
rather than optimistic. Another gentle number invoking 'Peace,
gentle peace', is a reminder that while Elgar was composing
the Ode, the Boer war continued. The finale, rightly for such
an occasion, does end in a blaze of hope and glory.

The *Coronation Ode* is far less pompous than might be expected.
The tone is one of thanksgiving. It begins and ends resplend-
ently, the call to arms is dull, but much of it is intimate and
devotional. 'We have crowned our King,' sings Benson, but
three days before the coronation was due it had to be postponed, because of the king's appendicitis. Elgar, out cycling,
heard the news 'at a little roadside pub', he told Jaeger, and

[42]   9 December 1901.
[43]   6 December 1901.

protested that *he* needed no sympathy. 'It gives me three blessed sunny days in my own country.'[44] The postponed first perform-ance was at the Sheffield Festival (the Sheffield choir would have sung at Covent Garden) on 2 October 1902, and it was performed in the presence of the king and queen on 25 June 1903.

Solo Songs, 1901–08

Owing to a temporary disagreement with Novello, the Marches and the *Coronation Ode* were published by Boosey. Promoter of popular ballads, they knew a good tune when they heard it, and suggested issuing 'Land of Hope and Glory' independently. Clara Butt sang the revised version, with the slightly changed words, in London on 21 June, so setting the song off on its career as a second national anthem. It gained Elgar his first substantial royalty. Hoping for a similar success, Boosey asked Elgar for more songs. He turned again to Benson's words. 'In the Dawn' is a love-song, conventional in style but for the key-changes that reflect the chances of parting and sadness, and ending with secret confidence 'among the stars'. He set 'Speak, Music' in 15/8, composing a charming, almost teasing little song to his own art. The piano echoes the last notes of the singer's phrases, only taking a two-bar initiative at the words 'music can say all that the poet, the priest cannot say'. 'Speak my heart', also to Benson's words, is an artless dialogue between a maiden and her suitor. (In fact, Benson produced words for a song Elgar had already composed to a text by 'Adrian Ross', who refused permission.) In 'Come, gentle night' (Clifton Bingham) Elgar chromatically inflects simple harmonies to add depth to the longing for rest. He was sent 'Always and Everywhere', verses by the Polish poet Krasiński (1812–59) by their translator Frank Fortey. The title recurs as a refrain to a declamatory song of doomed love. Arthur Salmons also hopefully sent verses to Elgar, who set his 'Pleading' ('Will you come homeward from the hills of Dreamland?'). Its simple phrases, beautifully shaped by the words, are highly charged

---

[44] 25 June.

with longing. As always, any reference to 'dreamland' inspires
Elgar to intimate expression.

ᘒᘒᘒ

In 1901 the Elgars met Edward Speyer (1837–1934), who
in Frankfurt had known Clara Schumann and Brahms. He
and his wife Antonia entertained the musical world at their
home 'Ridgehurst' in Hertfordshire. In 1902 Elgar first met the
violinist W. H. Reed (1876–1942) and the composer Arnold
Bax (1883–1953).

At the Coronation Ode in 1902 at Sheffield Elgar met the Stuart
Wortleys. Charles Stuart Wortley was called to the Bar in 1876,
and became Conservative MP for Sheffield in 1880. His second
wife was Alice Sophia Caroline (1862–1936), known to her
family as Carrie. She was the daughter of the pre-Raphaelite
painter Millais. She and her husband shared a passion for
music, playing the Grieg and Schumann concertos on the two
grand pianos at their home at 7 Cheyne Walk, Chelsea, though
she played only in private. A beautiful, cultivated woman,
she suffered some emotional insecurity, for her relationship
with her mother had been strained and her husband fostered
a strong attachment to his first wife's memory. She gathered
around her a circle of friends, among them Claude Phillips the
art critic, Frank Schuster, and Lady Charles Beresford. Known
to Elgar first as Alice, then as Windflower, she became his creative muse, and persuaded him to complete the Violin Concerto
when he was deeply despondent.

Elgar's mother died in 1902. She had instilled his ideals,
and had peopled his mind with 'heroes and poets'.[45] His father
died in 1906. In November 1903 Rodewald died at the age
of forty-two, suddenly after influenza. Elgar was profoundly
shocked. It was the first death among his contemporaries, of a
man he was musically close to.

An all-Elgar Festival was being planned for 1904. The idea
had come from Alice Elgar, who boldly proposed it to Frank
Schuster, who interested Harry Higgins of Covent Garden.

---

[45] J. N. Moore, Spirit of England (London, 1984), p. 52.

Richter was to conduct, and it was hoped Elgar would produce a symphony.

In the summer of 1903 the Elgars gave up Birchwood and decided to spend the winter of 1903–04 in Italy.

༺༻

1904 Concert Overture 'In the South' ('Alassio'), Op. 50

'Edward in Italy' this overture has been called, with some relevance and wit. Like Berlioz, Elgar found Italy an exhilarating, liberating experience, and revelled in its pungent colours and rhythmic exuberance. In both *Harold en Italie* and *In the South* the solo viola, that melancholy dreamer, is a haunting sound. Both composers found inspiration in Byron's *Childe Harold*.

The reference to Berlioz's symphonic-length work helps to move *In the South* out of the category of concert-overture (Elgar originally called it 'Fantasia Overture') and nearer to that of symphonic poem. Elgar at first estimated its length at twelve minutes, but it lasts for at least twenty; and its breadth, vitality, and range make for a grander and looser work than his previous overtures. He had promised a symphony for the Festival, but no symphony came until 1908. So *In the South* was first performed on 16 March 1904 at the Royal Opera House by the Hallé Orchestra under the composer's direction.

Though the subject suggests comparison with Strauss's *Aus Italien* (1886), the opening of *In the South* - bursting with energy, leaping up three octaves – is closer to *Don Juan*. Elgar and Strauss were exchanging courtesies. After *Gerontius* at Düsseldorf in 1902, Strauss hailed Elgar as 'the first English progressivist'. In his turn Elgar was to praise Strauss after he conducted his own music at Birmingham on 20 December 1904. Privately he told Jaeger 'S. puts music in a very low position when he suggests it must hang on to some commonplace absurdity for its very life.'[46] Elgar described the opening of *In the South* as being 'the exhilarating *out-of-doors* feeling arising from the gloriously beautiful surroundings'. He had written the bare theme – those pugnacious rising fifths, the dashing on-the-

[46] To Jaeger, 13 August 1904.

beat triplets – in 1899 in the Hereford organist's Visitors'
Book, calling it 'Dan, triumphant (after a fight)', Dan being
the bulldog of the eleventh 'Enigma' Variation. Now it became
'joy of living (wine & macaroni)', as Elgar called it.

Elgar's letters and his notes for the Covent Garden programme
provide some source details. At first the rain and gales in Alassio
seemed not to matter: 'we have such meals! Such wine!'[47] But
by January the Elgars were 'perished with cold', and he reck-
oned the visit 'artistically a complete failure'.[48] That afternoon
they made an expedition to the village of Moglio, which name
amused Elgar and Carice so much that it shaped a phrase in
the Overture (one bar after cue 11). Other excursions offered
a piping shepherd with his flock and a massive Roman bridge
– 'here a vision came of the old days of the grand, relentless
force' – that inspired the heavy chordal passage (cue 20) with
the prolonged crushing cadence. In the centre of the overture
(cue 34) is the magical song for solo muted viola – the shepherd singing his canto popolare. (Elgar sadly mangled words by
Shelley to fit the tune for the song 'In Moonlight'.) 'In a flash
it all came to me – the conflict of the armies on that very spot
long ago, where now I stood – the contrast of the ruin and the
shepherd – and then, all of a sudden, I came back to reality. In
that time I had composed the overture – the rest was merely
writing it down.'[49]

Elgar acknowledged literary sources as well. From Tennyson's
The Daisy: 'What hours were thine and mine, In lands of palm
and southern pine … What Roman strength Turbia showed In
ruin, by the mountain road.' Like many another composer, he
turned to Childe Harold, to the marvellous fourth canto in which
Byron describes his travels from Venice to Rome, and his inner
travels through his own soul. After four serious, introspective
stanzas come the two (xxv, xxvi) from which Elgar selected
words: '… a land Which was the mightiest in its old command
And is the loveliest … Wherein were cast … … the men of
Rome! … Thou art the garden of the world.' The quotations

---

[47] To Jaeger, 13 December 1903.
[48] To Jaeger, 3 January 1904.
[49] Interview with Miller Ular, Chicago Sunday Examiner, 7 April 1907.

The wind quintet in 1877. Elgar holds his bassoon, with Hubert Leicester and Frank Exton (flutes), William Leicester (clarinet) and Frank Elgar (oboe)

Elgar the violinist
in 1880

Elgar 'learning'
the trombone

Elgar at Craig Lea
in 1904, with the
manuscript of *In the
South* on the piano

Elgar rehearsing the Philharmonic Orchestra in
Queen's Hall for the première of his Violin
Concerto in 1910

Elgar and Beatrice Harrison at Severn House in 1919, preparing to record the Cello Concerto

Elgar at work at Severn House in 1913, photograph by Reginald Haines

Elgar and Yehudi Menuhin in 1932 before recording the Violin
Concerto. Photograph by Ivor Newton

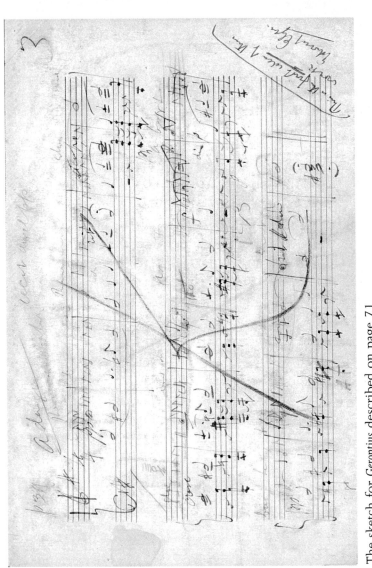

The sketch for Gerontius described on page 71

Elgar with his HMV gramophone

Elgar in 1932, photograph by Herbert Lambert

The postcard Elgar sent to William McNaught, described on
page 120

show that potent mingling of present beauty and the recollected past that brings out Elgarian exuberance and nostalgia.

The profuse invention falls roughly into sonata first-movement form, with two apparently self-contained episodes instead of a development. These do have tenuous links. The main feature of Dan's leaping diatonic theme, spanning three octaves, is the rising fifth, Example 2.6a. Elgar inverts, compacts, and compresses this for the grinding cadence of the Romans passage (2.6b). He opens it out for his *canto popolare*.

Ex. 2.6

(a)

(b)

The Overture has been criticized for being episodic and loosely constructed. Certainly the transitional passages between cues 17 and 20, cues 26 and 33 are the weakest. Thematically the most interesting music (cue 13) is what Elgar called 'EE and family musing'. Over it he wrote 'this is not bad', and indeed its troubled character – chromatics straining away from a pedal, double bass contradicting the even metre – suggests complicated relationships. The movement ends with Dan waltzing away in a happy augmentation of the opening springing theme into a broad flowing end.

Elgar dedicated In the South to Frank Schuster in gratitude for instigating the Festival. He wrote to him on 22 February 1904: 'The thing is not a picture of Italy: – one must not write the history, or epitome of a great country with an acquaintance of three months.' When Schuster died in 1927, Elgar wrote to his

sister, 'I have said in music ... what I felt long ago ... warm &
joyous, with a grave radiating serenity'.[50]

In February 1904 Elgar dined with King Edward and the Prince
of Wales at Marlborough House, and in June he was knighted.
In July 1904 the Elgars left Malvern for 'Plas Gwyn', Hereford.
Elgar's niece May Grafton came to live with them till 1909 as
secretary to him and companion for Carice.

In 1905 Parry, professor of music at Oxford, recommended
Elgar for an honorary doctorate, and engaged the newly formed
LSO to give a celebration concert. Elgar conducted them, and
agreed on future engagements. In November he accepted the
new professorship of music at Birmingham University, which
entailed giving lectures. In 1905 he was granted the Freedom
of Worcester.

Piano Music, 1901–05

When Elgar was a boy his extemporizing was much admired.
In mid-career he used the piano mostly as a composing tool; in
that way he found the 'enigma' theme. His friends agreed that
his playing was unusual (see p. 178). Dorabella remembered
that he seemed to play 'like a whole orchestra'. Yet nothing
could be further from an orchestra, or more pianistic, than
his *Skizze* of 1901. He dedicated it to Julius Buths in gratitude
for his Düsseldorf performances, and for translating the oratorios, which is no doubt why he called the piece 'skizze' and
not 'sketch'. He might indeed have called it 'whisper', for the
minute-long piece never rises above *pp*. Shadowy but daring,
it has Brahmsian figuration and almost Bergian harmonies. It
ends on a long pedal F, with chromatic contradictions in almost
every bar. His 'May Song' of the same year, on the other hand,
is pure tea-shop. It was honoured by the publisher Broome
with a limited edition on vellum with designs by Walter Crane,

---

[50] A. Schuster, 20 August 1928.

and printed on William Morris's press. It is better known in its orchestral garb.

Elgar left his only piano work for the concert hall unfinished. He composed it for Fanny Davies (1861–1934), a former pupil of Clara Schumann, who badgered him charmingly until he produced the *Concert Allegro*. She performed it on 2 December 1901 at St James's Hall, London, when *The Times* critic described it as 'a marriage between Bach and Liszt'. Elgar retrieved the autograph, and went some way towards cutting the repetitions, and also considered turning it into a piece for piano and orchestra. But as with his later piano concerto, it remained incomplete. He liked the *Concert Allegro* enough to suggest that Fanny Davies should play it for the Malvern Concert Club in 1906.

He had dedicated his song 'Pleading' to Lady Maud Warrender, his supporter since 1902 and a good amateur singer. The sister of the Earl of Shaftesbury, she was married to Sir George Warrender, Commander-in-Chief of the Mediterranean Fleet. Elgar and other friends were invited to join HMS *Surprise* for a fortnight during the autumn of 1905. They boarded at Athens. Off Constantinople Lady Maud sang 'In Haven' and 'Where corals lie' to Elgar's accompaniment. Smyrna (Izmir) was his 'first touch' with Asia, and he was enchanted. On board again after a visit to a mosque he extemporized *In Smyrna*. Its rippling opening might evoke the 'cymbals (small)', or the 'hundred' camel-bells. A passage with flattened supertonic was 'eastern' enough for him to reuse it in *The Crown of India*, though the *cantabile* section could just as well have been composed in Hereford.

Partsongs, 1902–08

In 1901 Elgar was visited by Canon Charles Vincent Gorton (1854–1912), the rector of Poulton-le-Sands in Lancashire and the founder of the nearby Morecambe Competition Festival for choirs. The festival movement had rapidly expanded since the first competition at Kendal in 1885. Test pieces were commissioned, Vaughan Williams composing his 'Sound Sleep' for East Lincolnshire in 1903. Morecambe was the most prestigious of

the festivals. Elgar first adjudicated there in 1903 and returned
for several years. Canon Gorton became a friend, and advised
Elgar on the texts for The Apostles and The Kingdom, writing
pamphlets about their interpretation.

Elgar's partsongs were test pieces from 'O happy eyes' of
1902 to 'Go song of mine' of 1910. Gorton asked Elgar to
compose a test piece for 1903 and Elgar supplied 'Weary wind
of the West' (T. E. Brown). It is well judged for its purpose,
beginning simply, with an energetic third verse taxing for the
tenors, and ending ppp in seven parts. Often sung at Morecambe were the five partsongs from translations of the Greek
Anthology, Op. 45, for four-part male voices, composed in
1902. Elgar cuts, repeats, or overlaps the words to gain his
effects. There is felicitous word-painting: 'Let the thunderbolt
strike me' in 'Yea, cast me from heights of the mountains', for
instance; the rustling grasshoppers and the wind in the pines
in 'After many a dusty mile'; twisting imitations for 'I wreathe
my hair' in 'Feasting I watch', and the lingering cadences in
the love-song 'It's oh! To be a wild wind'. In 'Whether I find
thee' the poet looks warmly ahead to when his love's bright
hair turns to grey; Elgar, as confident, lovingly extends his
melody to match the changes.

In 'Evening Scene' (Coventry Patmore, 1823–96, 1905) Elgar
makes a virtue of monotony. The opening 'sheep-bell tolleth'
through the song. The river flows gently in only two parts. The
tonality clings to D minor and there is hardly an accidental
until a D flat at the end for the old guard-dog. It is drowsy
and serene, and Elgar thought it 'my best bit of landscape so
far in that line'. He composed 'Love' (Arthur Maquarie) on
his fiftieth birthday and dedicated it to his wife ('Let me ever
gaze on thee'), which made her feel 'very unworthy & deeply
deeply touched'. He added it as No. 2 to his Op. 18, to join
'O happy eyes' to her words. 'How calmly the evening' (1907)
(T. T. Lynch) is appropriately hymn-like, as the editor of The
Musical Times invited it for their Church pages supplement. 'A
Christmas Greeting', 'from those in sun, to those in snow',
was sent from the Elgars (their joint production) in Rome
at Christmas 1907 to Sinclair and his Hereford choristers.
Like the early 'The Snow' it is for treble voices, two violins,

and piano. An instrumental prelude suggests something state-lier than the pretty lilting piece, quoting from the Pastoral Symphony in *Messiah*, that follows. The poem 'The Reveille' by the American Bret Harte (1836–1902) was suggested to Elgar by W. G. McNaught of Novello. It a fine remarkable piece for male voices (1907), more of a dramatic *scena* than a partsong. The insistent recruiting drum is interrupted by the introspective questioning, 'Let me of my heart take counsel', of a single voice against the herd, and the song ends nobly.

In Elgar's day choirs were big. Though authenticity in performance usually leads to a reduction of forces, Elgar wrote for large choirs. At Morecambe there were on average fifty voices. In 1907 he conducted more than two hundred male voices in 'Yea, cast me from heights', and in 1912 he had the three hundred voices of the Leeds Choral Society for 'Go song of mine'. It was an era when Granville Bantock could write the substantial choral symphonies *Vanity of Vanities* and *Atalanta in Calydon*; at one performance there were four hundred singers. It is not that *a cappella* works of this period can be effectively performed only by a big body of voices, but that is the context in which they were composed. Up to the outbreak of war Elgar's music and the competition festivals increasingly flour-ished. During the 1920s entertainments such as the cinema and the gramophone sapped the strength of the choral socie-ties. That Elgar's partsongs dropped from the repertory was as much to do with the disappearance of choral societies as with the decline in his reputation.

From his Op. 53 onwards, 1907–08, his choral songs are elaborate and expansive. They spread out richly into eight parts. He 'scored' his chorus like an orchestra, here dropping in note-clusters, there setting accompaniments to melodies, splitting the poem's lines across voice-parts. On the page he seems cavalier towards his poets, but the results are true to the poem's essence. His songs were to 'be listened to and not read', he declared; 'if you hear any one of them, the words flow on correctly.'

For three of his four Op. 53 partsongs Elgar chose great poets. 'There is Sweet Music' (Tennyson) alternates men's voices in G major with women's in A flat, at first apart, then intertwined and antiphonally. Sensuous, dreamy, drugged – 'the poppy hangs in sleep' – it inhabits that half-world between waking and sleep. The tender secret of 'Deep in my soul' (Byron) is described first by the basses, then by basses and sopranos in octaves, the other voices commenting sepulchrally. For so short a piece, the modulations are extreme. But all the voices join to swell the 'responsive heart'. Elgar's 'O wild west wind' is as tumultuous as Shelley's as the voices chase each other. For 'Owls', Elgar composed the words as well as the music. He told Jaeger 'it is only a fantasy & means nothing. It is in wood at night evidently & the recurring "nothing" is only an owlish sound.'[51] Unrelated thirds and sixths form a little dead march. He dedicated the song to Pietro d'Alba, his daughter's pet white rabbit. But there is nothing cosy or fluffy about this eerie and nihilistic song.

1905 Introduction and Allegro for Strings, Op 47

In 1905 Elgar composed a masterpiece: totally individual, compact, varied, and integrated. Yet it brought together many differing strands of his life. Historically it is based on the baroque concerto grosso, but it is godfather to Vaughan Williams's *Tallis Fantasia* and to Tippett's Double String Concerto. It is founded on Elgar's experiences when young, playing in provincial orchestras and chamber music groups, but was prompted by his becoming a sought-after conductor of a national orchestra. It was inspired by spontaneous amateur singing in the remote countryside, but it is technically sophisticated. It makes the most exhilarating sound imaginable, but recedes into secret visionary worlds.

In 1901 Rosa Burley took a summer holiday cottage at Llangranog, a seaside village in West Wales. Sensing that Elgar was depressed, she invited him to join her party. In her words, 'In the evenings a little company of men used to collect on the little quay in front of the pub ... someone would hum a note and they would all sing a hymn or song in four part harmony.'[52]

51   26 April 1908.
52   Percy M. Young, *Letters to Nimrod* (London, 1965), pp. 140–2.

In his words, 'On the cliff, between blue sea and blue sky, thinking out my theme, there came up to me the sound of singing ... One point [was] common to all ... the fall of a third ... I made the tune which appears in the Introduction ... and so my gaudery became touched with romance.'[53] He jotted down what he heard in a sketchbook of 1901, for cor anglais. Then he copied out a version, in the treble with only a few chords of piano accompaniment, headed 'pattern for Bag Poet', his homely name for Alice as wordsmith, so perhaps he meant it to be a song. The memory came back to him in 1904 when he heard singing in the Wye Valley near his new Hereford home. 'Although there may be (and I hope there is) a Welsh feeling in the one theme ... the work is really a tribute to that sweet borderland where I have made my home.'

Then came an invitation from the LSO for a new piece to include in the concert he was to conduct in March 1905. It would be mutually beneficial. The composer of the Variations and Cockaigne would endorse the newly formed orchestra, and Elgar would be honoured with a programme entirely of his music. Jaeger encouraged him, suggesting something brilliant for 'those fine strings only, a real bring down the House torrent of a thing'. He reminded Elgar that they had heard Steinbach conduct Bach's third Brandenburg Concerto in Cologne the previous May. Jaeger's declining health meant that he was wintering in Switzerland, where Elgar wrote to tell him, 'I'm doing that string thing ... no working-out part but a devil of a fugue instead. G major & the sd. divvel in G minor.'[54] He finished it on 13 February 1905.

Rich and free in invention, grand and poetic in resonance, the Introduction and Allegro is an intricate thirteen-minute-long piece. Its design is unique, as set out in words: Introduction, exposition, fugue, recapitulation, song-as-coda. First, a resplendent commanding theme in G minor of triplets with prominent fourths, plunging from on high down over three octaves. Next a questioning idea, reshaped in G major at cue 7 as the first subject of the Allegro proper. The second subject at

[53] Programme note for first performance.
[54] 26 January 1905.

cue 10 is a *Tapiola*-like pattering of equal semi-quavers, edgily shifting on the offbeat of each group. The fugue subject is related to it by rhythm but not by melody, having sharp angular outlines. By melody the ideas are linked by a phrase that first appears as a bass (after cue 1), then runs in the treble after cue 8 and sweeps in over the fugue at cue 17. So all is knit strongly together.

But what of the Welsh theme? Attempts to identify the original are scarcely profitable, for the falling third is common to many Welsh hymns and folksongs. More important is what it came to stand for in Elgar's imagination. He did not use it where it might have been expected, as the second subject of the Allegro. Instead, it seems to be a symbol of a secret unattainable goal, heard first as a fine *dolce* thread of solo viola, then (cue 5) dying away to nothing over falling chromatics, then (after cue 15) with all four soloists in unison, muted, but two plain and two *tremolo, ponticello*: shimmering, haloed by distance, as Elgar first heard it, and left incomplete. Not until the very end (cue 30) is it allowed a firm striding bass and a tutti statement.

Though the work reflects the baroque concertante and ripieno, Elgar does not often directly contrast the soloists with the group. At the beginning and the end they play together in splendid tuttis. Sometimes, as in the chattering second subject (cue 10), they are in antiphonal groups. But often they are meshed, perhaps the quartet's lower strings playing with the orchestra (after cue 1), or all four soloists topping and reinforcing the orchestra's phrases (after cue 22). Before he could afford to buy scores, if some passage struck him as particularly thin or sonorous, he would reconstruct it from the parts to see why. His string writing sounds composed under the fingers and the bow.

Elgar's title was abstract and unprogrammatic. He declared his First Symphony to be 'a composer's outlook on life'. On the same level, the Introduction and Allegro might ask where does certainty end and speculation begin? (That kind of proposition might well call for single voices within a group.) The work contains a striking sound-sequence that occurs often enough to seem special to it: a bold, formal statement yields to a gentler, more tentative impulse, coming to rest on a pause or an unclosed cadence. There is no evidence that Elgar had any such idea in mind (other than the *Cymbeline* quotation, 'A smiling with a sigh', Act 4, Scene 2, printed on the programme of the first performance). But there is surely some poetic attitude present, that comprehends the brilliant and the introspective moods, and finally resolves them into song.

At the first performance, on 8 March at Queen's Hall, the virtuoso writing was found difficult and the piece elusive. It soon took its distinguished place in the string music repertory. Elgar never recorded it, but Britten did.

∝❀∽

Elgar dedicated the Introduction and Allegro to Samuel S. Sanford (1849–1910), professor of Applied Music at Yale University. He and Elgar probably first met in 1900, on one of Sanford's many visits to England. A wealthy man, Sanford gave Elgar a Steinway upright piano, initiated his Yale honorary degree, and his first visit to the States in June and July 1905. There Elgar met Julia Worthington (1856–1913), who owned a flat in Manhattan, an estate up the Hudson river, and a villa at Careggi near Florence.

⌇❀⌇

Church Music, 1902–09

In 1902 Novello asked Elgar for music to 'O Mightiest of the Mighty' by the Revd S. Childs Clarke to be included in a set of eight hymns, the words and music newly composed for services to celebrate the coronation. He complained about the usual problem with hymn-texts – 'the words pause at end of third line in every stanza *except* 2 which requires to go on at once' ('while they/Yield Thee alway'). But he sent a sturdy tune framed with alleluias. It was sung at the postponed coronation on 9 August in Westminster Abbey.

Elgar's sister Helen Agnes, known as Dot, had entered the Dominican convent at Stroud, Gloucestershire, in 1903. In 1905 she asked her brother for a 'very simple & melodious tiny tune' for the organ, 'no pedal part because I could not do it'. The piece he sent was simple in the extreme – mostly minims – but not bland.

In 1907 he revised two 'tender little plants' from his St George's days, the *Ave Maria* as 'Jesu, Lord of Life and Glory' (Op. 2 No. 2), and the *Ave maris stella* as 'Jesu, meek and lowly' (Op. 2 No. 3) to join his Op. 2 No. 1. The *Ave Maria* he dedicated to Hubert Leicester's wife.

In 1909 Elgar published the carol 'Lo! Christ the Lord is born', originally composed as his Christmas card in 1897 as 'Grete Malvern on a Rocke'. Also In 1909 he contributed four chants to Novello's *New Cathedral Psalter*. Two single chants (in D and G) for the *Venite*, and double chants for Psalms 68 and 75, both in D. They stand out from their companions because most of them reach the dominant at their midpoint whereas three out of Elgar's four are still in the tonic, and the fourth modulates to the mediant.

1903 The Apostles, Op. 49 and 1906 The Kingdom, Op. 51

Elgar disclosed that the first stirring of his idea for his Biblical oratorios came when his school-teacher Francis Reeve made the casual remark: 'The Apostles were poor men, young men, at the time of their calling; perhaps before the descent of the Holy Ghost not cleverer than some of you here.'[55] That idea shaped his text. He wanted, he said, to look at things 'from the poor man's (fisherfolk etc.) point of view',[56] at a time when 'none of them had been sainted'. Perhaps the remark even shaped his life. As a young man with no worldly advantages, having for the most part to teach himself and then to keep himself, he was not regarded as 'cleverer' than his neighbours. It seems that it was the ordinariness of the apostles before they were *chosen* that struck Elgar; it is the same outlook as that of the pre-Raphaelites, who painted Christ's followers not as princes of the church, but in their workshops, among the tools of their trade. Elgar could identify with the young Galileans as they were before Pentecost. Without seeming sacrilegious, perhaps

55 Robert J. Buckley, *Sir Edward Elgar* (London, 1905), p. 8.

56 To Canon Gorton, 17 July 1903.

he even felt himself waiting for a call, for the musical descent of the Holy Ghost. What might happen after? The poor young men could speak with other tongues, could make themselves understood to foreigners – Galileans talking without inter-preters to Parthians and Medes, to Romans, Cretans, Arabians. They could prophesy, their young men could see visions, their old men dream dreams. Perhaps an unknown Worcester man, if he could find his own Pentecost, could communicate his visions to Londoners, Germans, Americans, in a language all could understand?

The Apostles was intended as the first work of a trilogy that should 'embody the calling of the Apostles, their teaching (schooling), and their Mission',[57] then the glorious outcome in the next world. It seems an astonishing, idealistic enter-prise, impossible for any man to commit himself to unless he was heart and soul bound up in it. But Elgar changed his mind several times about the shape and form of the orato-rios, and the third never reached completion. He had consid-ered composing The Apostles in 1899, when he received his first Birmingham commission, and he sketched the theme for Judas (see p. 66), which he used for the Angel of the Agony in The Dream of Gerontius. He was deflected because he had no libretto. In October 1901 the Birmingham Committee asked him for a major work for the 1903 Festival. In July 1902 he wrote to Ivor Atkins, now organist at Worcester, that he was plot-ting something 'gigantic'.[58] Later that month he saw the first three operas of the Ring at Bayreuth. At that point he planned to compose one work, running all the way from the calling of the Apostles to Antioch, where the followers of Jesus were first called Christians. He began seriously collecting material for the libretto, though he told Buckley he had been selecting the words for many years. In October 1902, still thinking of a single work, he designed what is now The Kingdom as part II of The Apostles, and in December he made a start on the vocal score. By May 1903, troubled with ill-health, he knew he was running out of time for the production in October. By June

[57] C. V. Gorton, The Apostles: an Interpretation of the Libretto (London, 1903).
[58] 2 July 1902.

he accepted that The Apostles would have to end with the Ascension, but proposed The Kingdom as a separate work to follow. On 17 August he completed The Apostles full score. The idea of a trilogy to end with The Last Judgment was formulated only after The Apostles première, though he wrote (in what might have been a face-saving expedient) to Alfred Littleton of Novello that his 'ideas now revert to my colossal scheme of year ago'.

Elgar's riposte in old age to Delius, who thought he had wasted his time and energy writing long-winded oratorios, was 'That is the penalty of my English environment'.[59] Had Elgar been born in Austria he might well have composed something like Bruckner's F minor Mass. But Elgar, like Bruckner a Roman Catholic, was living in England. The opportunities on his doorstep were essentially Anglican. He was nurtured on choral music, most of it with religious texts. Handel's Messiah and Bach's St Matthew Passion were stalwarts of the Three Choirs Festival. Musically, the birth, life, crucifixion, and resurrection of Jesus were over-familiar. So Elgar's idea was to focus on the men and women around Jesus. In The Apostles Jesus is the major presence, and Judas has the major role; but Jesus is crucified and Judas commits suicide. So it could be said that The Kingdom starts with the disadvantage that the main characters have left the stage. Pentecost is the central event in The Kingdom, with St Peter assuming the lead.

Elgar was blessed (sometimes he felt cursed) with immense talent. In that, he was 'chosen'. Some such conviction must have sustained him during the hard years before the 'Enigma' Variations brought him international fame. Did he consciously think of an allegory of the artist singled out by inspiration? His wife certainly wrote to Jaeger about 'O ye Priests' in The Kingdom: 'If you cannot feel the Sacerdotalism of any Church, there is the eternal priestdom of elect souls in all ages'[60]; by religion for believers, she went on, and for non-believers, by art. It is worth pondering what the opening words, 'The Spirit of the Lord is upon me ...' meant to Elgar the artist, as well as to Elgar the devout Catholic. It is when some internal

[59]   E. Fenby, Delius as I Knew Him (London, 1936), p. 124.
[60]   17 March 1906.

compulsion accords with external circumstances that the pressure comes from which an ambitious work is created.

As there was no ready text for his oratorios, Elgar had to compile his own. Wagner fashioned his (later Tippett was to do the same). Elgar, unlike Wagner, did not complete his libretto before he began composing, so he never had the total ground plan in his mind: text and music evolved together, and he was unsure of their final direction. He had taken on a double responsibility. That may be why he ran into trouble. On the other hand, Elgar's mind never worked in a methodical way but always impulsively, and too much forward planning might have brought his imagination to a standstill. His delays and false starts allowed him to sift out and retain what mattered most to him.

In Mendelssohn's *Elijah*, the Old Testament story is told in Old Testament words. Elgar spliced words from the Old Testament including the Psalms and from the Apocrypha into his New Testament story, in a more adventurous and intricate way than anyone had before. The main events are told simply and factually in the Gospels and the first four chapters of the Acts of the Apostles. A text that is reporting with no description gives a composer little chance for expansion, and plain words set up few overtones in him. Bach solved the problem in his Passions by inserting the reflective poems of Picander and Brockes. Elgar made the Bible amplify its own story. He used the New Testament as a synopsis and took the other words from all over the Bible, lifting sentences and even half-sentences out of context, selecting a bit here, a bit there. In that way he gave himself room for dialogue, comment, and reflection, for lyrical expansion within the narrative. As all came from the same period of translation, mostly from the King James Bible, the tone is consistent, archaic, and poetic. In part this was Elgar's reaction against anti-Catholic criticism of Newman's poem for *Gerontius*: words taken directly from the Bible would surely give sanctity and authority to the music and so satisfy the Church of England. Elgar studied everything he could lay hands on, 'no end of books on divinity'.[61] He used Pinnock's *Analysis of*

---

[61] To F. G. Edwards, March 1903.

New Testament History as a framework, Cruden's Biblical concordance, and E. Robinson's *Harmony of the Four Gospels*. He pressed his wife into service, even buying a typewriter as an aid (how he would have loved a computer!). Sometimes he changed a tense, or a pronoun, and sometimes a word depends on the translation he was using. Elgar adored puzzles: he had a sort of crossword, jigsaw mind, and he became absorbed in making his text. He was excitedly discovering the Bible, as generally at that time Catholics knew it, particularly the Old Testament, less well than Protestants. He consulted the Revd Capel Cure and Canon Gorton. He meant to publish his libretto separately, citing his references and his authorities. His sources, together with his drafts, are held in the British Library.

1903 The Apostles, Op. 49

Bach's Passions and Handel's *Messiah* have conditioned audiences to regard Jesus as the principal in any oratorio. Buckley (1905) says that Elgar was working along the lines of Greek tragedy: the stories are well known, so there must be a new angle. *The Apostles* is concerned with Jesus' influence on the people around him. It begins with a Prologue and ends with the Ascension. Part I comprises 'The Calling of the Apostles', Jesus' prayer at night, 'The Dawn', 'By the Wayside', 'By the Sea of Galilee', and concludes with the chorus 'Turn you to the stronghold'. Part II comprises 'The Betrayal', Judas's suicide, 'Golgatha', 'At the Sepulchre', and finally 'The Ascension'. Jesus' first entry is not until p. 49 of the vocal score, cue 55, at the end of a long ensemble for the chorus and the soloists John (tenor), Peter (bass), and Judas (bass). Jesus (bass) sings:

> Behold, I send you forth,
> He that receiveth you, receiveth me.

In other words, he transfers power to the Apostles. Peter is the impetuous activist, who makes things happen and uses verbs:

> Thou wilt show us the path of life ...
> will turn their mourning into joy ...
> then shall thy light rise ...

John is the peace-bringer:

> O blessed are they which love Thee, for they shall
> 　　　　rejoice in Thy peace ...
> The Lord shall give them rest ...
> Blessed are the undefiled ...

Elgar gave no unrecorded words to Jesus, but drew on the whole Bible for the subsidiary characters. The clearest result of this is in Judas. Elgar saw Judas as driven by greed and envy to force Jesus into assuming earthly kingship, never believing that He would voluntarily submit to crucifixion. Elgar cited several authorities for this view, that Judas aimed to compel Jesus 'to make what had seemed to His followers the too tardy display of His Messianic power'. Judas's vocal line, marked *deciso, ad lib.*, or *impetuoso*, has the thrust of earthly ambition behind it, in contrast to that of the peace-loving John or the sturdy Peter. So for Judas's aside 'Let Him make speed and hasten His work' (cue 154) Elgar drew on Isaiah v, 19; Zechariah vi, 13; and Judith ii, 5. In the Gospels Judas does not say any of the following phrases, which are scattered through Elgar's ensembles:

> We shall eat of the riches of the Gentiles,
> And in their glory shall we boast ourselves ...
> God exalteth by his power ...
> He poureth contempt upon princes ...
> Let Him make speed, and hasten His work ...

The Apostles and The Kingdom are musically linked. In both, as in *Gerontius*, Elgar uses leitmotifs, recurring easily recognized figures, standing for characters, ideas, and emotions, and by their modifications to offer structural cohesion. Motifs charged with association act on the musical memory and make allusions beyond the power of words alone. Whether or not they can be recognized and named, their import comes across. The Prologue begins with 'The Spirit of the Lord' motif, spread *pianissimo* from top to bottom of the strings, flanked by sombre timpani rolls: a concentrated image of spiritual power. The chorus enters reverently in unison. At the words 'anointed me', a crucial three-chord motif is heard, 'Christ, the Man of Sorrows', whose grinding dissonance in contrary motion contains the personal agony of God made man, in contrast to the consonant, numinous Godhead. Immediately after it, under the words 'Gospel to the poor', sounds the 'Gospel' motif. The feeling quickens with the 'Light' motif from *The Light of Life* (see Ex. 3.1). All this flowers into a lyrical melody which stands for the Church.

From his Organ Sonata onwards Elgar had shown ease in devising themes that dovetail and combine. Motifs to 'Gospel' and 'Preachers' are combined early on (before cue 5) and significantly at cue 213 when Jesus directs the Apostles 'Go ye therefore and teach all nations'. At cue 221 'Prayer' and 'Faith' are rolled out majestically together. Many of these themes are shaped by the Gregorian Gradual 'Constitues eos', promising power to the Apostles. Elgar had happily chanced on it (and on the antiphon 'O sacrum convivium', used in *The Kingdom*) during a visit to Rodewald in Liverpool in November 1902. From its limbs (Ex. 2.7a) he derived the motifs for the 'Apostles' and 'The Spirit of the Lord' (2.7b). The challenge he faced was how to integrate a modal single line in free rhythm into a tonal metrical work.

Ex. 2.7a and b

Not only did Elgar invent sayings for his characters. He made up whole episodes, shaping his own structure. These two verses as they occur in Luke vi are consecutive:

> And it came to pass in those days that Jesus went out into a mountain to pray, and continued all night in prayer to God./ And when it was day, He called unto Him His disciples.

Elgar imagined what happened in between. He composed a

nocturne, with remote pastoral reeds, and a 'prayer' theme whose incorporeal, unearthly quality comes from the self-cancellations of the root position triads – E flat major, A minor, F major, B minor, G major, A flat major – and from the strange scoring of two *tremolo ponticello* violas with muted horns over thrummed strings. Into the mysterious night floats the soprano voice, the angel Gabriel watching over Jesus.

A memo in Elgar's notes reveals how the next idea grasped him: 'Why not, after the prayer of Jesus (chos, orch. etc.) make the change – the waking-up – come from the Temple; the morning call to prayer?' And so comes the dawn, pierced with the rising sixth of the Shofar (the ram's horn) and heavy with the ritual tread of the morning psalm: splendid in itself and symbolizing the birth of the Church, as the 'Prayer' motif is blazoned out. The 'Apostles' motif, first slipped in unobtrusively during the night scene (two bars after cue 19), is now strait-jacketed for a chorus, 'The Lord hath chosen them', which retreats rather from the orient to the conventional Three Choirs, but broadens out as the disciples, now Apostles, join in.

As well as the Bible, Elgar studied Longfellow's *The Divine Tragedy*, a versified life of Jesus. For 'By the Wayside', Scene II, he conflated the Beatitudes with Longfellow's picture of Jesus teaching his companions as they walk through the countryside. The tranquil three-part opening is so simple as to be almost homely. Jesus recites eight of the Beatitudes; each begins the same, *quasi recit*, and keeps a narrow compass (Elgar reserved the ninth for Mary in *The Kingdom*). Mary (soprano) and the others respond. Judas is already showing his worldly side: 'The poor is hated even of his own neighbour' (Proverbs xiv, 20). Mary has a spurt of motherly pride and tenderness: 'Thou art of purer eyes than to behold evil' (Habakkuk i, 13).

Mary Magdalene (contralto) scarcely appears in the Gospels, and was certainly not one of the chosen twelve. Taking the idea from Longfellow, Elgar makes her, in an almost a cinematic device, the invisible spectator of the storm on the sea of Galilee, to reflect the storm in her own uneasy heart. For this he had theological and personal reasons. He was concerned to show two types of sinner: Mary Magdalene was to repent and be forgiven. So Elgar gives her a flashback to her earlier dissolute life: 'Whatsoever mine eyes desired I kept not from them', and in a dreamlike fantasy the chorus sings of costly wine, ointments, and rosebuds. Commentators differ about Elgar's music for this, some comparing it with Wagner's sensuous Venusberg music or the flower-maidens in *Parsifal*, others finding it disappointingly tame. In truth, the voluptuousness of Elgar's Magdalene lies in her remorse, not in her veiled erotic memories. But a great deal goes on in the continuous Scene III: her remorse, her fantasy, the storm, Jesus' and then Peter's walking on the water, Magdalene's repentance, Peter's impetuous affirmation, the proclamation of the Gospel, Magdalene's reappearance and absolution. All the episodes are ideologically significant, for Elgar needed the miracle to convert her, but the narrative demands too much of the half-hour span of music. Magdalene's aria, opened with a flattened second over parallel fifths, is glamorous. Her image for the scary walking on the water – the vast gap between treble and bass – is frighteningly precarious. Her aria when calm is restored is symphonically developed. After this, the return to the Wayside music and the song-like Church theme is at odds with the rest. The Virgin's comforting song is exquisite, but reverts to the style of *The Light of Life*. A final chorus was needed to consolidate the scene, but the predictable voice-leading of 'Turn you to the stronghold' is conventional. The whole act though interesting is over-ambitious, for the music itself lacks cohesive style.

The orchestral Introduction to Part II has been justifiably criticized for being no more than seven motifs laid end to end over forty bars. By Wagnerian standards there is no development. But the motifs themselves have such emotional power that the impact – with 'Christ's Passion' hugely augmented – is tragic. In both these oratorios the atmosphere is stronger than design. In Scene IV, The Betrayal, Elgar achieves the continuity that failed him in Scene III. Text and music move at same pace, the little refrain 'with lanterns and torches' acting as a ritornello. The muffled first entry of the chorus under the solo tenor (cue 146) indicates the suffering to come. The confrontation of the chief priests in choral recitatives against the solo voice of Judas is dramatic. At exactly the right moment comes the reproachful women's chorus 'And the Lord turned …', which by its intensity reflects and comments as well as narrates.

Elgar had a didactic reason for giving Judas prominence. 'To my mind,' he wrote, 'Judas' crime & sin was despair.' There was, he thought, 'a lesson to be learnt from him'. 'In these days, where every "modern" person seems to think suicide is the natural way out of everything (Ibsen &c.&c.), my plan, if explained, may do some good.'[62] Here is the dark side of Elgar, who also knew despair. He too was tempted by suicide. Ernest Newman, who met Elgar in 1901, considered him a self-divided and secretly unhappy man. 'I remember distinctly a dinner', he wrote, 'at which Mrs Elgar tactfully steered the conversation away from the topic of suicide that had suddenly arisen; she whispered to me that Edward was always talking of making an end of himself.'[63] For Judas's monologue Elgar found magnificent words from Wisdom and Jeremiah and composed some of his greatest music. Structurally the scene balances the morning hymn. The implacable psalm, with archaic harmonies and ritualistic small compass, is sung inside the temple. It drives Judas, his spinning thoughts caught in rhapsodic recitative, to extremity; the words seem directly to condemn him. The minor second of his 'Whither shall I go' echoes that of Mary Magdalene's aria, and here his recollection of the Wayside music is painfully apt. The jagged bass shows his perturbation, the fickle little phrase at 'for the breath in our nostrils' his studied indifference, but the warm phrase for 'a little spark' shows his humanity. Elgar's insight into him is powerful and sympathetic.

The Golgotha scene is the more intense because the trial and crucifixion of Jesus take place 'off-stage'. His last words on the Cross are written over the orchestral introduction, ending in the 'Agony' chord, and are reflected in the hushed chorus and the tender mourning of John and Mary, their winding chromatic sixths numb with misery.

The dawn 'At the Sepulchre' brings back the earlier Temple Watchers, but now all is water-colour freshness. The final scene,

[62] To Canon Gorton, 17 July 1903.
[63] *Sunday Times*, 23 October 1955.

the Ascension, stretches from earth to heaven in a complicated
but translucent texture for the male chorus, the four soloists,
a chorus of women, and a small 'mystic' chorus. A thundering
climax leads to the 'Spirit of the Lord' motif, with which the
work began, no longer hushed but in full majesty, and the
work dies away in gentle alleluias. To work out these climaxes
Elgar used to cycle from his Malvern home to Longdon Marsh,
and sit there among the reeds and willows. Except for the
skylarks, it is still a silent place today.

The Apostles was produced at the Birmingham Festival on
14 October 1903. In his notes, opposite the Ascension, Elgar
wrote: 'On leaving Birmingham after the Festival we (Alice
and I) went into St. Philip's Church, walked up it to see the
stained glass, and on turning round were struck by Burne
Jones' Ascension. (It is mine, or mine is it.) The sun shining
thro' it. Very impressive ending to our glorious week.' On his
score he quoted from William Morris's Earthy Paradise:

> To what a heaven the earth might grow
> If fear beneath the earth were laid,
> If hope failed not, nor love decayed

1906 The Kingdom, Op. 51

Some material, designed for Peter and the Lord's Prayer,
was ready for The Kingdom. In the two years since Elgar had
completed The Apostles the motifs had sunk deep inside him.
Now they reappear as familiar.

The grandeur and sweep of the Prelude make it the most
symphonic music Elgar had yet composed. It opens magnifi-
cently with the twin motifs 'Gospel' and 'Preachers'. They
were heard in tandem in The Apostles when Jesus directed 'Go
ye therefore and teach all nations', so here it is as if they
proclaim that His followers will now spread His word. Then
comes the 'Apostles' motif, but extended, as if renewed and
refreshed, and combining with 'Gospel'. The three-chord
'Peter' motif is heard impressively six times, followed by the
musical recall of significant events concerning him in The Apostles. There are two themes new to The Kingdom: the substantial

'New Faith' theme (ascending in sequence, strings only, with a triplet on the fourth beat), and the 'trust and hope' theme (triple time, groups of descending chords). Linked to a chromatic 'contrition' theme is a quotation from the chant 'O Sacrum Convivium'. So the train of thought in the Prelude might run: in joy and vigour the Apostles spread the Gospel; Peter emerges as leader, but bitterly recalls his denial of Jesus, His loneliness, His gentle reproach; Peter then finds a new steadier resolve. The way an inner part flares out, the delayed suspensions, the fluctuating tempi, the sudden lift from E flat to E major at cue 1, the moments of quiet anticipation, all reveal the range of the music. Without any need of leitmotifs, narrative, or doctrine, what comes over is the progress from initial fervour through shattering climaxes followed by a kind of inner collapse, which drains away in loneliness, to a quiet close. For Elgar's Kingdom is within: this is not Caractacus having to 'Go forth O king to conquer', but the music already looks towards the end, 'Thou art our Father and we are Thine'. Elgar was a man of complicated sensibility and this Prelude, notably in his own recording of 1933, is shot through with power and eloquence.

He divided The Kingdom into five sections. I and V balance each other: both are in 'the upper room' – that is to say, they are indoor scenes, and all the disciples are together. II and IV also balance each other: they are outdoor scenes, 'at the beautiful gate'; both of them lyrical, flowing music, with tender solo writing. Scene III is the 'hinge' of the work: Pentecost, the gift of the Holy Spirit. The most varied of the five movements, it is action-packed, but with stillness at its centre.

The first chorus begins quietly with the disciples and the Holy Women gathered together after the Ascension. The strikingly direct unaccompanied 'Seek first the Kingdom of God …' is answered by Peter's 'Peace … unto you'. Both are tailed by open-ended orchestral phrases, holding thematic significance to those who know The Apostles. The discursive music becomes graver, as Elgar introduces the antiphon 'O Sacrum Convivium' when Peter reminds his friends of the Last Supper. By purely musical means Elgar highlights certain important points: 'Thine almighty Word' in a sudden flashing soprano phrase;

'the true vine, the Bread of Life' in a strong choral unison at cue 31; 'wondrously' in an awed withdrawal. Peter now stands forward and addresses the group – 'Men and brethren' – in the half-declamatory, half-lyrical recitative Elgar had made his own. As idea follows idea in Peter's train of thought, the orchestra plays the appropriate motif. The disciples draw lots for a twelfth apostle to replace Judas. Their anxious, uncertain mood is reflected in syncopations, then released into the energetic wide melodic leaps of 'The Lord hath chosen you ...'. The scene ends with a formal chorus about vocation. The choir mostly takes the part of the other disciples, but here it administers an impersonal exhortation to the Apostles: 'O ye Priests' is a call to the elect through whom the Spirit speaks. Canon Gorton wrote of this chorus: 'The message the composer would have us to understand echoes down through the ages. The lot, on whomsoever it may fall, be he preacher, teacher, administrator or artist, is from the Lord.' So *The Kingdom* may be understood as an allegory of creative, as well as of religious, inspiration.

The following *Allegro piacevole* is in the nature of an intermezzo. As in *The Apostles* Elgar invented scenes. Here he imagined the two Marys at the Beautiful Gate, where Peter cured the lame man. He searched for words to describe the details: 'the singers are before the altar ...' (Ecclesiasticus xlvii, 9); 'to him that is afflicted ...' (Job vi, 14). The two solo women's voices twine and duet over a light orchestra. The music is chaste in feeling, limpid in sound, but with a dragging penitential pathos for the sighing of the lame and the blind.

Part III contains the spiritual crux of the work: the descent of the Spirit, which invests Peter with authority. In Acts ii, the story runs straight on:

> And when the day of Pentecost was fully come, they were all with one accord in one place.
> And suddenly there came a sound from heaven as of a rushing wind ...
> and they were all filled with the Holy Ghost

Elgar wanted music there to express the feelings of those waiting men. Not only must the music impart the power and exaltation brought by the Spirit, but also the patient waiting beforehand. Even the non-religious can respond to the symbolism: the time of quiet, in readiness for the creative idea. So must a composer wait in disciplined, attentive stillness when all his technique has been worked over and sharpened. Elgar gave the words from the Acts to the tenor and contralto in recitative, but found in Ecclesiasticus, Isaiah, and Exekiel the poetry of wonder for his disciples and female mystic chorus. He caught for a dozen or so pages that state of mind of rapt contemplation, awe, and ecstasy in which the invisible can be apprehended. From the 'Spirit of the Lord' motif he drew music, and to it he added new themes that harmonically seem to roll round and round a circle. Time stops. Out of this soft glow the flame-like 'Pentecost' motif flashes down through the orchestra at the contralto's recitative ('... a sound as of the rushing of a mighty wind ...'). The soaring high tenors are given vigour by martial rhythms.

Peter, now invested with authority, steps forward to face the crowd, calling at cue 95 for repentance and baptism. Under-pinning this is the 'New Faith' theme, not heard since the Prelude. At the climax Peter calls on the people 'to repent and be baptized' – 'Ye men of Judea...'. 'Pour upon us the Spirit of Grace', the people cry insistently, and the New Faith theme is emphatically confirmed.

Scene IV balances Scene II in returning to the lame man, and Peter demonstrates his new authority by performing a miracle. For this and for their subversive teaching he and John are arrested and imprisoned. Elgar does not set their questioning and trial. Instead, he saw the promise implicit in 'these all with one accord continued steadfastly in prayer with the women and Mary the Mother of Jesus.' Taking a hint from 'for it was now eventide ...' he created an intercession, a composite poem from half a dozen sources, for the Virgin Mary, and composed the ravishing meditation 'The sun goeth down: Thou makest darkness and it is night' (Psalm civ, 20). It has a strange exotic quality, the harp suggesting a lute, with a twining violin solo. This haunting nocturne of withdrawn, troubled sweetness is among the peaks of Elgar's output.

The final scene picks up from the first the music of warm-hearted friendliness, and also the antiphon at the mention of 'spiritual food and drink'. Peter and John relate their questioning and release, and Elgar picks up another hint, this time from a verse in the Acts, which he does not quote ('and when they had prayed'), and closes the work with the Eucharist. Not wanting to put a priest's actual words into the mouth of a layman, Elgar turned to a second-century church manual of prayers, The Didache. With this and with the Lord's Prayer, the work ends in quiet trust.

The Kingdom is less eventful than The Apostles. Instead of the grand set pieces – the dawn, the storm – it has idyllic interludes. It holds less action, more meditation. The finest music comes when waiting – 'and the patience' repeats the Virgin. Elgar evades chances for drama. Why does he not make more of John and Peter's defiance of the injunction after their arrest and release? Perhaps because the heart of this work is contemplation.

Jaeger, in his analysis of The Apostles, gave names to sixty-four of the ninety-two music examples, so much so that Elgar warned him against being too literal. Ernest Newman, in his cheerful debunking style, remarked that the 'ship' motif is 'no more suggestive of a ship than it is of a banana or a motor-car'.[64] Even then Elgar was wary of laying 'too great stress on the leitmotiven plan'. For The Kingdom, he discouraged Jaeger's motif-hunting zeal, and only twenty-nine of the seventy-eight music examples are labelled. There is, Elgar said, no theme for The Kingdom – 'the Kingdom includes everything'. Led by Jaeger, much emphasis has been placed on the motifs' extra-musical meanings, on how, in such a piece as Peter's sermon in The Kingdom, they can show his train of thought. But musically their function is organic. Some, met first separately, are then seen to be two halves of one harmonic idea. The combination of counterpoints seem endless. At cue 79 for instance, a new ecstatic theme combines vigorously with the 'Apostles' motif. This technique is nothing new in Elgar. He developed it in King Olaf (see p. 27), and it reached its height in the finale of Gerontius. As well as this vertical combining, some of the motifs

64   E. Newman, Elgar (London), p. 96.

– brief, without cadences – almost *need* others to fulfil them. For example, in *The Kingdom* after cue 70 the 'Spirit of the Lord' is followed melodically with 'Pentecost'.

Sustained work occupied Elgar between December 1905 and March 1906. During February, reduced almost to a nervous breakdown, he had again cut the plan by half. So in fact he had not finished what he had originally projected as one work. He then had to break off for a visit (6 April to 27 May) to the States, to attend a festival of his music in Cincinnati. There he conducted *Gerontius*, *The Apostles*, *In the South*, and the Introduction and Allegro but made time to continue scoring *The Kingdom*. He resumed work on that during June and July 1906, and completed the full score at Hereford on August 1909. The first performance was at the 1906 Birmingham Festival on 3 October under Elgar. The autograph score of *The Kingdom* bears this in Elgar's hand on the title-page from the Canadian poet William Bliss Carman (1861–1929):

I would write
'A music that seems never to have known /Dismay, nor
haste, nor wrong ...'
in Cincinnati, April 1906. E.E.

Many factors combined to prevent the third oratorio being composed. Elgar was disappointed at the financial returns of the first two. He frequently complained that English singers did not have brains enough to realize his intentions. Perhaps he blenched at composing music, which exists in time, for the end of the world, when time stops, but that did not deter Messiaen or Stravinsky. And he was turning more to instrumental music: the First Symphony appeared in 1908, the Violin Concerto in 1910, the Second Symphony in 1911. More significantly, it seems that his religious faith was failing.

CHAPTER THREE

The Symphonist 1907–1915

୶ৠৣ৶

At the end of 1906 Elgar was again plagued by ill-health. In December he and Alice left England for two months in Italy, spending time in Naples, Capri and Rome. In Capri he went to have his hair cut. The barber was playing a mandoline, so Elgar took up a violin, then a guitarist arrived, and the three played together. He wrote down the trio but left it unfinished. Another visit to the States (2 March to 27 April) was primarily to conduct. In New York he gave the American première of *The Kingdom*, then went on to Chicago and Pittsburgh.

In about 1906 Elgar came to know Sidney Colvin (1845–1927) and his wife Frances. Colvin was Keeper of Prints and Drawings at the British Museum, biographer of Keats and Landor, editor of Stevenson.

ఌৠৣ৾

1907–08 The Wand of Youth Suites, Op. 1a and 1b

Elgar's greatest music offers nobility, strong tensions, and profound spiritual experiences. But in it too can be found shy withdrawals to an inward, tender world. The *Wand of Youth* Suites belong to that world, and also to the playful, fanciful side of his nature. They were published in 1907 and 1908, but he designated them Opus 1. That is explained by the subtitle, 'Music to a child's play'. That child was Elgar himself, and the play was made up by him and his brothers and sisters. The stage was a dingle close to the cottage where he was born. He made of little Broadheath an image of pastoral innocence. Even after the family moved to Worcester, he was sent back to play on Broadheath common; and as an old man he delighted to drive close friends to see his birthplace. When he was sixty-four he wrote: 'I am still at heart the dreamy child who used to be found in the reeds by Severn side with a sheet of paper trying to fix the sounds & longing for something very great – source, texture & all else unknown. I am still looking for this – in strange company sometimes – but as a child & as a young man & as a mature man, no single person was ever kind to me.'[1] Though the letter was written soon after Alice died, soon after he'd moved alone into a London flat, the bitter contrast between the first and last parts of that statement suggest that Elgar's view of childhood was complicated. It is monstrously untrue that he found no kindness, but feelings have their own authenticity, and as an aging man his retrospective view was influenced by his more recent past. This music is not for children, but for a grown-up's memories.

In 1928 and 1929 Elgar recorded the Suites, and in the accompanying notes he gave this account: 'Some small grievances occasioned by the imaginary despotic rule of my father and mother (the Two Old People) led to the devising' of the play. The scene was a Woodland Glade. On the near side of a brook was 'our fairyland'; on the far side, ordinary life 'which we forgot as often as possible'. Though the play was unnamed and unperformed, it was meant to tempt the Old People to cross the brook to a transfiguring fairyland.

Elgar gave two dates – 1869 or 1871 – for the play (how many men of fifty can remember precise dates from their childhood?). Into his 1878 sketchbooks he had copied ideas as 'from the play (old)'. The origins of the waltz of the 'Sun Dance' (Suite I) and 'Moths and Butterflies' (Suite II) date from 1878; the opening of the March (II) was sketched in 1879, its central section in 1880; and the Minuet 'à la Handel' (I) in 1881. Into 1900 and 1901 sketchbooks he copied old ideas, which he now developed as the Overture (I) and the 'The Tame Bear' (II). The earliest tune is the start of 'Fairies and Giants' (I), which he dated 1867 and called 'Humoreske tune from Broadheath' (see p. 2). In his comment about the Suites to F. G. Edwards of *The Musical Times* in 1908 there may be some

---

[1]   To S. Colvin, 13 December 1921.

exaggeration: 'The music begun in 1871 was not completed until 1906–7; the orchestration is more or less of that date ... Occasionally an obvious commonplace has been polished but on the whole the little pieces remain as originally planned.' Some were composed for early chamber music or Powick combinations, so possibly Elgar's associating them with the earlier play was part of a nostalgic reinvention of his past. No doubt his early sketches provided stimulus, but as published the Suites are the work of a practised composer.

Elgar was conscious of reaching his half-century. He wrote to Jaeger, with that slightly distancing posture of his: 'I shall be fifty next week so they tell me, but I don't know it: I have my pipe & the bicycle & a heavenly country to ride in – so an end. I take no interest whatever in music now & just "edit" a few old boyish MSS – music is off.'[2] As a birthday present his brother in Worcester sent him an old sea chest that had belonged to the Dover family Elgars. Maybe that set him thinking of his boyhood. At first he meant to make the thirteen pieces into one long suite, then he divided them into two. He called them The Wand of Youth. Wherever did he find such an evocative title, with the double implication of a magic rod and of a conductor's baton? The work begun in June 1907 had no name in September. In early October he met Walford Davies, whose 'Holiday Tunes' for children had recently been performed. On 6 October Elgar had his title; might something Davies said have suggested it?

Baroque suites were generally composed of dances. In the nineteenth century composers found the suite a congenial form for a collection of character pieces. A suite was also an expedient way to rescue theatre music and bring it to the concert hall. The popular orchestral suites of Grieg, Bizet, and Tchaikovsky were mostly drawn from stage works. The Wand of Youth music has much in common with the Nutcracker. Mendelssohn's A Midsummer Night's Dream, Britten's Gloriana, and Adès's Powder her Face suites are other examples. What singles out Elgar's Wand of Youth is that the 'production' was a family affair, the composer only a boy.

[2]   28 May 1907.

Elgar was a master of musical architecture, at his greatest in the long spans of symphonic movements or in Part I of *The Dream of Gerontius*. But he also had a flair for the brief pregnant figure. In that the pieces of the Suites are separate, brief, and captivating, they might be young irresponsible relations of 'Enigma'; but unlike the Variations they have no common source.

Suite No. I

Miniatures need to be pithy and to make their effect by instant characterization, tunefulness, and vivid colour. None does so better than the Overture. It has swagger and panache, a great swooping tune, a sudden blare or two of horns, and that's that. The Serenade has a 'Dorabella' lightness. The gracious Minuet was composed for the entry of the Two Old People. In his sketchbook Elgar headed it 'Minuetto à la Handel from children's opera'. During the 'Sun Dance' mirrors were supposedly flashed at the Old People to rouse them: the witty syncopations and the waltz tune are once-heard-never-forgotten. Two 'Fairy Pipers' (clarinets in thirds) pass in a boat (rocking accompaniment) and charm them to sleep with caressing strings. 'Slumber Scene' makes a virtue of necessity (its young player could only manage open strings) and the soporific rhythm is built on an *ostinato* of three notes. Elgar's harmonic shifts over them are a tour de force, at whatever age he composed the piece. Perhaps to compensate the cellos and basses for this limitation, the 'tune from Broadheath' is given to them (as strangely growly Fairies), then the Giants stride in to brass and heavy percussion. Occasionally the sunshine is clouded over: in Serenade (cue 13) and 'Sun Dance' (cue 26) a timpani roll and a pedal note bring a sudden dark reminder of '* * *' in Enigma.

Suite No. II

The opening March is in G minor (two of the five *Pomp and Circumstance* marches are in minor keys). The chattering *staccato* episode is major, with a sonorous legato counter-melody. The airy, enchanting 'Little Bells' and 'Moths and Butterflies' lured the Old People in the children's play over the bridge into fairyland. The first is glittering, with whizzing scales. Of the opening of 'Moths and Butterflies' Elgar recorded, 'I do not remember the time when it was not written in some form or other.' In the 'Fountain Dance' the jet bubbles up over a drone bass (the fountain was in the Elgars' garden, the jet somehow controlled by a football). The 'Tame Bear' suggests, by the pathos of its awkward gait, that Elgar sympathized with the 'poor bear – captive, made to dance', as his wife recorded in her diary. The chain rattles on tambourine. The uproarious tune of 'The Wild Bears' had been used for an early Powick quadrille.

The two Suites together prove how early the swing of Elgarian melody showed itself, how instantly recognizable is the idiom of his 'boyish' pieces. But by no means all the *Wand of Youth* music, in its final form, is emotionally simple. Often there is a melancholy undertow, counter-melodies that would come easily to the composer of *The Kingdom*. But in general these pieces from the earliest stirrings of his imagination define and single out some of the feelings shortly to be combined in the symphonies. Elgar's nostalgia, his obsession with youth and dreams, is understandable in one whose middle years were so far removed from his childhood. For a sensitive man, ambitions must be achieved at some cost to continuity: memory, not actuality, becomes life's link. But to make too much of that belittles Elgar. He was not the only man of his time to move from cottage to court: so did Barrie and Hardy. Elgar's great works date from his forties and fifties, the products of a mature technique and imagination. Revisiting his early sketches allowed him to find the creative continuity within himself. The Suites are not only delightful in themselves; composing them may have given him the energy and confidence to embark on his First Symphony.

Henry Wood performed the first Suite at Queen's Hall, London, on 14 December 1907, while the Elgars were wintering in Italy. Elgar conducted the first performance of his Second Suite on 9 September in Worcester Public Hall during the Three Choirs Festival of 1908: he dedicated it to his boyhood friend, Hubert Leicester.

Some of the music found a later setting. During the 1914–18 war Elgar quoted parts of 'Little Bells' (cue 21) and 'Fairy Pipers' (cue 34) in *The Starlight Express*, both passages of the utmost tenderness drawn from simple but eloquent harmonies, as though for sheer affection he could not let them go.

The Symphonies

The two symphonies, in A flat (1908) and E flat (1911), are both long and powerful, without published programmes, only hints at some inward drama from which they derive their vitality and eloquence. A search for extra-musical 'meanings' should not obscure their strengths as musical structures, as adventures in tonality, and as explorations in motivic, thematic relationships. Both are based on classical form but differ from it to the extent that, compared with Brahms (then an accepted model in England), they have been considered prolix and slackly constructed by some critics. Of the First Symphony, the first movement alone is the length of many a complete Haydn symphony, the four movements together lasting fifty-five minutes. Elgar needed the passage of musical time as a novelist sometimes does, to uncover the significance of the past by looking back through subsequent experience ('with sad enough retrospections').

Elgar was a man of moods, of a temperament that swung quickly from high spirits to despondency. His quicksilver mind expressed itself in puns, verbal sallies, and allusions. So too in his music. He had the creative range and the technical equipment to write at length. And for a Romantic composer, the symphony was the summit of achievement. He could not undertake it lightly.

Elgar is a tonal composer, for though he writes long stretches where it is impossible to pin down the key, so that apparently tonality is weakened and obscured, it is this that opens up a harmonic hinterland beyond the immediate foreground. His musical language was broad, his vocabulary encompassing the chromatic extremes of his contemporaries in England and on the continent. He had absorbed the extended tonality of Liszt and Wagner, and this, together with his mobile basses and his habit of thinking in sequences, make it often more accurate to say that a theme is in a tonal region than in a key. His nervous instability of harmony, avoidance of root positions, and fluctuations from active to withdrawn tonal planes, all propose key relationships that need time and space for their resolution.

The invention in the symphonies is copious, almost recklessly and bewilderingly so. Ideas pour out, and their development is not confined to the 'developments'. The main lines are firmly laid down but in between there are sometimes shadowy spaces, filled with what sound almost like improvisations. Close acquaintance reveals all sorts of glancing cross-references. Even if, at a first hearing, the motivic relevancies are not all clear, Elgar's own character was forceful enough to hold the music together, sensitive enough for it to touch many a responsive nerve. Jaeger wrote of moments that 'bite like acid into my musical feelins'.[3] In all Elgar's larger works themes are subtly interrelated, internal references fleetingly revealed, sometimes as late as the restatement. This kind of allusiveness, by glancing cross-references, even by a texture or a colour, is more poetic than classically symphonic. This does not make the music simpler, for it is complex – poetry and rhetoric have their part in it; but the elusive moments become allusive.

Though Elgar has none of Bruckner's monumental patience and little of Mahler's self-parody, public familiarity with their lengthy symphonies helped to raise critical opinion of Elgar's. In Mahler and in Elgar an emotional narrative is held together by the force and sensibility of the composer's musicianship. Occasionally he takes a refined idea and subjects it to so much violence that it seems raw. Such inflation is common to many Romantic composers; in Elgar, a latecomer, it was intensified by a sophisticated technique at the service of a complex but unsophisticated man. At its most characteristic his music does not aspire to pure expression, but to a complex of rich, ambivalent, often conflicting emotions. If the symphonies are to some extent autobiographical, admitting frailties and doubts as well as strengths and visions, then their occasional over-workings,

[3]   4 December 1908.

rhythmic monotony, and inferior ideas can be accepted as part of a comprehensive and adult perception of his world.

1908, Symphony No. 1, Op. 55

I *Andante nobilmente e semplice* – *allegro* II *Allegro molto*
III *Adagio* IV *Lento* –*allegro*

Elgar was fifty-one when he produced his first symphony. Such tardiness was not for want of ambition. The idea of a symphony crops up in his letters as early as 1898, to be curtly dismissed since it would earn him no money. It was to have been inspired by General Gordon, whose religious zeal moved the committed Catholic composer that Elgar then was. But *Gerontius* deflected this. The 1904 Leeds and Covent Garden festivals expected a symphony, but received In *the South* instead. Sketches suggest that the work Elgar had on hand then became the Second Symphony. In the lectures he delivered at Birmingham University (1905–08), he attracted attention by comparing programmatic with absolute symphonies. He held, in that academic context, that 'the symphony without a programme was the highest achievement of the art'. It was an issue that faced serious composers in the early 1900s. It had probably been the cause of Brahms's delay in the previous century. It is unlikely that Elgar, like Brahms, felt overshadowed by a past great compatriot: there was no comparable Beethoven in English musical life. Neither Stanford nor Parry produced a symphony during Elgar's prentice years that was so highly acclaimed as to daunt him.

The reasons were more likely to have been circumstantial and psychological. Elgar did not have the backing of a private income or of an academic post. In 1898, *Caractacus* gave him the confidence to compose the uncommissioned variations, and in 1900 came *The Dream of Gerontius*. But the 'Enigma' Variations are self-contained except in their derivation from one theme, and *Gerontius* still depends from a poem. By 1907 Elgar had composed the march tune that made him a household name and also his two biblical oratorios, but he still had not

committed himself to a continuous orchestral work of more
than overture or tone-poem length.

As he worked on *The Wand of Youth*, Lady Elgar's diary for
27 June 1907 notes that he played a 'great beautiful tune'. If,
as is generally accepted, this was the opening theme of the
First Symphony, it might have come into his mind when he
was in Rome six months earlier, for after the first performance
he sent W. G. McNaught of Novello a picture postcard of the
Via Appia Antica, and written across the sky in his hand are the
first three bars (see illustrations). The ancient road stretching
away out of sight, the ruins of grand buildings bordering it,
and Elgar's noble tune – to look at them together brings a
sudden flash of illumination. The Elgars spent a further six
months over the 1907–08 winter in Rome, in a flat in the Via
Gregoriana near the Spanish Steps. There he worked on the
first movement and sketched some of the second, but the main
composition was achieved after his return home to Hereford
in May 1908. By 29 June he was, his wife noted, 'possessed
with his Symphony'. It was completed in September.

He wrote to Walford Davies: 'There is no programme beyond
a wide experience of human life with a great charity (love) & a
massive hope in the future.'[4] He told Ernest Newman, 'As to the
phases of pride, despair, anger, peace & the thousand & one
things that occur between the first page & the last, I prefer the
listener to draw what he can from the sounds he hears.'[5] He
declared the symphony 'to be "a composer's outlook on life"'.[6]
That is strikingly like 'a man's attitude to life', his comment
about his later Cello Concerto.

For all his denial of a programme, some kind of inner
drama works itself out in this Symphony. But what happens
operates purely on a musico-dramatic level. It opens with two
solo drum-rolls, which for him usually indicate dark emotions.
There is an austere but grand Andante motto-theme, which
occurs complete at the start and at the end. For a 'motto', it
is unusually long and self-contained. Elgar intended it 'to be

[4]   13 November 1908.
[5]   4 November 1908.
[6]   Programme note for the first performance.

simple &, in intention, noble & elevating ... the sort of *ideal*
call – in the sense of persuasion, not coercion or command
– & something above everyday & sordid things'.[7] It is a forty-
seven-bar sustained theme in A flat over a regular crotchet bass,
diatonic, with one passing D natural in bar twenty-nine. How
assured is it? Spacious certainly, but sounding oddly hollow
in only two parts. On paper, even played on the piano, it may
seem confident. Heard, the introductory drum-rolls, the tune's
syncopation and asymmetric phrase lengths (7 + 10 + 6 bars),
the shifting *staccato* bass with the third bass crotchet, D flat,
contradicting the C in the melody, the veiled sound of woodwind doubled by divided violas with no violins till cue 3, the
final drawn-out cadence fading and lonely, all make it more
tentative than confident.

This 'ideal call' is the structural and emotional core of the
Symphony (Ex. 3.1).

Ex. 3.1

Andante ♩ = 72
nobilmente e semplice

Its first four conjunct notes (C down to G, then A flat up to
D flat) are pervasive, and as if to draw attention to that pattern,
in the first twenty-five bars the only third strand is the horns'
four-note A flat descent to E flat before cue 2. The 'call' exerts
its influence sometimes spectrally (cue 18), and sometimes
consolingly (cue 48), when it steals in from the last desks
only of the strings (how like Elgar, a fiddler himself, to give
the *last* desks their moment). In the shadowy Lento of the last
movement it is hinted at mysteriously, then enters dramatically
(cue 129) to smooth out the march-melody, and lead to an
apotheosis.

In the opening movement the wrench from the Andante
into the Allegro brings violent tonal and rhythmic contrast.
Does the Allegro begin in D minor or A minor? Does it matter?
Both keys are distant from A flat, either sets up an imbalance,

and the drama lies in the ambiguity. The tonality of the Andante is stable, that of the Allegro, thick with accidentals, unstable. Certainly the Allegro is not atonal, for its power derives from its positive avoidance of a keynote. Subsequent movements begin in F sharp minor, D major, and D minor. Few symphonies spend so little time in their tonic key. Only the 'ideal call' being solidly in A flat grounds the symphony tonally. What does matter is the rift in the fabric between the Andante and the Allegro, mirrored in reverse in the last movement with an equally violent break before cue 129.

The rhythm, dynamics, and wide leaping melodies of the turbulent Allegro all oppose the Andante. The Allegro's opening theme, in propulsive duple dotted rhythm, is set against passages that mix two and three stresses. When six-four is established, under the soaring second subject there is a little dotted pendant, 'sad & delicate' Elgar called it (five bars after cue 11). This, after a massive work-up of the Allegro's upbeat and rising fifth, explodes at cue 17 into a fff anguished parody – 'despair, anger' indeed. That collapses before the wraith of the 'ideal call', which in turn seems to disintegrate. At cue 19 the development begins with what sounds like a new idea, but is built on to the skeleton bass of the Allegro's first bars. Arabesques flowering from a tied note, and a new stalking figure of fifths and sixths, swirl and flit through the atmosphere, and gather energy to blare out the second subject. At the recapitulation at cue 32, the new bass glides imperceptibly in under the Allegro, so putting together D/A minor and G major with what Elgar called 'a nice sub-acid feeling'.[8] At cue 48 the 'new' bass is counterpointed with the 'ideal call', and at cue 54 it is garlanded with the arabesques. The music seems to relax into A flat. But in the final bars the little pendant theme intervenes in A minor with remote and nostalgic effect, making the last A flat tonic chord seem an adventure rather than a homecoming.

The second movement, in effect a scherzo, is terse to the point of impatience. Two rumbles in the bass set the key of F sharp minor into which come flying even semi-quavers (first drafted

8   To E. Newman, 23 November 1908.

for a string quartet). At cue 59 a march-like tune brusquely truncates its final bar, and on its third repeat roughly syncopates it. Then comes the delectable B flat episode (cues 66–71), about which Lady Elgar wrote, 'You cd. hear the wind in the rushes by the water', and Elgar told an orchestra, as if disclosing a secret, 'play it like something we hear down by the river'.[9] The scurrying semi-quavers run underneath it, then (cue 75) underneath the march, so closely related it all is. The semi-quavers lengthen through triplets, quavers, crotchets, all the while shedding impetus, till at cue 91 the 'ideal call' sounds *ppp* on the bassoons. Only the keynote F sharp is sustained. With a 'W. N.' – 'Nimrod' link, the F sharp becomes the mediant of the D major Adagio.

So the flying semi-quavers are audibly transformed into the gravely exultant Adagio, its theme extended by suspensions, syncopations, and sequences. The transformation is note for note except that the seventh bar slips down a semitone in one of Elgar's sudden reticences. The opening of the 'ideal call' might be heard at bars 13–15, ff and *molto espressivo*, and as underpinning the expansive second subject (cue 96), though since all notes have to go up or down it is possible to find connections that are just coincidence. Better to appreciate the full-hearted main melodies, the wayward flickering woodwind filigree arabesques, the benediction of the coda. This (cue 104) is the earliest part of the whole symphony, composed on Sunday 21 August 1904. On the sketch is a quotation from *Hamlet*, 'the rest is silence'. Indeed it would seem that nothing would dare follow the finality and beauty of the muted brass triplets and the solo rising clarinet.

A troubled dream-laden Lento introduces the last movement. From dark recesses come memories of the 'ideal call' and the stalking figure that Dunhill called 'an enemy to complacency',[10] and Elgar described as 'restless, enquiring & exploring'.[11] The 'ideal call' becomes a stealthy sinister march. Elgar called the new rising clarinet theme 'romantico'. An

[9]   William H. Reed, *Elgar as I Knew Him* (London, 1936), p. 141.
[10] Thomas F. Dunhill, *Sir Edward Elgar* (London, 1938), p. 130.
[11] 4 November 1908.

abrupt key-change brings the determined Allegro, in obses-
sively dotted rhythm, and a Brahmsian second subject (aston-
ishingly, a late addition). The march takes charge, builds up,
in retrograde, inverted, compacted, turned upside down and
all ways, then is transformed into a refulgent *cantabile* in canon.
After the sudden fracture, at last comes the apotheosis of the
'ideal call'. Elgar has found the courage for his '*massive*' hope.
The whole symphony can be heard as the conflict between
reality and idealism. His 'ideal call' and his Welsh tune have
that in common.

Elgar dedicated the symphony to 'Hans Richter, Mus. Doc.
True artist and true friend', in spite of the fact that Richter, after
launching the 'Enigma Variations' excellently, had conducted
the none-too-good first performance of *Gerontius*. He gave the
première with his own orchestra, the Hallé, in Manchester
on 3 December 1908. At rehearsal of the LSO for the London
première on 7 December at Queen's Hall, Richter introduced
it with words that place it in the European tradition: 'let us
now rehearse the greatest symphony of modern times' and
then '*and not only in this country*'. At the performance people had
to be turned away. Jaeger wrote to tell Dora Penny that the
atmosphere was electric. At the end 'the audience seemed to
rise … I *never* heard such frantic applause … Five times he had
to appear.'[12] The critics saluted it as the finest masterpiece of its
type from an English composer, as a work of high endeavour
and extraordinary accomplishment, as a true solution to the
problem of fertilizing symphonic form by the symphonic
poem, and as a work of European significance. The musicians
present included Parry, Stanford and Fauré; and the young
Adrian Boult who was to become one of the Symphony's finest
interpreters. In just over a year it was played a hundred times,
in all the great musical centres and in places as far apart as the
USA and Sydney – Siloti conducted it in St Petersburg, Löwe
in Vienna and Munich, and Nikisch in Berlin – an astonishing
record, even allowing for the fact that Nikisch toured it with
the LSO.

---

[12]   K. Allen, *August Jaeger: Portrait of Nimrod* (Aldershot, 2000), p. 256.

1911 Symphony No. 2 in E flat, Op. 63

I Allegro vivace e nobilmente II Larghetto III Rondo: Presto
IV Moderato e maestoso

After the First Symphony's triumph, Elgar composed his
Violin Concerto, performed by Kreisler to high acclaim on 10
November 1910. The following month Elgar began sustained
work on his Second Symphony. He dedicated it to 'the Memory
of His late Majesty King Edward VII'.

In 1903–04 Elgar had wintered at Alassio. When his piano
arrived, he improvised the opening theme of the Second
Symphony's last movement. Another last movement idea is
strikingly like part of In the South, which he was then composing.
Later in life, he told Barbirolli that this (four bars after cue
155) was the germ of the whole last movement. It is right in
the middle of the development, which confirms Elgar's unorthodox way of composing. Sanford Terry recalled that 'in every
movement its form, and above all its climax, were clearly in
[Elgar's] mind ... It is the climax which invariably he settles
first'.[13] From the autumn of 1905 dates the last movement's
nobilmente theme at cue 142; he headed this 'Hans himself!', so
it may have been intended for the First Symphony, dedicated
to Richter.

In April 1909 the Elgars stayed with Julia Worthington
at Careggi above Florence. There, Alice wrote to the 'other'
Alice, 'in glorious weather, the world bathed in sunshine, the
air scented with flowers',[14] Elgar sketched part of the first
movement. Then they went on to Venice. He saw the sombre
magnificence of San Marco, and in the Piazza he noted down
the rhythm of some strolling musicians who took a 'grave
satisfaction in the broken accent' of what they played. He said
that the openings of the Larghetto and of the Rondo represented the 'contrast between the interior of St Mark's at Venice
& the sunlit & lively Piazza outside'. Home at Hereford in June,
he worked on the Concerto. Not till November did he look
at the Italian and older sketches, when his wife noted that he

[13] MS notes by Sanford Terry in possession of the Athenaeum Club.
[14] 4 May 1909.

'was quite inspired with Sym 2'. Some sketches may have been from the old 'General Gordon' symphony that had come to nothing. On Christmas Day he played sketches to their house guest, Alice Stuart Wortley.

In spring 1910 Mrs Stuart Wortley and her family were staying at Tintagel, of romantic Arthurian legend. Elgar, touring the West Country with Frank Schuster, visited them and saw the 'austere yet lyrical beauty' of the place. He associated the pastoral theme in the Second Symphony's Scherzo (cue 106) with her. No specific theme can be linked with Tintagel, though Elgar dated the score 'Venice–Tintagel 1910–11'.

Back in his rented London flat, Elgar played what 'Dorabella' recalled as a slow movement for his Second Symphony – 'the sound of a funeral march'. That was before Edward VII died on 6 May 1910. Elgar had been honoured by him, dined with him, composed the Coronation Ode for him. He offered to produce a march for the funeral, but there was not time enough for rehearsal. It used to be thought that the Larghetto was inspired by the king's death, but clearly much of it was composed before. When Elgar played the movement to his wife she heard a 'lament for King Edward & dear Rodey in it, & all human feeling.' Alfred Rodewald had died in November 1903 and Elgar, who arrived too late in Liverpool to see him alive, walked the streets distraught. He composed at that time a sketch for the passage of creeping chromatics that was destined for *The City of Dreadful Night*, a proposed sequel to *Cockaigne*, It now appears (cue 74) in the Larghetto.

Elgar had acquired a date-stamper, and this, together with Lady Elgar's diaries, make it possible to chart the final work day by day. On 28 January 1911 he finished the first movement, and the next day he wrote to Alice Stuart Wortley: 'I have recorded last year in the first movement to which I put the last note in the score a moment ago & I must tell you this: I have worked at fever heat & the thing is tremendous in energy.' He finished the Larghetto on 6 February; the Rondo on 15 February, and the complete Symphony on 28 February. On 1 February 1911 he first referred to it as 'the Spirit of Delight' symphony. On the published score he wrote from Shelley's 'Song': 'Rarely, rarely comest thou /Spirit of Delight!' To

Frances Colvin he added lines from Shelley's *Julian and Maddalo*: 'I do but hide/ Under these notes, like embers, every spark/ Of that which has consumed me.'[15]

Elgar told his publisher that 'the spirit of the whole work is intended to be high & pure joy: there are retrospective passages of sadness but the whole of the sorrow is smoothed out & ennobled in the last movement, which ends in a calm &, I hope & intend, elevated mood'. All Shelley's poem might be read, he said, though neither the poem nor the music wholly illustrate or elucidate each other. He told Ernest Newman: 'my attitude towards the poem, or rather to the "Spirit of Delight" was an attempt to give the reticent Spirit a hint (with sad enough retrospections) as to what we would like to have!'[16] So many experiences, such rich associations, went into this music. His turmoils, his extremes of elation and morbid despair, are at its heart, transfigured so that his private memories become universal.

The first movement breaks from a unison into a mettlesome long paragraph of which the third bar (the descent from the crest of the climax) may be the 'Spirit of Delight' figure. Its presence is felt at the end of the Larghetto and in the closing bars of the work. The profuse ideas are related by the plunge and soar of their outlines, and by the swinging trochaic metre. All is valiant, energetic, splendid; throughout the symphony most of the positive, assured themes have a prominent melodic perfect fifth. There are two second subjects, the first shifts waywardly between keys, the second is a yearning melody for cellos, but they do not stem the current. But a harmonic progression based on an augmented fourth carries seeds of introspection and apprehension (which Alice called 'ghost') for the exuberant vitality is often undermined by desolation and self-doubt. The vaunting themes strive to exult, but as the development begins, confidence ebbs away, and there are unnerving glimpses of wraiths and anxieties. At cue 28 comes a highly organized cello tune over a pedal, weird and disturbing – it was fully shaped, not in sketch, not even in

---

[15] 1 February 1911.
[16] 9 May 1911.

short score, but as late as full score. 'A sort of malign influence wandering thro' the summer night in the garden,'[17] Elgar called it. He also described it as 'remote & drawing someone else out of the everyday world'.[18] The passage 'might be a love scene in a garden at night when the ghost of some memories comes through it; it makes me shiver'.[19] The approach to the recapitulation is by way of part of the first subject, which is compensatingly shortened.

After the raw nerve-endings of the first movement, the grief of the Larghetto – a great solemn elegy – is the more powerful for being formally contained. It is enclosed by interlocking sixths for strings (from an early song sketch). The main theme is heard above a muffled processional tread; when it comes back a solo oboe twines lamenting triplets around it. Accumulated feeling wells up twice thrillingly into simple major diatonic climaxes. Just before the end the 'Spirit of Delight' seems a wan memory of lost happiness.

The fleet-footed Rondo theme drives impatiently across the barlines, with steep dynamics. The repeats of it, and the lyrical episodes, all attract fragments of counter-subjects, so nothing is clear-cut. There is a ponderous string tune (again trochaic) and a little pastoral figure. Then the movement settles grimly on to a tonic pedal and gathers itself together for an utterance of the 'malign' theme from the first movement – a desperate suffocating passage. The opening Rondo figure swirls round it. In later life Elgar told orchestras to think of 'a man in a high fever ... that dreadful beating that goes on in the brain'.[20] He wanted the percussion to drown the rest of the orchestra – Spirit of delight, indeed! Did ever a composer write more misleadingly for publication about his music? And this is not even in the 'funeral march' movement. He associated this, he told his friendly correspondent Canon Gairdner,[21] with lines from Tennyson's Maud: 'Dead, long dead,/ Long dead. /And

17 To Alice Stuart Wortley, 29 January 1911.
18 To Alfred Littleton, 13 April 1911.
19 To Ernest Newman, 29 January 1911.
20 B. Shore, *The Orchestra Speaks* (London, 1938), p. 135.
21 William H. Temple Gairdner, *W. H.T.G. to his Friends* (London, 1930).

my heart is a handful of dust/ And the wheels go over my head.'

The magisterial E flat finale would be 'the great serene movement', he told Alice Stuart Wortley. It opens positively. Its three big tunes all have one-bar repetitions, aspiring leaps, and sequences. The development begins with vigorous *fugatos* but the return to the first theme is poetic, by way of a melancholy C minor. After the sumptuous, rhetorical sequences towards the end, the mood relaxes to welcome the 'Spirit of Delight'. Here is the apotheosis of Elgar's expressive appoggiaturas and suspensions; their alternate flexing and relaxing propel his great themes, and form emotional crises all the way from the king's anguish in *The Black Knight* (1893) to the cadenza of the Cello Concerto (1919). There is no triumph, no certainty here, but a courageous and compassionate reconciliation of the extremes of this great work. The Symphony's final pages unforgettably mingle delight, regret, and acceptance.

The first performance, on 24 May 1911 as part of the London Musical Festival, did not attract a full Queen's Hall. Though after conducting it he was called to the platform several times, Elgar missed the true note of warmth in the applause. Perhaps the word 'delight' had led people to expect a gayer note; the black passages were disconcerting. The new king's coronation was only weeks away, and here they were listening to an elegiac movement dedicated to the dead king. In some ways their sober reaction was a true one, to a work that demands a thoughtful appraisal rather than carefree excitement. Canon Gairdner suggested, and Elgar agreed, that it is the 'passionate pilgrimage' of a soul.

It is absorbing to trace the growing complexity of Elgar's noble slow tunes. In 1888 came an indication of his grand processional manner, in the *Ecce sacerdos magnus*, composed for his own church. The previous year he had sketched a melody, which in 1894 became *Sursum corda*, hastily revived for his first royal occasion, the visit of future George V to Worcester Cathedral. Though the opening of its aspiring melody is over-regular, the second strain shows one of his mature characteristics: he repeats the rhythm of a couple of bars exactly but expands the intervals inside the basic shape (Ex. 3.2a). He uses the same device in the

Larghetto of the string Serenade, when bars 5 and 6, spanning
an octave, are repeated but spanning a ninth (Ex. 3.2b); in this
tune too he propels the melody forward by dissonance on a
strong beat, and balances the sixteen-bar tune by repeating the
opening bars to close it. (Similarly he 'balances' the twenty-
bar tune of the Second Symphony's Larghetto, with greater
sophistication, at a differing pitch level.) In 'Softly and gently'
he enriches the song by contrapuntal imitations and increasing
chromatic inflections. His most complex, intricate structure is
the Adagio of the First Symphony. Here the melody's syncopations and elaborate decoration create a *Tristan*-esque melodic-
harmonic tension in which delayed resolutions accumulate
force to build a sustained and sublime paragraph. The climax
is formed not only by a reference to the 'ideal call' but the
opening of the Adagio itself lies underneath (Ex. 3.2c).

Ex. 3.2

With rehearsals, premières, and the possibility of LSO concerts
to conduct, Elgar was finding living in Hereford inconvenient.
So during 1910, while composing his Violin Concerto, he took
a service flat in London at Queen Anne's Mansions, then in
March one at 58 New Cavendish Street.

1910 Violin Concerto in B minor, Op. 61

I Allegro II Andante II Allegro molto

This most Romantic of concertos is Classical in design. Elgar employed a standard symphony orchestra, and composed three separate contrasted movements. He laid out the first with a traditional exposition for orchestra alone, then brought in the soloist.

And yet ... was there ever a concerto about which analysis conveys so little? Ardent, sumptuous, but confessional, the music catches the listener by the throat. The first subject comprises three brief ideas, any one of which would have satisfied a less generous composer. As if to compensate, the second subject is one simple, almost childlike phrase, four times repeated. But it would be wrong to concentrate on the melody only, which might be considered short-winded. The flow of the Concerto comes from the frequent and fluid modulations, prompted by the sequential treatment of the brief ideas. The Concerto is in B minor, but Elgar begins it tonally off-centre, on a dominant chord with a flattened leading note; A natural sounds in the first bar, and the orchestral exposition leans towards the 'flat' side of the key. Between cue 4 and cue 6 the keys of E major, A minor, C sharp minor, B flat, and E flat are touched on. That, combined with the movement's rhythmic drive, creates a strong momentum but some tension. Not once in the intro-duction is there a tonic in the bass on a strong beat: every-thing is ambiguous, and melancholy underlies the grandeur: all possibilities are open. Not until the soloist steals in with the phrase that concludes the first subject does the music settle on to a tonic pedal, giving a sense of expectancy fulfilled.

At once the soloist rhapsodizes freely, almost improvising. A single voice can be more flexible, personal, wayward, than a group, and a good concerto uses this principle. Elgar writes a virtuoso violin part, but the bravura is seldom just decora-tive: almost every twist and turn is organic and poetic. Also, all three movements are thematically connected. In Example 3.3, (a) and (b) are the first and third ideas from the first move-ment, (c) comes at cue 47 in the Andante and (d) at cue 56. For all the first movement's energy and warmth, there is an occasional sense of desolation, caught in the persistent semitone call of F sharp–G natural. This is derived from bar 1 (Ex. 3.3a) and cue 6. In the final movement, for four bars before cue 101, the semitone F sharp–G natural calls into being the cadenza.

Ex. 3.3

The Andante in B flat begins in all innocence, but in bars 5 and 7 it takes an introspective turn, and swivels on the note F, changing it from the dominant into the mediant of D flat. The violin enters as an inner part but soon soars. D flat is explained when it becomes the key of the intense, sustained second subject, which again has a tonal adventure, supported by solemn trombones. In the development the transition theme at cue 47, at that point modal, floating, and motionless, becomes propulsive and modulating, to merge in a bar at cue 56 from the first movement (Ex. 3.3d). This is a more complicated and passionate movement than its naïve opening would suggest. In old age, listening to a recording, Elgar said about the coda, 'This is where two souls merge and melt into one another.'[22]

The finale opens with the F sharp–G natural oscillating like a whirlwind, bringing high spirits and resolution. Ostensibly it is the most brilliant and decisive of the three movements, until that melancholy semitone calls back the past in the famous cadenza (cue 101), in which muted orchestral strings thrum a mysterious *pizzicato tremolando* background. While most cadenzas throw a spotlight on the soloist, Elgar withdraws his

[22] Kevin Allen, *Elgar in Love* (Malvern, 2000), p. 75.

into the twilight while the violinist weaves his yesterdays. He told Ernest Newman that the sound of a distant Aeolian harp fluttered around the soloist (Elgar had one fitted into his study window at Hereford; the wind blowing through it made an 'ethereal and mystic' sound). Over this, he brought in 'the real inspired themes from the 1st movement' (his words) and the music 'sings of memories and hopes'.[23]

Much of the Concerto's richness lies in what in other composers might be called 'accessories'. Rubato, dynamics, register, compass, colour, are an integral part of the invention. There are subtle lingerings and hastenings that a fine performer makes sound spontaneous. *Crescendos* and – particularly – the shading down of *diminuendos* seem part of the structure, and so is a sudden hush before a new theme. As to colour, horns hurtling down *con forza* just before the soloist's entry are unforgettable! Horns frequently sound the concerto's first two notes (the rising semitone) as a call to attention. The gentle opening theme of the Andante is flavoured by the extra tang of wind on the last chord of each phrase. When the violin sings it, it leaps up rapturously two octaves. As the movement gains intensity, timpani rolls deepen the emotion.

Elgar dedicated the Concerto to Fritz Kreisler (1875–1962), who made his London début in 1902 and had recently soared to fame. He and Elgar met at the 1904 Leeds Festival, Kreisler playing the Brahms concerto, Elgar conducting his *In the South*. Both were to appear at the following year's Norwich Festival. Before this, Kreisler was interviewed, and, placing Elgar as an equal with Beethoven and Brahms, wished he 'would write something for the violin'.[24] Immediately Elgar made sketches for the first movement. That Christmas he was given the scores of the Beethoven string quartets, and in his thank-you letter, his mind going back to his violin-playing days, he wrote: 'I renew my growth in reading some of the old dear things I played when a boy.'[25]

Further ideas had come during his Italian holiday in 1909,

---

[23]   16 June to Alice Stuart Wortley.
[24]   *The Hereford Times*, 7 October 1905.
[25]   To Edward Speyer, 15 December 1909.

then he turned to the Second Symphony. Serious work on the Concerto took place between January and June 1910, much of it in London or at Frank Schuster's house on the Thames near Maidenhead. The Andante was finished first, and played through to friends on 6 February. Then Elgar seemed to lose heart. At that point the encouragement of Alice Stuart Wortley became crucial. She became deeply, romantically, involved in the Concerto. On 7 February he composed the linking passage in the first movement at cue 2 and annotated the sketch he sent her with the date and time (6.30 pm), adding 'When Love and Faith meet/ There will be Light'. He called her 'Windflower', after the delicate white spring woodland flower, and attached her name to tender themes in the Concerto. He referred to her as the work's 'stepmother' and gave her further sketches. On 27 April he wrote to her: 'I have been working hard at the Windflower themes but all stands still until you come & approve!'

In May he finished the first movement, and found the man to help him with technical details. This was W. H. Reed (1876–1942), a violinist in the London Symphony Orchestra and soon to become its leader. Reed played over variants of the fiddle part, suggested bowings and fingerings, and wrote valuable accounts that give insights into Elgar's way of composing.[26] Kreisler was playing that year at the Three Choirs Festival (Elgar was conducting his *Gerontius*), and the two rehearsed at Gloucester. Robin Legge, the critic of the *Daily Telegraph*, was present and recorded: 'Elgar is quite a good pianist of his kind, but Kreisler is a better! Now & then K. would stop Elgar & show him how this passage or that should be played & was always right ... At the end of [the Adagio] the tears were pouring down [Elgar's] face. The whole man & his life is in his composition.'[27] Reed was at Gloucester too, and, in a charming gesture, Elgar asked him to perform the Concerto, himself playing the piano, before a private, distinguished audience. In London Kreisler suggested revisions, often simplifications, which were sent to Novello as late as 16 October. The interest

---

[26] William H. Reed, *Elgar as I Knew Him* (London 1936), pp. 170–1.

[27] R. Legge to his wife, 8 September 1910.

generated was exceptional. Even before the public première the Concerto was scheduled for performances at home and abroad. On 10 November 1910 the Queen's Hall was packed. Kreisler came on 'looking as white as a sheet' and Elgar was 'very much strung up'.[28] The applause lasted a quarter of an hour. It was such a triumph as to make it a sad loss that Kreisler in later years was elusive about recording the Concerto, even though Elgar was prepared to go to Berlin to conduct it.

Elgar placed an additional superscription on the score, a quotation in Spanish: 'Aquí está encerrada el alma de .....' (herein is enshrined the soul of .....). The quotation comes originally from the introduction to Le Sage's *Gil Blas*. Instead of the name there, of the student Pedro Garcias, Elgar placed the five dots, and checked on the correct grammar for the female gender with a Spanish-speaking friend, later confirming to Basil Maine that he had in mind a feminine spirit. Suggested candidates have been Alice Stuart Wortley, Julia Worthington (in whose villa the Concerto was begun), Frank Schuster's sister Adela, Elgar's early love Helen Weaver, or Alice Elgar herself. The mystery has prompted speculation, and it is strange that, having appeared distressed at the curiosity aroused by his 'Enigma' of 1899, Elgar should have invited it again in 1910. Perhaps the impulse partly to conceal, partly to reveal, lies at the heart of his music, with its compelling mixture of passion and inhibition. The Concerto is grand and noble, spacious in design however intimately it speaks; as taxing as Bartók's, as romantic as Berg's. Whoever was the 'soul' Elgar wished to enshrine, he has enshrined his own, and the violin's. Ernest Newman found that 'human feeling so nervous and subtle as this had never before spoken in English orchestral or choral music'.[29] To Alice Stuart Wortley, Elgar wrote on 25 October 1910 'What a wonderful year this has been! ... the radiance in a poor, little private man's soul has been wonderful & new & the Concerto has come!' To Albert Sammons his comment

---

[28] Mrs Richard Powell, *Memories of a Variation* (4th edn, Aldershot, 1994), p. 113.

[29] *The Nation*, 16 November 1910.

was more earthy: 'It is a b—— romantic theme and I b—— well
know because I b—— well wrote it.'[30]

Short Orchestral Works, 1909–11

In June 1909, at the request of Alfred Littleton of Novello,
Elgar composed the Elegy for Strings, Op. 58, in memory of a
member of the Worshipful Company of Musicians. But there
is nothing 'written to order' in the muted sound, harmonic
tension, and concentrated melody of this Adagio. The control
of phrase-lengths and internal imitations is masterly. August
Jaeger had died on 18 May, having lost his long battle with
tuberculosis. Elgar's grief must have informed this dignified and
deeply felt Elegy. He inscribed it 'Mordiford Bridge', a narrow
old bridge over the river Wye within easy cycling distance of
'Plas Gwyn', where he fished and made pencil sketches.

Elgar composed his Romance for bassoon and orchestra Op.
62 in 1910 for Edwin James (1861–1921), principal bassoon
of the London Symphony Orchestra, and soon to become its
chairman. James gave its first performance, Elgar conducting,
on 16 February 1911 at the Herefordshire Orchestral Society.
James was a founder member of the LSO, an orchestra with
which Elgar now had close associations. He had first conducted
them in a concert in 1905, when he gave the premières of
the third Pomp and Circumstance march and of the Introduction
and Allegro. In 1911 he was to succeed Hans Richter as the
LSO's conductor, so composing the Romance for James may have
been a diplomatic move. Richter described James's playing
as 'very fine, beautiful sound, good technique'. James must
have been delighted with such an addition to the bassoon's
scanty solo repertory. There were, of course, Mozart's and
Weber's concertos; of English works he might have possibly
have known Capel Bond's concertos, or Hurlstone's sonata. The
famous opening of The Rite of Spring was as yet unperformed.

Elgar played the bassoon in the wind quintet of his
Worcester boyhood (in the photograph in the plate section he

---

[30] RCM Magazine, Spring 1995, p. 12.

is seen with his four fellow wind players). He was working on his Violin Concerto when he composed the *Romance*, and the two works share some ideas. It is also reminiscent of the accompanied vocal recitatives in the oratorios, having the same flexible style, with tenutos and rubato. Elgar enjoyed testing the bassoonist, using the sonorous low notes (at one point reaching B below the bass stave) and the plaintive high notes. The orchestral scoring is tactful. A few years later he humorously used the bassoon's 'buffoon' image in the tavern scene in *Falstaff*, when it 'somewhat unsteadily but encouragingly' represents the drunken knight's speech, then becomes 'vague and somnolent'; but this *Romance* is a sympathetic and poetic piece.

Though Elgar was a Roman Catholic and was not to become Master of the King's Musick for another thirteen years, by the time of George V's coronation in 1911 he was the obvious man to compose a march and an anthem for the Westminster Abbey service on 22 June. The *Coronation March* is one of his finest 'laureate' works. It must have amused him to open it in three-four, with music planned for a 'Rabelais' ballet.

❧

In 1911 Elgar joined a Commonwealth tour by the Sheffield Chorus to celebrate the coronation. He admired the choir, trained by Henry Coward, which had given the first performance of the Coronation Ode. He was away from 25 March to 9 May, and conducted his own works in Toronto, Cincinnati, Indianapolis, Chicago, and St Paul.

In June he received the Order of Merit. His increasing conducting engagements with the LSO meant more time had to be spent in London. During May 1911 the Elgars took a furnished house, 75 Gloucester Place. They then found an imposing house in Hampstead. In order to raise money to buy it (it would be the first house they owned) Alice had to break her family trust. They moved into Severn House, 42 Netherhall Gardens, on 1 January 1912.

❧

Anthems, 1909–14

Sir Walter Parratt, Master of the King's Musick, asked Elgar for an anthem to be sung at the Royal Mausoleum at Frogmore, Windsor, on 22 January 1910 for the tenth anniversary of Queen Victoria's death. This would be a private occasion. Elgar turned again to Cardinal Newman for the words 'They are at rest', and composed a quiet unaccompanied setting. The key signature is two sharps, and the piece begins in B minor, moves to a blissful D major for the river as it 'murmurs by' and the Seraphs as they 'chant above', and ends – 'they are at rest' – on a chord of F sharp major. So Elgar achieves by tonality a poetic effect of apartness and peace.

His next anthem, 'O hearken thou', Op. 64, was for the grandest of royal occasions, George V's coronation on 22 June 1911. But again it was for a private moment, the preparation for the king's communion. Elgar's music is intense and devotional. The twining chromatics and suspensions of the opening *pianissimo* four bars for organ end with an upward figure, like prayers or incense rising, that recurs four times. This beautiful supplication – 'my King, and my God' – enshrines the essence of Elgar's spirituality.

'Great is the Lord', Op. 67 (Psalm 48), was composed in 1912 for the foundation of a church (or for general use) and was first performed in Westminster Abbey on 16 July 1912. It is broad and plain, with a sturdy striding opening for lower voices in unison. There is a graphic illustration of the assembling of the dismayed earthly kings, a queasy four bars for the woman in travail (a very short labour), a bass solo for God's loving-kindness, a dancing six-four for Zion's rejoicing, and a grand recapitulation for 'everlasting' God.

In 'Give unto the Lord', Op. 74, composed for the Festival of the Sons of the Clergy at St Paul's on 30 April 1914, Elgar has no difficulty in reconciling a sequence of awesome chords for the Lord's voice with contrapuntal rampaging as He destroys the poor cedars and forests, but comes down sweetly on the side of peace at the end. There is easier imagery in the harvest anthem for parish use, 'Fear not O Land' (1914), when pastures, figs, and vine all flourish, and Elgar writes a simple happy piece of rejoicing.

Solo Songs, 1909

In 1909 Sir Gilbert Parker (1862–1932) sent *Embers*, a volume
of his poems to Elgar, who planned a cycle of six songs with
orchestra as his Op. 59. It might have been another integrated
cycle like *Sea Pictures* but only Nos. 3, 5, and 6 were completed.
All three are love poems, intricately worked and attentive to
the words and declamation. 'Oh, soft was the song' begins
gently; the phrase for 'thou wert mine own' rises up a seventh,
and returns at the end to close on the tonic. 'Was it some
golden star?' is a lovers' fantasy, in another land ('Malabar?
Italy?') and another age ('Charlemagne? Dido?'). Elgar's singer
begins almost in recitative, with the romance in the accompaniment, but with roles reversed at 'You were a queen'. In
'Twilight' the drooping phrases and dragging rhythm mourn
the past and 'things … that might have been'. The Parker songs
were first performed at the memorial concert for Jaeger on
24 January 1910, sung by Muriel Foster (by now Mrs Goetz).
Elgar composed 'A Child Asleep' for her infant son. He took
four verses from Elizabeth Barrett Browning's poem, and set
them simply with loving stress on 'summer', 'music', and
'peace'.

The strangest songs – raw, declamatory, jagged, full of
longing – Elgar composed are his Op. 60, 'The Torch' and 'The
River'. He disguised them as Eastern European folk-songs, the
words paraphrased by Pietro d'Alba, Carice's pet angora rabbit
(see p. 92), whose death in 1910 he sincerely mourned. He
further made them sound exotic by concealing their place of
composition as Leyrisch-Turasp. In fact, he himself wrote the
words and their place might be an anagram of Tupsley Parish
near Hereford. There is a further mystery in the identity of
their dedicatee, Yvonne.

1912 The Crown of India, Op. 66

Of all Elgar's compositions, the most firmly tied to its time is
the Imperial Masque, *The Crown of India*. It was commissioned
by Oswald Stoll to honour the visit in December 1911 of the
King-Emperor and Queen Mary to India for the Delhi durbar.
The imperial couple made their entry in a five-mile proces-

sion, and then appeared in full coronation finery to receive the homage of the princes. Stoll had opened the Coliseum theatre in 1904 for music-hall entertainment. The Masque took its place in a programme that included gymnastic equilibrists, a ventriloquist, a Russian harpist, a scene from Barrie's *The Twelve-Pound Look*, continental mimes, and with the *Tannhäuser* Overture as interval music. Henry Hamilton, who wrote the text of the Masque, was prolific and versatile, turning out everything from a pantomime to a version of Mérimée's *Carmen*, excoriated by Bernard Shaw. Elgar was commissioned to compose the music and conduct two performances a day for two weeks, from 11 March 1912 at the London Coliseum.

The invitation came opportunely. The Elgars had moved into their London house on 1 January. Their expenses were high; so was Stoll's commission fee. To Frances Colvin he was frank: 'It was an inoffensive thing & some of the music is good! When I write a big serious work e.g. *Gerontius* we have had to starve and go without fires for twelve months as a reward: this small effort allows me to buy scientific works I have yearned for and I spend my time between the Coliseum and the old bookshops ... I found a lovely old volume *Tracts against Popery* – I appeased Alice by saying I bought it to prevent other people seeing it – but it wd make a cat laugh ... My labour will soon be over ... & then for the country lanes & the wind sighing in the reeds by Severn side again & God bless the Music Halls!'[31]

Alice Elgar had been born in India. Her father, Sir Henry Gee Roberts, had joined the East India Company in 1818, served on the northern frontier, and reached the rank of major-general in his military career. In the Indian Mutiny he captured the town of Kota. Alice, who was eleven when he died, brought Indian furniture and momentoes to Elgar's homes. Elgar's initial reaction to the Masque was that it was going to be 'very gorgeous & patriotic'. His later comment that there was 'far too much of the political business' in it seems to have been directed at the rivalry between Delhi and Calcutta, rather than any criticism of the British Raj. He cut some lines from the libretto, and raided his sketchbooks.

[31]   14 March 1912.

The Masque was in two tableaux, 'The Cities of Ind' and 'Ave Imperator!' In the first, Calcutta and Delhi both pleaded to be made India's capital, and in the second the King-Emperor diplomatically settled their differences: 'Delhi to be his capital he names/ And of his Empire further makes decree/Calcutta shall his premier city be.' 'Happy Britain – that above all lands/ Still where she conquers counsels not commands … Who spread her Empire not to get but give/ And free herself bids others free to live.' There were singing roles for Agra and St George; speaking parts with melodrames for India, Delhi, Calcutta, and Benares; processions, dances, marches for other Cities, Emperors, Courtiers, Attendants, Natives. The Times critic stressed that it was symbolic: 'it is necessary to remember this when a smooth-faced female figure heralded as "George, by the grace of God, of that great name the fifth" enters in triumphal procession. Any other arrangement would be likely to be a still greater shock to local sensibilities.'

The work begins – suitably enough for British triumphalism – with a theme composed in 1903 for Sinclair's bulldog – 'the sinful youth of Dan'. Elgar used up ideas rejected from the oratorios. Music for dervishes from In Smyrna provided an all-purpose decorative orientalism for Agra's song. The 'Sacred Measure' charmingly if ineptly recalls 'The Tame Bear' from The Wand of Youth, from which the pretty 'Dance of the Nautch Girls' might also have strayed. 'March of the Mogul Emperors' and 'Warriors' Dance' are maybe Elgar's idea of the primitive, vigorous though rather coarse. St George could fittingly have been part of his Banner of 1897: 'Lift aloft the Flag of England! … Keep her ancient Honour bright, her manhood ever glorious/ Her valour still victorious …'. The jewel in this Crown is the Interlude, an exquisite violin solo comparable with 'The sun goeth down' in The Kingdom.

The Times found no number in the masque to excel or even to equal Elgar's already published best popular work. Elgar put together a suite, which was performed at the Three Choirs Festival in 1912, and later recorded it. Much of the orchestral score and parts are missing. The complete score was published only in a piano reduction by Hugh Blair, who was now the organist of Holy Trinity, Marylebone. Two big numbers are

complete: Agra's song 'Hail, Immemorial Ind', which is rather
like a study for the contralto part of *The Music Makers*; and *The
Crown of India March*, which has a splendid central tune and is a
better piece than the *March of the Mogul Emperors*.

As for the music, 'the subject of the Masque', Elgar wrote,
'is appropriate to this special period in English history.'[32] As
sensible a summing-up as any.

1912 The Music Makers, Op. 69

Soon after completing *The Wand of Youth* in 1907 Elgar had
sought copyright permission for Arthur O'Shaughnessy's Ode
The Music Makers. O'Shaughnessy (1844–81) came to notice as
a poet in 1870 with his *Epic of Women and other Poems*. Though he
worked in the zoological department of the British Museum
specializing in reptiles, his temperament, according to the
Dictionary of National Biography, was 'that of a genuine poet. His
slender frame and spiritual expression recalled Chopin.' He
died young. His Ode appeared in *The Athenaeum* of 30 August
1873, and the following year in his collection *Music and Moonlight*. Elgar's interest was first announced[33] at the time of the
Elgar Festival at Covent Garden: that had set the seal on him as
a music maker. But it was not until May 1912 that he began
serious work on *The Music Makers*, which he conducted on 1
October at the Birmingham Festival.

Shelley's contention that 'poets are the unacknowledged
legislators of the world' lies behind the Ode. The idea of the
artist as dreamer, alone at the water's edge, apart from the
world yet inspiring every generation, is wonderfully appealing.
'The soldier, the king, and the peasant/ Are working together
in one' was an ideal Elgar could share. His early life, if not
among the peasantry, was among cottager country folk. His
Pomp and Circumstance marches idealized the soldiers' profession
before the carnage of the Great War put an end to all that. He
had dined with royalty and dedicated his Second Symphony
to the king's memory. The atmosphere of the whole poem is a

---

[32]   *The Standard*, 1 March 1912.

[33]   Edward Baughan, *The Daily News*, 25 March 1904.

heady mixture of aspiration and melancholy. It contains unforgettable lines: 'each age is a dream that is dying' – 'sitting by desolate streams' – 'a singer who sings no more'. The alliteration, cadences, and imagery are deeply evocative. Elgar had an unerring instinct for the sentiment that would release his creativity. How could he fail to identify with 'We are the music makers, And we are the dreamers of dreams ... Our souls with high music ringing ... '. The words seem as much written for his artistic creed as *The Dream of Gerontius* was for his religious creed.

On a more mundane level O'Shaughnessy's poem has been dismissed as Swinburne and water,[34] derided as self-conscious, as Victorian escapist verse. Some line-endings are limply contrived: 'Gleams/it seems'; 'As they may/yesterday'; 'Deathless ditties/great cities' (though Shakespeare's lark welcomed daylight with her ditty and Milton could write of 'amorous ditties all a summer's day'). The verses do not bear close examination as to exactly who 'we', 'they', 'you' are at each point. Ernest Newman had to provide a footnote to his *Musical Times* article in September 1912 explaining that 'they' in verse 5 referred to 'soldiers, kings, peasants, and other of the world's workers'. But these drawbacks did not deter Elgar, and can be overlooked by a listener who wants to understand his outlook.

Besides his article, Newman contributed the programme note for the first performance. O'Shaughnessy's contention is that artists are the 'movers and shakers' of the world, the true makers of history, inspirers of men and their deeds. They can foresee in vision what others must work out through struggle. Today is the realization of yesterday's dreams, tomorrow will bring into being the dreams of today. So all is continuously renewed. Elgar wrote of the artist's 'tremendous responsibility' and of the 'unending influence of his creation'; and acknowledged that 'the mainspring of O'Shaughnessy's Ode is the sense of progress, of never-ending change'.[35] Yet the

---

[34] Thomas F. Dunhill, *Sir Edward Elgar* (London, 1938), p. 119.
[35] To Ernest Newman, 14 August 1912.

pervasive motto of his music is the gentle, withdrawn choral opening, 'We are the music makers/ And we are the dreamers of dreams.'

The orchestral prelude is almost an anthology of Elgar's characteristics. It presents two themes, alike in their typically Elgarian sequences, and alike rhythmically, each having semi-quavers on the last of three quaver beats to a bar. The first theme, which returns as an instrumental ritornello, may symbolize the artist's 'sadness and spiritual unrest': under the sinuous melody the horns probe chromatically and insistently. The second theme, more reposeful, is associated with the artist's 'mission' and climbs diatonically upwards. Then, thrusting up with absolute naturalness through the texture, comes the 'Enigma' theme, marked *affretando*, the first of Elgar's self-quotations.

He sets the first six lines ('We are the music makers …') quietly, chordally, unaccompanied (he called it simply the 'artist' theme). A quotation from *The Dream of Gerontius* deftly illumines 'dreamers of dreams', and one from *Sea Pictures* the 'lone sea-breakers'. But such details must not destroy an appreciation of the sweep, the continuity, and integrity of this opening paragraph. Elgar's style was so homogenous that these and the 'Enigma' theme follow seamlessly within the opening twelve choral bars. One of the admirable qualities of this work is the large-scale design and firm placing of climaxes.

At 'an empire's glory' he quotes not his own music but snatches of 'Rule Britannia' and the 'Marseillaise', and pointed out to Newman 'the deadly sarcasm of that rush in horns & trombones (deliberately comicalizing it)'. 'Trample a kingdom down' is set to a whole-tone passage, which will eerily recur. A lyrical theme for 'to the old of the new world's worth' is worked up into grandly sustained counterpoint: this is Elgar in his Parry-esque style. Then, in a masterly stroke, he recapitulates the first two lines of verse, emphasizing 'music' and 'dreams'. At cue 39 as the 'mission' theme reaches its highest note, the orchestra falls silent and the chorus breathes '… our inspiration'; the phrase is almost the one under the words 'and he worshipped Him' in *The Light of Life* (see Ex. 1.10) and will recur in the Cello Concerto at the *con passione* climax at cue 69.

It is an inspired moment. Elgar's music is sometimes its own best interpreter.

So far the soloist has been silent. An unexpected side-slip from major to minor suggests her serious import. Elgar composed the part for Muriel Foster, the Angel in the 1902 Düsseldorf performance of *The Dream of Gerontius*. Her classical, intense style could be deduced from this solo, a twenty-bar quotation from 'Nimrod', so achingly intense that formally it overbalances the whole work. It is a tribute to Jaeger ('Nimrod'), whose look and word 'wrought flame' in Elgar's heart. 'Amongst all the inept writing and wrangling about music, his voice was clear, ennobling, sober and sane, and for his help and inspiration I make this acknowledgement'.[36] At cue 53 'Nimrod' slides into the close of the Second Symphony.

There is an allusion to the most withdrawn moments of the Violin Concerto at 'in our dreaming and our singing/ A little apart'; and, blazingly, to the 'ideal call' of the First Symphony at 'infinite morning'. Both reveal something of those works besides this one. The most 'advanced' passage, indeed some of the most original sounds Elgar ever created, that might well have been inspired by 'the dazzling unknown shore' was in fact adapted from a 1907 sketch. In contrast to that, and as though to affirm the artist's influence, the words 'you shall teach us' are declared in broad, strong, diatonic chords. A final heartrending allusion to the death of Gerontius at 'a singer who sings no more' is often taken to refer again to Jaeger. Perhaps it could also symbolize Elgar's awareness of his own mortality, or more widely, of the short human span of all artists.

He set the poem with no cuts, but not unchanged. He repeats the 'artist' theme as a refrain, and in the final stanza quotes words from stanzas 7 and 8. It is almost as if he undermines the poet, who with brave optimism greets the dazzling unknown, the glorious future, which will renew the world in spite 'of a dreamer who slumbers, And a singer who sings no more.' That conclusion will not do for Elgar, and his work ends as it began with 'We are the music makers…' '*ma più lento*'. For all the grand, forceful passages of music, the impression that

---

[36] To Ernest Newman, 14 August 1912, for the programme note.

remains is of the artist's apartness: music can influence only the inner life of the individual, not politics, nor empires, nor the building of great cities.

Elgar's self-quotations may have been prompted by the 'works of peace' section in Strauss's *Ein Heldenleben* in which he quotes his own music; Elgar had heard the work in 1902. Since it takes longer to read about the quotations than to listen to them, they can assume too much importance. Elgar himself begged for not too much insistence 'on the *extent* of the quotations which after all form a very small portion of the work'.[37] Some of the new music, and that discarded from his previous works, is less distinguished by comparison. The repeated sequence of diminished sevenths for 'dream' is almost too facile, the conquering, trampling men are too obvious. Nor is Elgar quite convinced that 'today is thrilling'. All through the work, the optimistic sentiments seem strained rather than authentic.

But the quotations *were* significant to Elgar. Some early writers found them superficial and obscure, and searched for 'some allusion which may not really be there at all'. Nowadays few can be unaware of their relevance, and the backward glances to Elgar's life through his art constantly enrich this music. As he wrote to Newman: 'I am glad you like the idea of the quotations: after all art must be the man, & all true art is, to a great extent egotism.' More formally, he wrote: 'I have used the opening bars of the theme (Enigma) of the Variations [at the words 'sitting by desolate streams'] because it expressed when written (in 1898) my sense of the loneliness of the artist as described in the first six lines of the Ode, and to me, it still embodies that sense; at the end of the full score of the Variations I wrote: 'Bramo assai, poco spero, nulla chieggio (Tasso)' [see p. 53]. This was true in 1898 and it might be written with equal truth at the end of this work in 1912.' In linking these two works Elgar gives the strongest possible hint that the 'enigma' is himself.

The quotations turn this music from being just a setting of O'Shaughnessy's Ode into Elgar's autobiography. The theme is

---

[37] To Ernest Newman, 16 August 1912.

surely inspiration. He quotes his own great published works (complete lists are given in Kennedy's *Portrait of Elgar*, appendix II and in the Elgar Collected Edition, Vol. 10). He used ideas discarded from *Gerontius*, from *The Apostles*, and from projected but unfinished works: the 1907 string quartet, a Callicles song by Matthew Arnold. All are from his maturity. In The *Wand of Youth* his early unpublished pieces, though acknowledged, were a matter for the professional composer. Now he went public. But the curious thing is, *The Music Makers* seems even more personal, more confessional and introspective. Elgar's music often suggests some intimate coded message. O'Shaughnessy's poem is about music's possible influence on grand affairs. Elgar reveals more about the process of creation than about its effects. The positive words inspire the least good music.

When he finished the vocal score, he felt desolation. Wandering alone over Hampstead Heath, he experienced the 'usual *awful* day which inevitably occurs when I have completed a work'. All he could then quote was 'World losers & world-forsakers for ever & ever.'[38] This was to Alice Stuart Wortley, to whom he had sent sketches during the composition: the opening page headed 'the complete understanding', the strange chords at 'Yea, in spite of a dreamer...'. By 29 August he could confess to her 'I have written out my soul in the concerto, Sym II & the Ode & you know it ... in these three works I have *shewn* myself.'

༄

In early 1913 Elgar was again unwell and depressed, so his wife suggested a holiday in Naples. That did little good, so he went for the cure to Llandrindod Wells for a week in March, then spent the first part of April with his sister Pollie in Worcestershire.

༄

---

[38]   19 July.

1913 Falstaff: Symphonic Study in C minor, Op. 68

Falstaff, commissioned by the Leeds Festival, has always challenged commentators and divided Elgar's admirers. He told
Delius[39] he considered it his best work. Gerald Cumberland
recorded his saying that he had 'enjoyed writing it more than
any other music I have ever composed ... I shall say "good-
bye" to it with regret, for the hours I have spent on it have
brought me a great deal of happiness.'[40]

Yet in the year of its first performance it played to half-
empty halls. The fact that Elgar published his own 'analytical
essay'[41] before he conducted it on 1 October 1913 at Leeds
seems to have put people off. Jaeger wrote analyses of *The
Dream of Gerontius* and the two oratorios. With Jaeger dead, who
better than Elgar to write about his *Falstaff*? His knowledge of
Shakespeare went back to his boyhood, and was not gained
only from the printed page. Ned Spiers, his father's handyman
and retired hack actor, would not have declaimed from a text
in the back parts of the Worcester shop. But the work has been
faint-praised for being too learned, for smelling too much of
the midnight oil and the study.

It is a problem common to all programme music. In his
Birmingham lectures Elgar declared that the abstract symphony
was the highest development of art. That provoked Ernest
Newman into demanding why, if Elgar rated absolute above
descriptive music, he had composed so much in a medium that
his judgment condemned. At the time there was a general view
that descriptive music was inferior, even improper. Towards
Falstaff, then, Elgar's attitude was mixed. He was careful not
to call it a symphonic or tone poem, but a 'symphonic study'
(the word study to be taken 'in its literary use or meaning', as
a consideration of Falstaff's character). He defensively pointed
out 'it must not be imagined that my orchestral poem is
programme music – that it provides a series of incidents with
connecting links' such as in Strauss's *Ein Heldenleben* or *Symphonia*

[39]   Eric Fenby, *Delius as I Knew Him* (London, 1936, 1966), p. 113.
[40]   'Gerald Cumberland' [C. F. Kenyon], *The Daily Citizen*, 18 July 1913.
[41]   *The Musical Times*, September 1913, reprinted as a booklet in 1933, the
source of Elgar's comments unless otherwise noted.

Domestica. 'Nothing has been farther from my intention. All I have striven to do is to paint a musical portrait – or rather, a sketch portrait.'

But in *Falstaff* things happen. Incidents of dramatic sequence are paralleled in musical sequence. The study is not a portrait, not a timeless reflection of a man's qualities such as 'Nimrod', or Hans Sachs in the Act III prelude of *Die Meistersinger*. Falstaff is not the same man at the end as at the beginning. Elgar's *Falstaff* is remarkable just because it combines portraiture and narrative in symphonically developing music that deeply satisfies several opposing criteria.

How can a composer best reconcile narrative and character study, descriptive and musical values? Incidental music needs short self-contained pieces, each setting a single atmosphere: Mendelssohn, Sullivan, and Finzi, in *A Midsummer Night's Dream*, *The Tempest*, and *Loves Labour's Lost*, did not have to shape the extended structural framework that Elgar (or Strauss) did. Opera has demands and opportunities of its own, but a symphonic work must make its own stage. Elgar was aiming high. Falstaff is English, but before Elgar it was a German and an Italian who had notably portrayed him in music. Shakespeare demands a double standard: how does a work measure up to its source, and how fine is it in itself? The greater the composer, the more strongly he may bring out his own interpretation.

Elgar considered the Falstaff of the *Histories* only. 'The caricature in *The Merry Wives of Windsor* which, unluckily, is better known,' he said, 'must be forgotten.' In dismissing *The Merry Wives* as an afterthought written at Queen Elizabeth's request, he was following scholarship of his time. As A. C. Bradley declared in 1902, Falstaff is 'to be found alive in the two parts of *Henry IV*, dead in *Henry V*, and nowhere else'. Though Verdi's *Falstaff* is based mainly on the *Merry Wives*, it is curious that Elgar made no reference to it. Boito borrows half-a-dozen passages from *Henry IV*, and in design and characterization his libretto is far superior to *The Merry Wives*. Verdi's music, for all its merriment, brims over with tenderness for middle-aged folly and young love. It is just conceivable that Elgar had not seen the opera. Though it reached Covent Garden in 1894, the year after the Milan production, it was not revived there until 1914. There were, however, student performances at the RCM, Stanford having been at the première and written enthusiastically about it.

Absolute fidelity is not only impossible in moving from one medium to another but is no more automatically to be praised than is the suppression of details or episodes. Elgar used much the method he had to make his *Apostles*. There he took a hint from 'and continued all night in prayer to God' and expanded it into a nocturne. Here he takes a hint from Shallow's reminiscence, 'Then was Jack Falstaff, now Sir John, a boy and page to Thomas Mowbray, Duke of Norfolk,' and composed his delectable Dream Interlude. Similarly Boito gave 'Quand'ero paggio del Duca di Norfolk' to Verdi, who made it into one of the tiniest, freshest arias ever composed.

In his Analysis Elgar quotes Maurice Morgann (1726–1802), whose celebrated *Essay on the Dramatic Character of Sir J. Falstaff* was published in 1777, reprinted in 1903, and again – perhaps significantly – in 1912. Morgann was Under-Secretary of State with a special knowledge of American affairs, which accounts for such charming excursions as 'When the hand of time shall have brushed off [Shakespeare's] present Editors and Commentators … the Appalachian mountains, the banks of Ohio, and the plains of Sciota shall resound with [his] accents.' The passage where he breaks away from Falstaff into general praise of Shakespeare's comprehension and poetry is superb.

Elgar quotes his paragraph beginning Falstaff 'is a character made up … wholly of incongruities', also quoted by Elgar's second authority, Edward Dowden, in his *Shakspere – A Critical Study of his Mind and Art* (1875). It raises two points: 'incongruities': 'want of accordance or harmony'. How can such a state best be indicated in music? For composers of Elgar's period 'accordance' still meant reference to the diatonic system. A glance at his *Falstaff* themes shows how many of them are characterized by chromatic contradictions. The very first (Ex. 3.4), because it is unharmonized, does not properly establish its C minor key but is full of implications, of Falstaffian shifts of attitude. Each complete bar could be parsed as belonging to a different key: bar 1 in E flat major, bar 2 in C minor, bar 3 in G minor.

Ex. 3.4

Falstaff 'cajoling' (cue 7) and Falstaff 'boasting' (cue 25) are equally prone to accidentals. Most significant of all is the singing Falstaff at Eastcheap (cue 19), the chordal passage on lower strings and wind, where the first bassoon part, for instance, runs: F sharp, F natural, F sharp, F natural, G sharp, G natural, E, F natural, G sharp, G natural, and so on. A series of contradictions indeed! '... A man at once young and old, enterprising and fat, a dupe and a wit, harmless and wicked.'

Elgar relished Morgann's splendid extravagant prose, and between them they hotly defended Falstaff from charges of cowardice. Morgann's essay, a vindication of Falstaff's courage, was directed against the ignominious clowning he received on the eighteenth-century stage. Elgar repeats Morgann's 'knight, gentleman, soldier', but without his qualifying lack of 'dignity, decency or honour'. 'I could have better spared a better man./ O, I should have a heavy miss of thee,/ If I were much in love with vanity!' mourns Prince Henry at Shrewsbury, thinking Falstaff dead. The first line is more often quoted than the following two, but they reveal the Prince's changing heart and mind. 'The feeling of pleasantry which runs through the dialogue is almost courtly,' writes Elgar of the opening scene between the Prince and Falstaff. 'Prince Henry apostrophises him as "Thou latter spring! All-Hallown summer!"' Yes, but also as 'fat-witted with drinking of old sack'.

Elgar's view was that of his period, and no doubt he, like Bradley, would have regarded the Prince's dismissal of his old companion as 'The Rejection of Falstaff', with all the unfairness and hard-heartedness that the phrase implies. But Samuel Johnson, whose estimate of Prince Henry was that 'the character is great, original and just', had seen that Falstaff's influence was the more corrupting because it was seductive. 'No man is more dangerous than he that, with a will to corrupt, hath the power to please; and that neither wit nor honesty ought to think themselves safe with such a companion when they see Henry seduced by Falstaff.'[42] Elgar nowhere quotes Johnson. George Brandes, editor of the copy of *Henry IV Part 1* that Elgar owned, accounted for Falstaff's downfall in a passage Elgar marked:

> In the second part he falls more and more under the suspicion of making capital out of the Prince, while he is found in ever worse and worse company. The scheme of the whole, indeed, demands that there shall come a moment when the Prince, who has succeeded to the throne and its attendant responsibilities, shall put on a serious countenance and brandish the thunderbolts of retribution.

The essence of Falstaff as Lord of Misrule was that his reign must have an end, that when the reformed Prince becomes King he must side with Law, and the audience would accept the 'rejection' as both just and inevitable. Elgar's attitude to Falstaff was defensive. He noted 'almost with pain' Falstaff's fall, and musically he works on our sympathies in the two interludes when he imagines Falstaff in idyllic innocence. But nothing in Elgar's music shows, as Shakespeare does in Part II of *Henry IV*, that gradually, while Falstaff is over-reaching himself and becoming bumptious, the prince is growing into kingship and authority. Elgar's *Falstaff* leaves us no choice either: we must be absolutely and gloriously on Falstaff's side.

The vividness of Elgar's musical imagery is proved by Tovey's analysis,[43] made before seeing the composer's own: the two tally extraordinarily. Nearly all Elgar's 'corrections', which Tovey footnotes, are more specific than Tovey's guesses. The important point at which Tovey misread Elgar's intentions is not a matter of action but of sentiment. The theme at cue

---

42 W. K. Winsatt (ed.), *Dr Johnson on Shakespeare* (London, 1969), p. 118.
43 D. F. Tovey, *Essays in Musical Analysis*, Vol. IV (Oxford, 1937).

19 was described by Tovey as 'blown up like a bladder with sighing and grief'. 'Not at all!', responded Elgar. 'A goodly, portly man, of a cheerful look, a pleasing eye and a most noble carriage.' The misunderstanding is fundamental. For all that Elgar was attracted to Falstaff the libertine, he himself could only go so far. He chose to identify himself creatively with a character of gusto, liberality, and lawlessness who comes to be 'rejected' by the new regime, but only by idealizing him.

There was in Elgar a little part, as there was a large part in Falstaff, that kicked against convention. It comes out in his love of japes, in his punning letters to Jaeger, and his occasional outrageous or cutting remarks. Not for nothing did he once contemplate a Rabelais ballet. Rosa Burley noted how much more at ease he was abroad, away from a society where he had to keep his place. 'Why,' he had said one day, 'can't one live this free and happy life in England?' 'Why,' she had asked herself, 'had the Genius been so much happier in Munich than in Malvern?'[44] For *Falstaff*, Elgar quoted Dowden: 'From the coldness, the caution, the convention of his father's court ... Henry escapes to the teeming vitality of the London streets, and the Tavern where Falstaff is monarch.'

Elgar's *Falstaff* has no conventional 'form' though the two interludes add up to a lyric movement, there is a virtual scherzo and trio, and the ending recapitulates much of what has gone before. The music is without a distinct break but falls into four divisions. It opens with Falstaff and the prince in conversation. Then comes a scene at the Boar's Head Tavern, Eastcheap. Night at Gadshill brings an 'out-of-door ambling' theme, of the kind familiar since the 'Shed' days: spooky night sounds (a reminder of the partsong 'Owls'), the ambush and the struggle for booty (a *fugato*). Back at the tavern the chatter is suggested by pattering staccatos, and the 'honest gentlewomen' are coquettish with trills and teasing triplets (developed into a scherzo and trio). Elgar admitted that Alice was 'horrified' with his honest gentlewomen – 'do you think I

---

[44]   R. Burley and F.C. Carruthers, *Edward Elgar: The Record of a Friendship* (London, 1972), pp. 71, 72.

have overdone them?'[45] Indeed no, they are dainty rather than common or vulgar. Falstaff falls into a drunken sleep (exaggerated and repetitive bassoon) but dreams sweetly (Interlude 1) of his youth. A call to arms spurs him to march with a scarecrow army to the Battle of Shrewsbury. Coming back through Gloucestershire they rest in Shallow's Orchard (Interlude 2). Henry is proclaimed King, and Falstaff rides joyfully to London, but King Henry rejects his old companion. Falstaff sinks to death.

Falstaff's character is limned in Example 3.4 as 'in a green old age ... gay, easy, corpulent, unprincipled, and luxurious'; then as witty, then (in six-four) as 'cajoling and persuasive'. The Prince is lordly in E flat major. During the work many of these themes are shown to be related. The 'cajoling' and the chief Falstaff theme can follow each other as one melody (cues 15 and between cues 21 and 22). The 'boastful' and 'singing' themes work in counterpoint (cues 27 and 48). The 'cajoling' and 'honest gentlewomen' also go together, as well they might (cue 60). Themes are resourcefully transformed, the 'boastful' theme into drunken speech before cue 72, and into a fiery *fugato* at cue 44. The Prince's theme is outlined in wind over running triplets at cue 41 and similarly at cue 122, in both cases to herald his approach. The 'scarecrow army' before cue 86 is tenderly transmuted at cue 98 to lead into Shallow's orchard. Elgar's study is strong in having so many and such sharply defined themes, which can be run together as countermelodies to make dramatic points. They all 'tell the story' but also integrate the long work symphonically.

Elgar was thinking of *Falstaff* as early as 1901. Then among sketches for *The Apostles* and the projected *Rabelais* ballet come the first two bars of the theme at cue 119. That does not occur until near the work's end, occurs only the once, and is not mentioned, let alone quoted or titled, in Elgar's analysis. That theme can next be traced in 1913, when Elgar and Alice Stuart Wortley were guests of Frank Schuster at 'The Hut' near Maidenhead. She left first, and that evening he copied the now eight *espressivo* bars to send to her with the words '(Farewell

---

[45] To Troyte Griffith, 2 September 1913.

to the Hut) July 1913 written on Tuesday after you left /&
now – Good night'. 'Farewell' not only to a loved place, a
loved companion (The Hut, the Windflower) but in its final
context, Falstaff's full-hearted but objectively honest farewell
to his prince, now to be his king.

Elgar several times extended the coda. The score ended
originally at Falstaff's death, eight bars after cue 146. He had
to finish the piece before leaving for a holiday at Penmaen-
mawr. He came downstairs at 4 am and his wife made him tea.
He finished 'his great work'. But it was then an afterthought
to add those last, spine-chilling bars – the strict rhythm, the
hollow chord, rattling side drum, *pizzicato*, 'the man of stern
reality has triumphed'.

Holst in his opera *At the Boar's Head* (1924) covered the same
Eastcheap scenes as Elgar. The means the two men used to
suggest 'Englishness' are very different. Elgar's music was original ('I write the folktunes of this country!'). Holst acknowledged nearly forty old English melodies. (Vaughan Williams
sought to make an English opera combining his love of Eliz-
abethan drama and of folksong, but *Sir John in Love* is based
on *The Merry Wives* only.) Elgar gains sympathy for Falstaff by
giving him idyllic interludes. Holst gains it for the Prince by
setting the monologue that ends 'Redeeming time when men
least think I will' and also by giving him two of Shakespeare's
reflective 'time' sonnets, lyrical poetic passages that tip the
balance well towards the Prince.

Falstaff 'is the name but Shakespeare – the whole of human
life – is the theme & over it all runs – even in the tavern
– the undercurrent of our failings & sorrows'.[46] Elgar's 'failings & sorrows' theme occurs as the second half of a *cantabile e
Largamente* theme at six bars after figure 64. It is not one of the
main themes but appears as a counter-melody in what Elgar
described as 'a trio section of vitality'. Elgar gives a variant of
it as the dying Falstaff's final thought at cue 146: no longer
a counterpoint, but at the last a prime, expressive melody,
serenely accepted. How much his comment reveals, made as
it was about a work based on one of the great comic figures

[46] To E. Newman, 26 September 1913.

of European literature! So in his own way Elgar gives the old rascal a philosophical depth and craves our compassion. If there is as much Elgar in *Falstaff* as Falstaff, it has total consistency; it is subjective, and emotionally authentic. It ranks with Verdi's *Otello* and *Falstaff* and Britten's *Dream*.

Elgar dedicated *Falstaff* to Landon Ronald (1873–1938), who had conducted the first Rome performance of the First Symphony in 1909.

Solo Songs, 1914–16

In 'The King's Way' Elgar set Alice's words to the trio theme of *Pomp and Circumstance* No. 4, to celebrate the thoroughfare recently opened in London. Though Clara Butt gave the première, the song never gained nor deserved the popularity of 'Land of Hope and Glory'. Hardly better (though Boosey paid a hundred guineas for it) is 'The Chariots of the Lord' (1914, Revd John Brownlie), a beefy example of muscular Christianity, also sung by Clara Butt. 'The Birthright' (1914, G.A. Stocks) is a plain marching song for boys, with fetching bugles and drums. 'Fight for Right' (1916) is Elgar's only setting of William Morris, from *Sigurd the Volsung*, a sturdy verse and refrain.

Partsongs, 1909–14

If some of Elgar's solo songs deserve to be forgotten, his unaccompanied partsongs do not. On his Italian holiday in 1909 he composed a beautiful little 'Angelus' to words he adapted from the Tuscan. The Stuart Wortleys had recommended him to see a monastery near Fiesole, and the middle two voices of this SATB piece imitate its bells, till at the end of each of the two verses the tenor takes up the Latin 'Sancta Maria'. Elgar dedicated 'Angelus' to 'Alice/ Mrs Charles Stuart-Wortley' (this was before she became his Windflower) though he wondered whether the 'simple words might be too papistical for you – or for your family'. On the same holiday he composed the great six-part 'Go Song of Mine', to words by Guido Cavalcanti (1259–1399), the Florentine friend of Dante, translated by D. G. Rossetti. The poem, sent to soften man's hard heart, speaks of how life begins and ends in dust. Elgar reflects this with a subdued opening and close over the pedal tonic B, but the *crescendo* and harmonic tension as the 'spirit of grief' guides man's soul to 'seek its Maker' glows with the radiance of the Second Symphony, or perhaps even of Isolde's 'Liebestod'.

In 1914 he set passages from two poems by Henry Vaughan (1621–95) as his Op. 71. 'The Shower' speaks also of a hard heart, comparing a shower of rain with softening tears. Elgar ruffles the chordal song with inner part pattering for raindrops, then reaches a blissful cadence at 'sunshine after rain'. For 'The Fountain' he chose stanzas six and seven of Vaughan's 'Regeneration'. He has no compunction in sounding words from different stanzas at once. The little fountain from stanza seven trickles from one part to another, supported by chords murmuring 'all the earth lay hush' from stanza six (Vaughan actually wrote 'all the ear' to contrast with 'eye'). Finally Elgar repeats the 'music of her tears' six times. Such word-setting breaks all conventional rules, but because he 'scores' the voices instrumentally, the layering of melody and accompaniment probes the poem's emotional core.

Op. 72 and Op. 73 are translations from the Russian by Rosa Newmarch, 'Death on the hills' and 'Love's Tempest' by Apollon Maikov, 'Serenade' by 'Minsky' (Nikolai Vilkenkin). Death leads his shadowy train, refusing to pause lest the living might by 'their claspings' reclaim his victims. Elgar's obsessive rhythm never lets up, even when Death speaks ponderously in the basses. He described the 'very sad Russian poem' to Windflower as 'one of the biggest things I have done'.[47] In 'Love's Tempest' billows on the sapphire ocean (rich eight-part chords) symbolize the storm (fiery counterpoint) in the poet's heart. 'Serenade' is no light romantic song, but a plea to find in dreams happiness not to be found in waking. The *staccato* repeated rhythm of 'dreams all too brief' contrasts with two melodious passages.

[47] 22 January 1914.

Short Instrumental Pieces, 1912–15

Elgar still had the 'Shed' books of wind quintet music that he had borrowed from Hubert Leicester for the *Wand of Youth*. In November 1912 he revised the Andante Arioso from the 1897 Harmony Music No. 6, as *Cantique*, his Op. 3, and arranged for it organ, piano, or small orchestra. Landon Ronald included it in one of his regular concerts, but Elgar found himself disappointed, perhaps because in truth the music is rather anonymous. *Carissima* of December 1913 had the distinction of being composed with recording, then in its infancy, in mind. Landon Ronald was musical adviser to the Gramophone Company (HMV), and contrived a meeting between Elgar, W. W. Elkin, the publisher of light music, and Jeffrey Stephens, also of the Gramophone Company. Elgar dedicated the piece to Mrs Stephens, Muriel Foster's sister. *Rosemary (That's for Remembrance)* began life as the trio tune of a Menuetto written in 1882 for family music-making with Charles Buck in Yorkshire, then became a piano piece as *Douce pensée*. New in 1915 was the introduction and extended coda. Such light pieces need to be played with elegance and style.

In another category altogether is *Sospiri* (1914), which Elgar dedicated to Billy Reed, the LSO violinist who played Joachim to his Brahms when he composed the Violin Concerto (1910). It might almost be a 'sigh' left over from that work, the first violins' part is so eloquent, the accompaniment so intense.

CHAPTER FOUR

The Music of Wartime
1914–1920

Music of Wartime

When war broke out on 4 August 1914, the Elgars were on the west coast of Scotland. He had almost agreed to compose the last part of his oratorio trilogy, and was taking a long holiday before starting work. When he returned home he put that idea aside, and within weeks was sworn in as a special constable.

His first musical reaction was to compose on 6 September a 'Soldier's Song: The Roll Call', which Clara Butt sang on 10 October 1914. But he must later have found this an inappropriate response, and withdrew it. Then, as Belgium was overrun, Elgar was invited to contribute to a fund-raising anthology by leading artists, musicians, and writers. In *The Observer* he found a poem (*Après Anvers*) by the Belgian Émile Cammaerts (1878–1953), translated by his wife Tita Brand Cammaerts, the daughter of Marie Brema, the first Angel in *Gerontius*. He composed it as *Carillon*, Op. 75, in memory of the ruined bell towers of Flanders. At Rosa Burley's suggestion, he did not set the words to music, but composed a prelude and brief entr'actes between the recited verses.[1] The four-note bell *ostinato* rings out from tonic down to dominant against an upward-thrusting three-in-a-bar figure, making an effective tug of rhythmic war. To 'cover the graves of our children', as the dying leaves scent the autumn air, Elgar tenderly begins his carillon figure in the treble on the mediant and augments it;

---

[1]   Rosa Burley and Frank Carruthers, *Edward Elgar: The Record of a Friendship* (London, 1972), pp. 197–8.

then inverts it against the original to usher in the hoped-for triumphant entry into Berlin – to 'sing of hope and fiercest hate ... and charity'.

Carillon was performed at the Queen's Hall on 7 December by Tita Brand (and was later taken up by Réjane). At that threatening moment it incited tremendous enthusiasm. Thomas Dunhill recalled a 'poignant and unforgettable experience'. However askance later generations might look at the work, it caught the mood of the moment, when Rupert Brooke's 'Now, God be thanked Who has matched us with His hour' was also rapturously received. Henry Ainley's abridged recording with Elgar of 1915 captures a little of the period. Attempts to revive Carillon during the Second World War with new words by Binyon failed; the rhetoric then apt was to be found in Churchill's broadcast speeches.

After the success of Carillon, Cammaerts persuaded Elgar to set two more of his poems as recitations with orchestra. Une voix dans le désert, Op. 77, was devised for the stage and produced at the Shaftesbury Theatre on 29 January 1916. The desert is of scarred battlefields, made by man. A narrator describes the desolation and loneliness over Elgar's fragmented accompaniment of drumtaps and muted strings. From a shell-torn cottage a girl sings a self-contained lyric, hoping for a future Spring when once more the land will be cultivated and all will flower again. The girl and her father, says the narrator, would die rather than leave their fields. The piece could not differ more from Carillon, being restrained and bleak, with homely courage. The slightest of the three Cammaerts settings, Le drapeau belge, Op. 79, failed to make an impact. Composed in 1916, it was not produced until King Albert's birthday concert in 1917. The verses deal in the symbolism of red, black, and yellow, and the only interest of Elgar's strophic setting is the little half-jaunty, half-sad 'recruiting' phrase, cousin to 'They went with songs to the battle' in For the Fallen to come.

Poland had long ago lost its independence in the partition between Russia, Germany, and Austro-Hungary. In early 1915 Paderewski, who was becoming increasingly political, launched a Relief Fund for the Polish refugees in London. Elgar and Paderewski had met in 1899. It was Paderewki who made the famous crack about Elgar's teacher being 'Le bon Dieu'.[2] Basil Maine recounted that while living in Hereford Elgar had come to know a descendant of the Lubienski family, and heard 'much of Polish history, thought and feeling'. So he agreed when the composer-conductor Emil Młynarski asked for a work for a charity concert that would include a movement of his own symphony *Polonia*. Elgar borrowed the title, and incorporated several Polish national airs into his symphonic prelude *Polonia*, Op. 76, performed on 6 July 1915. It is a substantial work lasting about fourteen minutes, scored for a big orchestra including harps, organ, and much percussion. He opens it in A minor, grandly, with his own themes but with the muttered hint of the 1905 uprising march, and shortly brings in, *cantabile* in E major, the hymn 'With the smoke of the fires'. A tranquil episode introduces Chopin's G minor Nocturne (Op. 37, No. 1), wraithlike in its new harmony and sound-palette, and over this comes a gentle theme from Paderewski's *Polish Fantasia* – so bringing together Poland's two greatest composers, as Elgar tactfully wrote to Paderewski. This the march stealthily infiltrates, and is strongly developed, till near the end comes the national song 'Poland is not lost', clinching the piece sturdily rather as Brahms does with 'Gaudeamus igitur' in his *Academic Festival Overture*. *Polonia* is a curiosity, a efficient product of Elgar's workshop but not to be ranked with his overtures.

In January 1916 a request came from Lord Charles Beresford to set some verses by Kipling. Elgar had enjoyed his Mediterranean cruise in 1905 as Admiral Beresford's guest. They chose four pieces from *The Fringes of the Fleet*, 'fringes' because the vessels concerned were little merchant ships commissioned into war service. 'The Lowestoft Boat' was built for the herring trade, and the 'five damned trawlers with their syreens blowing' had become 'The [mine]Sweepers'. Elgar set three of the four poems to bluff, hearty tunes, in a 'broad saltwater style', as he told Ernest Newman. All three have refrains: 'The game is more than the player of the game, And the ship is more than the crew!' from 'Fate's Discourtesy' is a typical Kipling sentiment. But one song, 'Submarines', is strange and

[2]   Letter from Schuster, 26 November 1902.

imaginative: not much more than a rising and falling minor arpeggio ('we arise, we lie down') over a heaving *ostinato*, oily and sinister ('in the belly of Death'). These were the 'little ships' of 1914–18, like those that went to Dunkirk in the later war.

Kipling at first objected to his verses being set but was persuaded to grant permission, and Oswald Stoll staged the songs for four baritones at the Coliseum with the singers in sou'westers and fishing boots. Elgar conducted two performances a day from 11 June 1917. He added a new song, 'Inside the bar' by Gilbert Parker, for the four baritones unaccompanied. He toured the performance in the provinces, at Chatham to a realistic background of Zeppelin raids, and he recorded the five songs in 1917 with the original singers. In 1918 he set another Kipling poem, 'Big Steamers', this time a unison strophic song for children.

1915 The Starlight Express, Op. 78

Of all Elgar's scores, *The Starlight Express* is among the most tantalizing. It has sentiment, comedy, delicious music, basically a good story, and magic. It is however that awkward and improbable mixture of speech, song, dance, mime, and melodrama (at a good many removes, like another English work, Purcell's *Fairy Queen*), forming the sort of producer's problems best looked squarely in the face and then cheerfully ignored. The play was drawn from Algernon Blackwood's novel *A Prisoner in Fairyland* (1913) by its author and Violet Pearne. Lena Ashwell, actress and manager of the Kingsway Theatre, decided at short notice to stage the play at Christmas 1915. Blackwood (1869–1951) visited the Elgars at Severn House, and Elgar found him 'an unusual man and sympathetic to me'.[3] Blackwood's upbringing had been comfortable and privileged, in a country house with attendant servants. As a young man he had knocked about in Canada and America, making and more often losing money, but keeping always his cherished violin.

---

[3]   To S. Colvin, 20 November 1915.

His story-telling to friends led to the publication of his first book in 1906.

His novel is a fantasy, an allegory, rambling and muddled but idealistic (for the play a love story with an 'amber-eyed' Countess was cut). The theme is not unlike Elgar's own childhood play: children transforming prosaic, 'wumbled' grownups. 'Daddy' is a frustrated author, who has taken his family to live cheaply in the Jura mountains, where at night it is possible to find Stardust (sympathy or vision), and so become unwumbled. 'Cousin Henry' boards the starlight express to visit him, with the Dustman, the Sweep, the Head Gardener, the Lamplighter. The cast includes Sprites, fantasy figures of a Victorian nursery. The Tramp/Organ Grinder links the action, with his wheezy barrel-organ. The Laugher, who sings 'I'm everywhere', whisks away trouble, and calls on the Sprites to 'unwumble' the sleeping parents. The Little Night Winds blow the enormous Woman of the Haystack into the Star Cave. The daughter Jane Anne has a Dawn Song and 'Oh, think beauty'. Finally the Organ Grinder and the Laugher sing a duet, when 'The First Nowell' joins the *Wand of Youth*.

Elgar used *The Wand of Youth* as his starting point, some of the pieces ('Sun Dance', 'Moths and Butterflies') as entr'actes. Caressing passages from the trios of 'Little Bells' and of 'Fairy Pipers' sound through the play, bringing sleep with its healing dreams ('till I sleep and dream That I'm lost in your Fairy-lands'). He became more and more engaged in the work, and when *The Starlight Express* was put on at the Kingsway Theatre, London, on 29 December 1915, there was over an hour's music, much of it original. The captivating songs are only a part of it. At the end of the score the fifty-eight-year-old Elgar signed his name and – touchingly – his age as fifteen.

In the course of the production changes were made. O. B. Clarence, who played the father, recalled that 'during rehearsals there were constant bickerings and difficulties ... disagreements about the symbolism ... even dissensions among the orchestra'.[4] The designer was Henry Wilson, president of the Arts and Crafts Society, who had to be dissuaded from depicting

4   O. B. Clarence, *No Complaints* (London, 1943), p. 145.

the Sprites as Greek gods. Blackwood was so frustrated after the dress rehearsal that he complained to Elgar 'this suburban, Arts & Crafts pretentious rubbish stitched on to your music is really too painful for me to bear'.

Elgar at first hated the sets, and commented in 1921 that 'the drama (not by my friend A. B.) did not seem to hang together'. Perhaps this was a straightforward reaction to a poor production, or perhaps he had become so involved in memories of his own childhood that he would have found any staging a travesty. There was unfavourable criticism of the play, and praise for the music. The young Wulstan Atkins, son of Ivor, remembered being completely absorbed from the moment 'the Organ-Grinder, Charles Mott [one of the *Fringes* baritones], appeared on the apron of the stage to sing his first song, "O children, open your arms to me".'[5] The show ran for four weeks. Elgar was delighted to have the chance to make eight records of the music in February 1916. Then by a series of mischances both scenario and score were lost, and *The Starlight Express* was not revived until the BBC broadcast a version in 1965. Were it less whimsical, it would make perfect Christmas television.

Apart from the songs and dances, the music is not in closed forms, so it needs the dramatic context. Much of it is fragmentary, some nimble, much musing, some improvisatory. One or two all-too-brief passages are profoundly stirring. Most of the set pieces have a charming Edwardian light music touch. Over it all waves the wand of Elgar's own youth. The whole conception of qualities special to childhood is essentially an adult one. Who is this entertainment for, children or adults? On Elgar's part, surely for himself.

1916 The Spirit of England, Op. 80

I *The Fourth of August* II *To Women* III *For the Fallen*

Although at first it was hoped that the Great War would be over by Christmas, some of the serious journals began printing

---

5   E. Wulstan Atkins, *The Elgar–Atkins Friendship* (Newton Abbot, 1984), p. 271.

the leading poets' responses to it. One such poem was John Masefield's 'August, 1914', in *The English Review*: 'How still this quiet cornfield is tonight! ... So beautiful it is, I never saw/ So great a beauty on these English fields ...'. Elgar wrote to Ivor Atkins in Worcester: '*That* is the best thing written yet ... We are fighting for the country, & I wish I could see it ... look over the valley towards Malvern – bless my beloved country for me.'[6] He might easily have set Masefield's words; instead, Gerald Finzi, ten years later, set them in his *Requiem da Camera*.

As the ravaging of Belgium went on, more than half of those who crossed to France in August became casualties, and one in ten was killed at Mons and Ypres. Elgar asked A. C. Benson for extra words for 'Land of Hope and Glory', 'since', he said, 'the people have adopted our effort as the 2nd National Anthem & it does good.' But the 'people' preferred the original words. Sales of Elgar's old *The Banner of St George* soared. The popularity of 'Land of Hope and Glory' was exceeded only by that of 'Tipperary' and challenged by Parry's 'Jerusalem'. In January 1915 Sidney Colvin wrote to Elgar, 'Why don't you do a wonderful *Requiem* for the slain – something in the spirit of Binyon's "For the Fallen".' Colvin and Laurence Binyon both worked at the British Museum, where Binyon specialized in oriental art. Elgar had met him in 1901 at the home of their mutual friend Edward Speyer. Binyon's poems were published in *The Times* in August and September 1914, and then in *The Winnowing Fan*. Elgar at once began sketching music for three of them.

Then he heard that Cyril Rootham was setting 'For the Fallen', to be published by Novello, Elgar's own publisher. Rootham (1875–1938) was organist of St John's, Cambridge, and a university lecturer; he was making a name as a composer. His orchestral rhapsody *Pan* had been performed at Queen's Hall in 1913. But compared with Elgar, he was unknown. Elgar met him to discuss matters, and then withdrew: 'I have battled with the feeling for nearly a week but the sight of the other man comes sadly between me & my music.'[7] He lapsed into

---

[6]   26 October 1914.
[7]   To Binyon, 24 March 1915.

his all-too-frequent complaint that his music was unwanted, which brought the encouraging but severe retort from Colvin: 'You take far too censorious & jaundiced a view of your countrymen.'[8] Elgar's friends then persuaded Novello to publish both settings. Rootham's, though longer, was designed for small local choral societies. It is dignified music, but lacks the passion and sensibility of Elgar's. Rootham composed finer works later but his For the Fallen deserved its 1987 recording.

Elgar was persuaded to go ahead, and completed his 'For The Fallen' during June 1915. Lady Elgar, who showed partisan feelings in most situations, became increasingly vicious in her diary entries about the Hun, calling them 'brutes', 'uncivilised fiends'. 1915 ended with her comment: the 'Germans are more diabolical than ever'. Elgar orchestrated 'To Women' in February 1916. He conducted the two movements at Leeds on 3 May 1916, then Clara Butt sang them for a week's series of charity concerts during May at Queen's Hall. 'The Fourth of August', the first in the set, was the last to be composed. Its sixth stanza, beginning 'She fights the fraud that feeds desire on Lies', held Elgar up. He kept hoping for some sign of chivalry from the enemy, 'that some trace of manly spirit would shew itself'.[9] It was, after all, musicians from Germany who had most generously recognized his own genius – Jaeger, Richter, Buths, Strauss. But as the war dragged on, Elgar's heart hardened. Perhaps remembering his wife's 'diabolical' Germans, he pressed into service the demons' music from The Dream of Gerontius, and in March 1917 finished the remaining movement. He grouped the three under the collective title The Spirit of England, from the second line, 'Spirit of England, ardent-eyed'. He dedicated it to 'the memory of our glorious men, with a special thought for the Worcesters'. He conducted the complete work at Leeds on 31 October 1917, then in London on 24 November 1917. Gervase Elwes, who sang, described the experience as harrowing: almost every member of the choir had lost a relation or close friend.

The orchestral prelude to 'The Fourth of August' (the day

[8]   3 April 1915.
[9]   To Ernest Newman, 17 June 1917.

war was declared) opens with a diatonic upward-leaping melody, Elgar's signature for 'courage and hope'. The chorus entry is directed 'grandioso', denoting dignity, with largeness and nobility of spirit. Almost at once the soloist brings a personal note to the nation's collective voice. Sadly, the temperature drops with the secondary themes: 'we step into the grandeur of our fate' provokes weak syncopation, and the tune is worked in limp imitation, though the demons from *Gerontius* are subtly introduced. Another memory from *Gerontius*, the Angel's soaring phrase 'the sight of the Most Fair', becomes 'Endure, O Earth'. Then comes a soft, unaccompanied reflection on suffering, breathing the atmosphere of *The Music Makers*, before the opening returns, now purged, as it were, by experience.

In the second movement, women take a passive but inspiring role, 'in the watch of solitude ... to bleed, bear, and break'. The situation and the atmosphere – a woman set apart from violence, but devotedly meditating to the sound of the harp – is close to the Virgin's song in *The Kingdom*. This is about sympathy for the living, not commemoration of the dead. Nowadays, when women are sea captains and airline pilots, it needs to be remembered how much time was spent in the Great War nursing, or just waiting. A threatening hum in the cellos and basses brings 'the hawks of war'; on his sketch Elgar wrote 'aeroplanes stanza III' – is this graphic image of aeroplanes the earliest in music? The 'courage and hope' theme from the first movement now supports the resolve 'but not to fail'.

'For the Fallen' is the longest, and the finest, movement. The poem contains the lines, spoken on Remembrance Sunday, 'at the going down of the sun and in the morning we will remember them', which have been described as 'poetry aspiring to the anonymity of the Prayer Book'. The opening bars set up tension, as chords tug heavily against each other in a sombre processional. A minor modulates through contorted chromatic sequences to B flat, and a *cantabile* rising scale melody (originally the 'wistful' bulldog Dan) 'sings sorrow up into immortal spheres'. Elgar described the third stanza as 'a sort of idealized (perhaps) Quick March, the sort of thing which ran in my mind when the dear lads were swinging past'.[10] But this is no military cheer. The pacifist Britten heard 'in the grotesque march an agony of distortion'.[11] Rootham set 'they went with songs to the battle' straight, cheerfully. Elgar set the words to a monotone, gave the orchestra a jiggy tune with awkward augmented intervals, such as B flat to E natural. There is irony of situation here, a sardonic collision between innocence and awareness. It brings to mind the march of the scarecrow army in Elgar's own *Falstaff* (or even of Shostakovich to come). Twisting, sliding chromatic harmonies underline the ambiguities of 'they shall not grow old', and with unbearable poignancy there is an isolated diatonic chord on the soloist's 'we will reMEMber them.' (Binyon wrote 'they shall grow not old'; Elgar transposed the two words.) The climax at cue 31 is formed from a passage – Elgar called it 'a premonition' – from cue 11 of 'To Women'. The grand arching themes return with more complicated modulations, moving towards the chastened ending. After the war, Elgar made a simpler version of 'For the Fallen' called 'With Proud Thanksgiving' for the unveiling of the Cenotaph in 1920. In the end it was not performed until 7 May 1921, at the Royal Albert Hall.

Before and for some time after the 1939–45 war, *The Spirit of England* was performed every year near Armistice Day at the Albert Hall. Then it fell from fashion. For younger listeners, it was a highlight of the Cambridge Elgar Festival in 1994. The music's objectivity and compassion are remarkable. There is no jingoism here. There is patriotism, certainly, and nationalism. Binyon wrote an extra verse about the young soldiers for the musical settings:

> They fought, they were terrible, nobody could tame
> them,
> Hunger, nor legions, nor shattering cannonade.
> They laughed, they sang their melodies of England,
> They fell open-eyed and unafraid.

No-one today would accept sentiments like 'They fell with their faces to the foe ... open-eyed and unafraid.' A. C. Benson's

[10]   To Ernest Newman, 15 April 1916.
[11]   Aldeburgh Festival programme book, 1969.

novelist brother Fred wrote his semi-autobiographical *As we Are* in 1932. The core of the book is a shocking scene after the war, a dinner given to three young ex-officers, volunteers in 1914, now maimed and jobless. It culminates in their hysterically singing 'they shall not grow old … as we that are left grow old' to a trivial waltz-tune, shouting 'sing up, you cripples … think of the fallen! Aren't we lucky?' Understandable bitterness, but idealized courage is essential in wartime, with its appalling demands and distresses. In 1934 Edmund Blunden wrote about the ghastly events of July 1916: 'Neither race has won, nor could win, the war. The War had won, and would go on winning.'

Would any composer now be able to use the title *The Spirit of England* without irony? Much has recently been written about that war, the trenches, the shell-shock and its rudimentary treatment: books such as Pat Barker's *Regeneration* trilogy and Paul Fussell's *The Great War and Modern Memory*. Patriotism and idealism seem out of place today. There was a time when Elgar's music was identified with the less sensitive aspects of the British Empire. The year before Elgar died, Constant Lambert, reacting to the shift in culture since the 1914 war, wrote of 'the aggressive Edwardian prosperity that lends so comfortable a background to Elgar's finales', and 'much of Elgar's music, through no fault of his own, has for the present generation an almost intolerable air of smugness, self-assurance and autocratic benevolence'.[12] Osbert Sitwell described Elgar on his seventieth birthday as looking 'every inch a personification of Colonel Bogey'. 'Colonel Bogey' was the popular military march, not by Elgar; but the inference is obvious. *Pomp and Circumstance*, the *Imperial March*, the *Coronation March*, the *Empire March*, all add up to allow the automatic charge of jingoism, the word taken from the old music-hall song of 1878:

> We don't want to fight, but, by jingo, if we do
> We've got the ships, we've got the men, we've got
> the money too.

[12] C. Lambert, *Music Ho!* (London, 1933), pp. 283–4.

Unlike, say, Bliss's *Morning Heroes* (1930) or Britten's *War Requiem* (1961), composed some years after their respective wars, Elgar's *Spirit of England* was written in the middle of hostilities. Elgar was too old to fight, but he was in the nation's capital, not in some country retreat (he did not find his country cottage, Brinkwells, till 1917). The horror and misery of the war moved him to a deeper utterance than the songs and marches of peacetime pageantry. All good art made in response to a crisis enlarges and transfigures that crisis. Binyon's poems and this music are lofty, involved, rhetorical: unfashionable qualities in today's detached, laconic, laid-back – sometimes sentimental – Britain. But nothing can detract from the haunting benediction of Elgar's falling cadence 'at the going down of the sun …'. Direct and eloquent, *The Spirit of England* still speaks to the heart.

Strangely, a comparison might be drawn with *Metamorphosen* by Richard Strauss, composed in 1945. Ostensibly, Strauss mourned the destruction of the Dresden opera house, Elgar mourned the death of young soldiers, but both composers, in exalted music, lament the loss of their cultural worlds.

In April 1916 Elgar was taken ill on a train journey and spent two days in a nursing home. He was often in poor health during these years, suffering from colds, giddiness, noises in the ears. Though Severn House represented the height of his social ambition, he seemed restless, depressed, and unhappy. He made frequent visits to his sister at Stoke, always without his wife. Much of 1917 was taken up with conducting *The Fringes of the Fleet*, at the Coliseum and on tour.

1917 The Sanguine Fan, Op. 81

All his life Elgar loved the theatre, from his Worcester boyhood when he heard touring opera companies, through his pilgrimages to Bayreuth, his delight in Jack Hulbert revues, to his last years and friendship with Bernard Shaw. His *Rabelais* ballet came to nothing, as did his frequent ideas for an opera. Perhaps his intricate style of symphonic development was unsuited to major stage drama, but when Beecham snorted 'ballet music, my dear sir' about the Variations, his condescension concealed some truth: Ashton's 'Enigma' ballet (1968) showed an artist's insight into Elgar and his music. Elgar admitted having learnt scoring from Delibes, and his touch in Edwardian-style light music is infallible. When he was asked to compose music for a ballet in 1917 he produced *The Sanguine Fan* in a matter of weeks.

It was probably his 'Windflower' (now Lady Alice Stuart of Wortley) who thought of inviting him to compose for a society charity matinée called 'Chelsea on Tiptoe' in aid of Concerts at the Front, with which she was involved. The ballet was to be organized by Mrs Christopher Lowther, the daughter of Canon Raymond Pelly, vicar of Malvern and so known to the Elgars. Ina Lowther was an amateur dancer, and it was her scenario.

The fan was coloured in reddish shades by the Chelsea painter Charles Conder (1868–1908) and it belonged to Mrs John Lane, the publisher's wife. One side showed Pan playing his pipes to Echo, the other showed couples in Louis XV costume in a sylvan setting. The scenario traced mixed mortal and mythical amours. Eros ('a somewhat disfigured statue') shoots the wrong arrow to the lovers. 'Pan, believing himself deserted for the mortal, in a mad outburst of jealousy, utters his wild shout summoning the shepherds, who at his command kill Echo.'[13] But the immortal voice of Echo still haunts him.

Elgar turned to early material, and by 19 February 1917 he was beginning the orchestration. He asked for a modest minimum – one each of wind, two horns, harp, percussion, strings, no brass – and though he finally scored it for a fuller orchestra, his music is light and transparent, with hardly a trace of his usual doubling. Never has a page of his shown so much white or sounded so delicate. Pan's clarinet and Echo's flute set the mood. Elgar conducted at the Chelsea matinée on 20 March 1917 when the leading roles were taken by Ina Lowther herself as Echo, Gerald du Maurier as Pan, Ernest

---

[13] David Lloyd-Jones, *The Sanguine Fan*, study score (London, 2002).

Thesiger and Fay Compton as the mortal lovers (stylish mime rather than ballet?). There was a further performance at the Palace Theatre. Echo's dance was published for piano, and Elgar recorded excerpts in 1920. Then the music was silent, until the discovery of the score by the Elgar scholar Jerrold Northrop Moore. At his prompting Boult recorded it in 1974. Then, for London Festival Ballet, Ronald Hynd choreographed an elegant new work, set on an Edwardian summer evening, and concerning twin brothers, two women, and a fan. Neither plot is necessary to enjoy the delectable fifteen-minute-long score. Continuous, but for the ballet's sake episodic rather than developmental, it opens and closes with a courtly minuet. *The Wand of Youth* suites, and 'W. N.' of 'Enigma' are relatives of this music, which is Elgarian in every bar.

The Chamber Music

'I wish somebody would write an account of people to whom music has been dedicated (I would have written dedicatees, but I scorn to be pedantic) – there are so many names which don't seem to exist apart from some quartet or other small composition; and then I should like to know all about the Grosshändler TOST to whom Haydn dedicated a whole string of IVtets – nearly a dozen. I expect it is all in Pohl but I haven't got P. Do ENCOURAGE, say Selfridge, as a useful Grosshändler, to order some quartets from me.'[14] A characteristically entertaining but down-to-earth suggestion, at a period when there was more private patronage than commercial.

1918 was Elgar's chamber music year. In no field was English music at that time more flourishing. Audiences were large, interest had been encouraged by the patronage of W. W. Cobbett, and composers such as Ireland and Bridge were producing fine work. Chamber music seemed like a new departure for Elgar, composer of oratorios and symphonies. In fact, it was a throwback to his early days. His Op. 8 and Op. 9, which he destroyed, were a string quartet and a violin sonata, and many unfinished sketches from 1878 onwards are

14 To William McNaught, 25 March 1918.

trios and quartets. On 20 March 1900 he wrote to Jaeger, 'I should *dearly* love to get out some of my chamber music!' His wife's diaries show that in autumn 1907 he was engaged on a string quartet. Sketches from that were absorbed by the First Symphony (the Adagio) and by *The Music Makers* (cue 42).

Miserable in London during the war, in May 1917 the Elgars leased a 'lovely cottage in the woods, high above the world in peace, plenty and quietness'.[15] This was Brinkwells, near Fittleworth in West Sussex. In March 1918 Elgar had to have infected tonsils removed; in those days, such an operation on a man of sixty-one was severe. Returning to Severn House, he at once made tentative sketches. Later that year, when victory was assured, he refused Laurence Binyon's suggestion to set his 'Peace' Ode. 'The whole atmosphere is too full of complexities for me to feel music … The last two divisions [of Binyon's poem] are splendid altho' I regret the appeal to the Heavenly Spirit which is cruelly obtuse to the individual sorrow & sacrifice – a cruelty I resent bitterly & disappointedly.'[16] The war had changed his world. Lady Elgar was failing, friends were dying: the baritone Charles Mott, William McNaught of Novello, Marie Joshua, patron of musicians including Richter in her early days, Richter himself, Hubert Parry. Brian Trowell believes Elgar knew about and was profoundly shocked by the death on the Somme of Kenneth Munro, the son of his early love Helen Weaver, now in New Zealand.

In May 1918 the Elgars settled in to Brinkwells and in August he had a piano delivered. Ideas crowded in: for a Violin Sonata (composed during August and September), a Quartet, a Quintet, and a Cello Concerto. He was aware that he was not breaking new ground as in *Gerontius* or in the First Symphony. 'I know it does not carry us any further,' he wrote of his summer's music, 'but it is full of golden sounds. I like it. But you must not expect anything violently chromatic or cubist.'[17] Was he perhaps thinking of Schönberg's *Pierrot Lunaire* (1912), or Stravinsky's *Rite of Spring* (1913)? He charted the

---

[15] To P. Hull, 2 June 1918.
[16] To Binyon, 5 November 1918.
[17] To Marie Joshua, 6 September 1918.

changing seasons in his letters: 'heavenly ... nightingales in May ... young birds hatching ... high summer, rich full & perfect ... wheat cut ... the sun climbing over our view in golden mist ... cold but vividly bright.'

There is indeed a retrospective feeling to his chamber music. It is more Brahmsian than anything he composed. Recognizing in himself no wish to absorb recent idioms, he went his own way easily. From his present delight and his cherished memories he created music of harvest and fulfilment.

1918 Sonata for Violin and Piano, Op. 82

I *Allegro* II *Romance — Andante* III *Allegro, non troppo*

Ivor Atkins described Elgar's playing in the Three Choirs Orchestra at the 1890 Worcester Festival, the year *Froissart* was produced: 'There he was, fiddling among the first violins, with his fine intellectual face, his heavy moustache, his dark hair, his nervous eyes and his beautiful sensitive hands.'[18] So it goes without saying that the Sonata is beautifully crafted. It may also be that the established Elgar could look back on that young fiddler with affection (he looked back on the young fiddler's *circumstances* often enough with bitterness).

A composer's words about his music are sometimes notable for what does not strike him. 'The first movement is bold & vigorous,' Elgar told his Windflower. Yes, but remarkably conservative. 'The last movement is very broad & *soothing* like the last movemt of the IInd Symphy'[19] – but not magisterial, which the Symphony is. What is unusual for Elgar is how precisely the outer Sonata movements fulfil the promise of their opening bars: no less, but no more. The Allegro begins strongly, the main theme leaping over two octaves, the fifth bar providing a three-note figure that generates much later development. Violin and piano are good partners, with shared thematic give and take. Tonally the movement is evasive. It begins by suggesting A minor, and ends on a chord of E

---

[18]   E. Wulstan Atkins, *The Elgar–Atkins Friendship* (London, 1984), p. 25.

[19]   11 September 1918.

major reached by a plagal cadence. What at first sounds like an expressive second subject turns out to be a transition theme (cue 3). When the second subject is indeed reached at cue 5, it is crossing strings passage-work for the violin and static treble chords for the piano, outlining just four notes. Described like that, it sounds dull. Heard, it is poetic and reflective, reminding Reed of the 'rise and fall of the wind'[20] across Elgar's Aeolian harp at 'Plas Gwyn'. There is a similar oscillating passage at cue 43 in the last movement.

Cobbett, in a letter to The Times on 2 March 1934, said that the Sonata was generally considered to be influenced by Brahms, but perceptively found the middle movement 'far removed from the influence of anything but the composer's own subconscious self'. For in the Romance, Elgar uses the clichés of his salon music – descending chromatics, harped chords, pizzicatos, snatches of seductive 'Spanish' rhythms, sprays of fioritura – idioms he took at their face value in, say, Sevillana or The Black Knight. But here, he 'uses' them creatively, compressed elliptically into this intense and personal Romance. It is strangely like the Serenade of Debussy's Cello Sonata (1915) called 'Pierrot fâché avec la lune'. In both Elgar and Debussy the elements are symbols, the treatment stylized. On 24 August Lady Elgar called the new music 'different from anything of his ... wood magic. So elusive & delicate.' The expansive central episode would be almost too beautiful, too strong a contrast, were not the sustained melody subtly undermined by harmonic sideslips. It was sketched, 'made at that sad moment', to told his Windflower, when the news came that she had badly broken her leg. He recalled the melody in the last movement, in immediate response to hearing of the death of his old friend Marie Joshua. Elgar's composition was always closely bound up with his personal life. Ernest Newman said that his music came 'straight out of some highly vitalized experience'.[21] But such literal inspiration is disconcerting. Perhaps the events released music already latent in him.

[20] William H. Reed, Elgar as I Knew Him (London, 1936), p. 149.
[21] Sunday Times, 25 February 1934.

1918 String Quartet, Op. 83

I *Allegro moderato* II *Piacevole (poco andante)* III *Allegro molto*

The Quartet's first movement is intricate, with subtle internal consonances and references. For the first two bars the strings move in close harmony, rhythmically at one, with a spurt of energy in the second. They quickly fan out to ff over four octaves in a loping twelve-eight figure, checked at once by a series of fanfare-like chords whose hollow irresolute harmonies are at odds with their formal square-cut gestures; the impetus is dissipated. The second subject sounds smooth and lyrical, but turns out to be an expansion of the jerky first. At the fiery climax of the development the viola has the second subject between soaring violin and plunging cello. In the reprise it returns sad and inarticulate, in broken phrases (on a tiny scale it is what happens to the Arioso in Beethoven's late A flat piano sonata). When it is miraculously made whole, it is withdrawn to a remote E flat. All through the movement the tonality is fluid. The first two bars are in E minor but rise to a D natural, giving a modal flavour. Often root position chords are avoided, and the final major close at the end of the movement is achieved without emphasis or drama. The tone of voice is unlike anything else in Elgar, experienced and undogmatic. Compared with the Serenade for Strings of 1892 (Ex. 4.1a), which the opening closely resembles, the movement is sophisticated (4.1b). There is a coming-to-terms with life here, which might have proved a point of departure for a third period.

Ex. 4.1

(a)

Allegro piacevole

(b)

Allegro moderato

The second movement, often considered the gem of the three, is more conventional. The comfortable relationship between metric and harmonic values makes it a perfect complement to the first movement, and, though poignant, it is undemanding. The artless, winsome melody is heard at the start without the first violin. At its reprise Elgar seamlessly quotes from his *Chanson de matin*. Much of the movement's charm lies in its colouring. 'Piacevole' Elgar directed it – 'agreeable, pleasant' – a term he had used for the Serenade. His wife likened the movement to 'captured sunshine'. Perhaps the long spells of drowsy repetitions against pedal points (cues 28 and 33) made her think of 'the sound of bees and insects on a hot summer's afternoon'. As in similar spells in the Violin Sonata, the play here is with minute pitch variables of a pattern. There are also stabs of pain (cues 20–1) slightly reminiscent of Mozart's G minor string quintet. The sound, though sweet, is thin, sprinkled with harmonics and finally muted. This sunshine is fitful and autumnal.

Of the Finale, Lady Elgar wrote, 'Most fiery & sweeps along like Galloping of Squadrons'. It has more of the dash and flow of the pre-war orchestral works, and combines the characters of a scherzo and a last movement. The opening has thrust and resolution, the ending has breadth. The second subject allows some relaxation, but a phrase from it then vigorously propels the development, so bringing together the motor power of the first subject and the lyricism of the second.

Elgar dedicated the Quartet to the Brodsky Quartet, in fulfilment of a promise made in 1907. He finished it on Christmas Eve 1918, the Quintet some weeks into 1919. What is remarkable, in view of their closeness in time, is how unalike the works are. The Quartet is nervy, inward, plaintive; the Quintet is spacious, noble, a little sinister. Elgar told Ivor Atkins that it 'runs gigantically in a large mood'.[22]

[22] E. Wulsan Atkins, *The Elgar-Atkins Friendship* (London, 1984), p. 291.

1919 Quintet, Op. 84

I *Moderato* – *Allegro* II *Adagio* III *Andante* – *Allegro*

A surprise for the 1919 audience was that Elgar in the Quintet and the Violin Sonata composed for the piano. He left his only major piano piece, the *Concert Allegro* of 1901, unfinished. Though when he was young he impressed people with his improvisations, 'the violin is my instrument, not the piano', he used to say. 'I can read any old or new rhythmic pattern on the fiddle. I never play the pianoforte. I scramble through things orchestrally in a way that would madden with envy all existing pianists.'[23] Bernard Shaw, after hearing Elgar play the piano part of the Quintet, said the same thing to him, wrapped up in blarney:

> There are some piano embroideries on a pedal point that didn't sound like a piano or anything else in the world, but quite beautiful, and I have my doubts whether any regular shop pianist will produce them: they require a touch which is peculiar to yourself, and which struck me the first time I ever heard you larking about with a piano.[24]

Shaw thought the Quintet 'the finest thing of its kind since *Coriolan*. I don't know why I associated the two; but I did: there was the same quality – the same vein. Of course you went your own way presently.' It *was* an unexpected association, a quintet and a theatre overture, which do not begin alike in any literal way. The 'of its kind' might have meant that Shaw was alert to the compressed force in Elgar's introduction.

The 1919 *Musical Times* reviewer drew attention to the 'monastic cold plainsong melody' that opens the work. Only the first four notes, D, C, D, G, make a thematic link with the *Salve regina*, but the austere atmosphere pervades the piano theme. It is given out in octaves, while under it strings make insistent agitated stabs. Then an imploring chromatic passage,

[23] P. Hull, 'Elgar at Hereford', *RAM Magazine*, 1960, p. 6.
[24] 8 March 1919.

with cello rising against the drop of other strings, holds human anguish (Ex. 4.2).

Ex. 4.2

The confrontation of the emotionally blank piano theme with the personal chromatic passage (Ex. 4.2) indicates the serious intent of this work. (In the last movement, those ideas return as ghostly presences; confidence falters, as memories and presentiments play out some interior drama.)

After the introduction, the first movement sets off in a resolute Allegro. But Example 4.2 reappears, then the plainchant (cue 9), now generous and *cantabile*. A *fugato* on the Allegro theme opens the development. Shaw protested at this 'relapse into the expected'. Elgar defended himself saying 'it was meant to be square … and goes wild again – as man does'. He does indeed build it to a powerful altercation between the piano and the strings before the reprise. In this the 'Spanish' second subject and its pendant are inflated beyond their worth, though the movement closes with the return of the introduction.

The sublime slow movement opens with an eight-bar melody for viola. This is gloriously extended to a forty-two bar paragraph. Echoes of Example 4.2 link the Adagio to the first movement, but do not impede either its flow or its ripe serenity. Example 4.2 opens the last movement, but is brushed aside by the impetuous Allegro. But as in the first movement the quality drops with the jazzy second subject. At last the plainchant returns, with piano and strings now in accord, but everything disintegrates into ghostly, disillusioned fragments. The reprise is crowned at cue 72 not, sadly, with the great plainchant but with the jazzy second subject, though the sheer

impetuosity is almost convincing. Even if flawed, the Quintet
is an ambitious, remarkable work.

Elgar dedicated it to Ernest Newman, who referred to the
'quasi-programme that lies at the base of the work'. Elgar
admitted to him that the Quintet was 'ghostly stuff'.[25] It has
a Spanish, or at least an exotic, flavour, mostly in the second
subject of the first movement (violins in thirds over a languid
piano accompaniment, A major with G naturals and B flats).
Reed described Elgar as being fascinated by a group of twisted
dead trees on a nearby plateau. Basil Maine (1933) talks of a
legend of an early settlement of Spanish monks there, who,
while carrying out their ungodly rites, were struck dead – the
trees were their dead forms. Research by Michael Pope found
no Spanish monks, and the legend has no basis in local tradition. However, Maine published the story when Elgar was alive
and he did not contradict it. Lady Elgar seemed to corroborate
it at the time: she wrote of the 'sad' and 'dispossessed' trees,
referred to their dance, their wail for their sin. She also thought
that the 'weird beginning' of the Quintet has the same atmosphere as the eerie partsong 'Owls' for which Elgar wrote the
words – ('what is it? … nothing' (see p. 92). In July Algernon
Blackwood, a friend since *The Starlight Express*, came to Brinkwells.
He had a taste for the macabre and the occult, and he may well
have recommended Bulwer Lytton to Elgar, for on 3 September
there is a note that 'Lytton's novels arrive'. Bulwer Lytton was a
prolific nineteenth-century novelist, famous for *The Last Days of
Pompeii*. Lady Elgar thought that Lytton's *Strange Story*, which Elgar
was reading, sounded through the Quintet. Wulstan Atkins was
'satisfied that Blackwood invented the legend … Elgar talked a
lot about Blackwood … and their visit to the haunted trees …
the legend [would have been] an unconscious background in
Elgar's mind.'[26] Elgar had mourned as his young countrymen
were massacred in the trenches, and the image of trees blasted
in their prime must have held contemporary resonance. It was
not the first time that some spectre had stalked through his
music; the Second Symphony gives evidence of that. For all his

[25]   5 January 1919.
[26]   To McVeagh, 30 September, 1999.

outward jocularity, Elgar was a haunted man. Maybe the blas-
phemous dance of the Spanish monks, the lightning blast of
retribution, were fastened by his imagination onto the twisted
trees; and who can be sure whether the music, shaping itself
in his subconscious, suggested the 'legend', or the 'legend' the
music?

At Brinkwells through the autumn of 1918 Lady Elgar seemed
unwell, with many coughs and colds. In late October she had
an operation for a wen on her forehead. The Elgars were back at
Brinkwells for Armistice Day, 11 November 1918. In December
Severn House was burgled. Its upkeep was becoming more
difficult and expensive, and in September 1919 they put the
house on the market.

1918 Concerto for Cello in E minor, Op. 85

I *Adagio* – *Moderato* II *Allegro molto* III *Adagio* IV *Allegro, ma non troppo*

Elgar had long had a cello concerto in mind. He had suggested
one for the 1913 Leeds Festival. There was talk of Casals playing
it (he was then at the height of his reputation); that came to
nothing, possibly because the fee Casals asked was too big.
Instead Elgar produced *Falstaff*.

The night he returned home in March 1918 from his
tonsils operation he wrote down the 9/8 theme of the Concerto's first movement: a long wandering single line of melody
which, taken in isolation, has the qualities of tiredness and
resignation. Neither instrument nor context was defined. Back
at Brinkwells he improved. The Elgars returned to London for
the winter, and the public premières of the Violin Sonata, the
String Quartet, and the Piano Quintet on 21 May 1919. The
cellist of the performing quartet was Felix Salmond. Then the
Concerto gripped Elgar, and he worked through May and June
1919, partly at Brinkwells. Salmond made several visits for
technical try-outs, and Elgar offered him the first performance.

The Concerto can be grouped with Elgar's chamber music in period and to some extent in mood. The orchestra is the same size as for the Violin Concerto, but is sparely used. The four movements are short, and none is cast in fully traditional concerto-sonata form, though the second corresponds to the symphonic scherzo, which most concertos omit. Perhaps writing for a low-toned instrument conditioned Elgar to simple expression. At any rate, the Cello Concerto is quite unlike Dvořák's or Schumann's (or Walton's or Prokofiev's), or even Elgar's own Violin Concerto. It has gathered round it symbols of sadness, of the autumn of civilization as Elgar knew it, of the autumn of his own life, of bonfires and falling leaves. It is his Autumn Meditation rather than his *Rite of Spring*.

Nevertheless it is a work in which Elgar takes surprising risks. Is there another concerto with such a strange start? The whole work is braced by the opening commanding double-stopped recitative for the soloist, which returns *pizzicato* as a link to the second movement, and melodically to shape the fourth. The amplitude and panache of the opening gesture lead one to expect something more emphatic than the rising *ad lib.* questioning phrase that follows. The six-bar main theme, almost featureless, sinking over two octaves, is played for first time on the violas, the least assertive of instruments. It has no harmony and only a monotonous rhythm. In its six presentations, it shifts position so as to begin first on the supertonic, then on the dominant, then with full orchestra on the tonic, and back wanly to the supertonic: emotionally from unease to confidence and back again.

There is a warmer middle section in the lyrical 12/8 that often in Elgar's past music suggested prettiness. Here it is deeper, with the soloist and the orchestra engaged in serious conversation. On the return of the 'featureless' melody the soloist breaks boldly into the tonic statement as if in desperation, and the movement ends bleakly. Many passages in this work end less expansively, less confidently, than they began. That is not a failure of technique, but a moving complex of disillusion and compassion.

A haunting link, a 'try-out' passage, casting backwards and forwards, leads to a fantastic *moto perpetuo* in G. As in a similar passage in his Introduction and Allegro, Elgar places the melodic shift just off the beat. That, together with the frequent chromatic self-cancellations (is the B natural or flat?), gives the movement a precarious balance. The cello, skittering high through flecks and wisps of orchestral colour, sounds brilliant but unstable. The two-bar second subject has an eloquent first bar, a couldn't-care-less second bar. The coda whizzes manically away to A flat minor, before defining G major.

Three probing questions open the Adagio, and return at its end having found no answer. The cello pours out forty-five bars of heartfelt song, silent only for two orchestral bars. First it reaches out in octaves and sevenths; then contracts into painful semitones; then quotes the 'inspiration' figure (Ex. 1.10, see p. 33), ending on an interrupted cadence. The great arching opening is repeated in A major instead of B flat major, the lower pitch, the *stringendo*, and the increased dynamics making passionate what was expressive. This is one of the world's great elegies.

The orchestra abruptly dismisses it for the finale. The cello casts the new theme in the style of the opening recitative, but is swept aside. The *risoluto* marking does not disguise some nervousness beneath the swagger. This ambivalence is further exposed in the second subject when a moment's sweetness is peremptorily dismissed. The full pain of the work is gathered in a passage that begins by developing a passing counter-melody with abstruse harmony, and moves through passion and regret to die out with a quotation from the Adagio. Self-command is restored and summation achieved with a full statement of the soloist's opening recitative, and the work ends brusquely. Even people who shun what they hear as the 'imperialist Edwardian' strain in Elgar respond to this searching Concerto.

The first performance was at Queen's Hall, London, on 27 October 1919. Elgar was to conduct only his own work, the rest to be directed by Albert Coates, in the opening concert of the post-war season with the London Symphony Orchestra. Coates included the demanding *Poem of Ecstasy* by the recently dead Skryabin and – wanting to justify his new appointment – overran at both rehearsals. Elgar and Salmond went short of time. As a result, the performance was indifferent, the orchestral playing a muddle. Lady Elgar did not mince her words: 'brutal, selfish, ill mannered bounder A. Coates'. The nineteen-year-old John Barbirolli played among the cellists, and would not have blamed Elgar had he walked out. In such circumstances, Salmond, still a chamber music player, might well have projected his part wanly. In spite of the poor performance, the Gramophone Company invited Elgar to record the Concerto (abridged) with the young Beatrice Harrison, who then became his chosen soloist. In 1929 Lionel Tertis arranged it for viola, which Elgar approved.

He dedicated the work to Sir Sidney and Lady Colvin: their friendship he called 'a real and precious thing'.[27] Colvin was close enough to Elgar to receive some of his most intimate confidences and understood his sometimes violent despondency. After Alice Elgar died, it was to the Colvins that Elgar wrote most simply. When he left Brinkwells for the last time, for instance: 'inscrutable nature goes on just the same – young larks six, in a nest on the lawn & many other birds; nightingales sing; but I miss the little, gentlest presence & I cannot go on'.[28] And on Severn House: 'I am rescuing a few papers and a few books and go forth into the world alone as I did 43 years ago – only I am disillusioned and old.'

Early in 1920 the first number of *Music & Letters* appeared, in which Bernard Shaw grandly saluted Elgar. Of recent English composers, 'so far, Elgar is alone for Westminster Abbey'. Lady Elgar was able to read this, and to hear Adrian Boult conduct the Second Symphony. She had been too unwell to attend the recording of the Cello Concerto, and during March she grew weaker. She died, probably from heart failure, on 7 April 1920. Elgar gave up Brinkwells. In 1921 his daughter Carice became engaged to Samuel Blake, and they were married on 16 January 1922. When Severn House was sold, Elgar moved into a service flat at 37 St James's Place, London.

[27] Letter of 26 June 1919.
[28] 26 May 1921.

CHAPTER FIVE

The Last Years 1920–1934

Arrangements and Transcriptions, 1921–32

As a young man Elgar arranged much music, from Handel's *Ariodante* overture in 1878 to Wagner's *Good Friday Music* in 1894, scored for whatever local group he was involved with. Before radio and gramophone, the dissemination of orchestral works was mostly through arrangements or the domestic pianist. Brahms composed his Haydn Variations for two pianos and for the orchestra. In the present day, Howard Ferguson did the same for his Partita. Often the motive was the publishers' financial reward. *Salut d'amour* was arranged for every imaginable combination – and some unimaginable. Karg-Elert's transcriptions of Elgar's symphonies for piano are remarkable in their own right, and Elgar's reduction of his 'Enigma' Variations is a delight to play.

Nowadays, when authenticity is expected, there is seen to be an aesthetic, even a moral, issue in changing the medium. In Elgar's time not even the distinction between transcription and arrangement was clear. For most of his life he did not arrange other men's music. In the 1920s and 1930s he transcribed Bach, Handel, and Chopin, telling Eugene Goossens that he depended on 'people like John Sebastian' for inspiration now that his wife was dead.

Long before, he had written to Ivor Atkins that Bach 'heals and pacifies all men & all things'.[1] In April 1921 his daughter noted that he was playing Bach fugues on the piano. Perhaps, at this sad time, his mind went back to his organist days. In April

[1]   2 July 1902.

and May 1921 he transcribed Bach's C minor Organ Fugue (BWV 537) for orchestra, as his Op. 86. Eugene Goossens gave the first performance, on 27 October 1921 at the Queen's Hall. The following January Richard Strauss visited London, and Elgar gave a lunch for him and some young British composers. They discussed the Bach fugue, which Elgar had already recorded. Strauss favoured a more restrained approach than Elgar's. Elgar challenged him to orchestrate the Fantasia, but Strauss declined. So the next year Elgar did so himself, and conducted both pieces at the Gloucester Three Choirs on 7 September 1922.

Elgar would have heard Bach performed by large forces and on the great Cathedral organs, not on baroque instruments. In his sumptuous arrangement he sets the romantic tone at the start by his atmospheric treatment of the Fantasia's long pedal note, with timpani and bass drum pulsing alternately against the basic triple rhythm. The first harp *glissando* marks an interrupted cadence; brass shines through the climax. Bach's fugue is unusual in having two subjects, not ultimately combined but with the first section recapitulated. Elgar marks the entry of the second subject (rising semitones in equal minims) with the tambourine, and from then on he lets rip – percussion, syncopations, whizzing scales, and trills produce what he called a 'vibrating shimmering sort of organ sound – I think'.[2]

Ivor Atkins had collaborated with Elgar in 1911 on an edition of Bach's St Matthew Passion. Elgar told Atkins that he had treated Bach's Fantasia and Fugue 'in *modern* way – largest orchestra … you may not approve … many arrgts have been made of Bach on the "pretty" scale & I wanted to shew how gorgeous & great & brilliant he would have made himself sound if he had had our means'. Later he told Atkins 'it's a "wild wark" '. Elgar's arrangements reveal as much about Elgar and his period as about Bach, but that in itself is valuable. They are creative, filtered through the imagination of a great composer.

All his life Elgar venerated Handel. Since 1736, when Handel was first heard at a Three Choirs Festival, he reigned

[2] To E. Newman, 26 October 1921.

there supreme. Although in most cases only selections from his oratorios were played, his *Messiah* was performed at every festival since 1757 except two until 1963. In 1869, when Elgar was twelve, he persuaded his father to get him into a *Messiah* rehearsal. The Elgars' music shop supplied the orchestral parts, and while Elgar Senior was preparing them, Elgar wrote into them a little tune of his own. When played, 'the thing was an astonishing success', he recounted, 'and I heard that some people had never enjoyed Handel so much before!'[3] But when he listened to 'O thou that tellest', he was so impressed that he determined to learn the violin, and at the end of a fortnight he had mastered the aria's violin part.

He was asked for a new work for the 1923 Three Choirs festival, but was adamant he could no longer compose. So Atkins persuaded him to provide orchestral accompaniments for two anthems, Battishill's 'O Lord, look down from heaven' and S. S. Wesley's 'Let us lift up our hearts'. (In 1929 he scored Purcell's 'Jehovah, quam multi sunt hostes mei.') Elgar also transcribed Handel's Overture in D minor to the second Chandos anthem, 'In the Lord put I my Trust', and conducted its first performance on 2 September 1923. Though he did not give it an opus number, he valued it enough to record it the next month (taking it faster, more athletically, than some later conductors). Sending the score to Novello he wrote: 'I have known the overture from the old two stave organ arrangement since I was a little boy and always wanted it to be heard in a large form – the weighty structure is (to me) so grand – epic.'[4] Reed wrote of the 'thrills' Elgar derived from Handel: 'he would speak of Handel with tears in his eyes'. 'He would rub his hands gleefully and look up to heaven at the thought of old Handel's genius.'[5] Herbert Howells remembered Elgar's telling him that the sonority and brilliance of his Introduction and Allegro derived from Handel's concertos. Maybe Elgar thought of Bernard Shaw's comment in his *Music & Letters* article, that Elgar's 'range is so Handelian'.

[3] J. N. Moore, *Edward Elgar: A Creative Life* (Oxford, 1984), p. 43.
[4] 16 July 1923.
[5] William H. Reed, *Elgar as I Knew Him* (London, 1936), p. 43.

Handel composed his eleven Chandos anthems for James Brydges, Duke of Chandos, who built himself a grand house in Palladian style, near what was then the village of Edgeware. Though Elgar described the piece he chose as 'epic', Handel scored the anthems for a modest orchestra without violas, and they were performed at the parish church of St Lawrence. 'In the Lord put I my Trust' has a substantial two-part orchestral introduction, which Handel used again in his Concerto Grosso Op. 3 No. 5 and as the third movement of his sixth clavier suite. Elgar conflated Handel's instrumental and keyboard version, made a four-bar cut, and brought back the opening Largo to form a Maestoso close. Lively though it is, his scoring is less colourful, less opulent, than that for the Bach.

In 1930 the BBC founded its own Symphony Orchestra, under Adrian Boult. Fred Gaisberg, the far-sighted recording manager at HMV who was responsible for Elgar's own recordings, quickly put the new orchestra under contract. It was thought a good idea to involve Elgar. So in March 1932 he was invited to arrange Chopin's Funeral March from the B flat minor sonata. Of his three transcriptions that of the Chopin is the least 'Elgarian'. That was deliberate: the work is among the few scored with recording in mind. Boult remarked how 'open chording' in the Classics with nothing 'obscured by duplication' made for brilliance of sound. That, he said, Elgar recognized in scoring the Chopin 'specially for gramophone reproduction', when he 'took pains to keep a very open and clear score and resisted the temptation' of richness and thickness of the texture.[6] Elgar uses his large orchestra lightly; and though one need not go so far as *The Record Guide* ('it cannot be too often said that arrangements of Chopin's music for orchestral or other combination are always to be deplored'), the trio naturally suggests *Sylphides*.

Elgar's reactions to Chopin were not always so agreeable. 'Dorabella' once unwisely pointed out a similarity between a place in *Gerontius* and the *Polonaise Fantaisie*, to be told 'I don't care

6   *The Listener*, 28 December 1932.

for Chopin and I never heard the piece you mention'.[7] But no composer enjoys having his music likened to anyone else's. In *Polonia* he quoted from Chopin's G minor Nocturne. In his retirement he loved listening to the gramophone, and, writing to HMV, said 'I *should* like the Chopin *Ballades*'.

In 1921 Alice Stuart of Wortley made her will, and asked that her gifts from Elgar since 1905, and her portrait painted by her father, should be given to Worcester in the hope that the cottage where Elgar was born should be acquired and that her gifts could find their place there. Lord Stuart of Wortley died in 1926.

In 1923, keeping his London flat, Elgar took a lease on Napleton Grange, Kempsey, near Worcester. 'In my own land I am a boy again,'[8] he wrote to Ernest Newman. Lonely and looking for diversion, he boarded the *Hildebrand* on 15 November 1923 for a cruise '1000 miles up the Amazon'. Its furthest point was Manaus, where they stopped for five days. Elgar was struck, as are all visitors, by the opera house, completed in 1896.

Stage Works, 1923–28

In January 1923 Laurence Binyon asked Elgar to compose music for his play *Arthur: a Tragedy*, based on Malory. Elgar, who had set Binyon's poems in *The Spirit of England*, was attracted by the idea. He replied, 'I *want* to do it but since my dear wife's death I have *done nothing* & fear my music has vanished.'[9] A visit to Carice and her husband, now settled at their farm near Guildford, produced thirty minutes of music, introductions, and entr'actes for the nine scenes, and motifs under the speech and action, some of it from old sketchbooks. The play was

---

[7] Mrs Richard Powell, *Edward Elgar: Memories of a Variation* (London, 1937), p. 52.
[8] 1 May 1923.
[9] 31 January 1923.

produced by Lilian Baylis at the Old Vic on 12 March 1923, and Elgar conducted the first night. He began rehearsing on 2 March, which prompted the *Sunday Times* into commenting: 'Fancy the greatest composer in England rehearsing ten musicians in the Waterloo Road ... He sat about for hours ... his face half-lit by the light in his pipe, waited at the conductor's desk while the stage hands struggled with the scanty properties, and Lilian Baylis sat in the box admiring him.' In fact, Elgar paid for extra musicians himself.

Binyon seems more concerned with Launcelot and his love for Arthur's queen, Guenevere, and the young Elaine's love for him, than with Arthur himself. The plot plumbs deceit, suspicion, passion, and betrayal, and the scenes demand a banquet, a battle, a convent, and two funeral barges. The score was not published, and in a suite drawn from it edited by Alan Barlow the orchestration is not Elgar's for the original Old Vic production. Elgar showed no interest when Ivor Atkins wanted to perform some of the music at the 1926 Three Choirs. Perhaps he had already laid other plans. The proud 'chivalry' theme, Example 5.1, would have found its way into the finale of the third symphony, and the banquet music would appear in its second movement. The battlefield trumpet call would go into *The Spanish Lady*. There were links too with his past. Among his early works was the processional *Ecce Sacerdos magnus*, and here he uses the traditional chant for that. In some respects *Arthur* looks back to *King Olaf*, particularly with the tolling of the convent bell.

Ex. 5.1

In 1928 Elgar moved into Tiddington House, near Stratford-on-Avon, and often went (sometimes with Bernard Shaw) to Shakespeare. He came to know the actor-manager Gerald Lawrence who asked him for music for a new play by Bertram Matthews. *Beau Brummel* presented an idealistic view of the character 'as a gentleman who is ready to sacrifice his life, his career, his friendship with the Prince Regent, to save a woman's honour'.[10] Elgar seemed to enjoy working in the theatre, and was content to dig into his sketchbooks for a Minuet (all that was published) and to use some of the Brummel material later for The Spanish Lady. He conducted the first night at the Theatre Royal, Birmingham on 5 November 1928.

On Sir Walter Parratt's death, Elgar was made Master of the King's Musick at the end of April 1923.

Pageant of Empire, 1924

The British Empire Exhibition aimed 'to make the different races of the British Empire better known to each other, and to demonstrate to the people of Britain the almost illimitable possibilities of the Dominions, Colonies, and Dependencies together'. It was also, of course, 'to find ... new sources of Imperial wealth'. The site at Wembley Stadium covered two hundred acres, and was visited by twenty-seven million people.

Elgar conducted the massed choirs and bands in Parry's 'Jerusalem' and his own 'Land of Hope and Glory' for the opening ceremony on 23 April 1924. At the rehearsal the huge choir 'cheered the veteran conductor as he mounted the steps' though he seemed a 'lonely figure in black poised in his lofty pulpit', and he found, he wrote to his Windflower, 'no soul & no romance & no imagination'.[11]

The Pageant itself ran from 21 July to 30 August. Each of the three parts began with Elgar's Empire March, forceful and brilliant, the melody of 'Song of Union' making a memorable trio section. He composed eight songs to words by Alfred Noyes. 'The Islands' (New Zealand) and 'Sailing Westwards' ('adventurous captains') share the same tune, and it serves too for 'are

---

[10] The Birmingham Post, 6 November 1928.
[11] 16 April 1914.

there worlds beyond the darkness' in 'The Immortal Legions', which grieves for the victorious dead. So the complete set might be thought of as a suite. There is nothing to match 'Land of Hope and Glory' or *The Spirit of England* in quality, but it is all decent community music. *Sursum corda, Imperial March,* 'Land of Hope and Glory', selections from *The Crown of India,* and *With Proud Thanksgiving* were also played, among the eighty items of music. In 1928 Elgar wrote to Leslie Boosey, 'I think the pronounced praise of England is not quite so popular as it was; the loyalty remains, but the people seem to be more shy as to singing about it.'[12]

In 1927 Elgar turned seventy. He conducted a birthday concert for the BBC on the day, 2 June. In December Frank Schuster died, leaving Elgar £7000. In 1928 Elgar was appointed KCVO, and in 1931 he became First Baronet of Broadheath. His lease at Napleton Grange ending, he rented Battenhall Manor. For the 1929 Worcester Three Choirs Festival, he took a house called Marl Bank, which he liked enough to buy. So at the end of the year he moved into his final home in the city where he had been born. In 1931 Basil Maine approached him about his proposed book. On 7 November 1931 he met Vera Hockman, a young amateur violinist to whom he became romantically attached.

☙❦☙

Severn and Nursery Suites, 1930

1 Introduction (*Worcester Castle*) 2 *Toccata* (*Tournament*) 3 Fugue (*Cathedral*) 4 Minuet (*Commandery*) 5 *Coda*

Elgar had long been asked for a piece for brass band. He accepted the invitation for the twenty-fifth annual National Brass Band Championship at the Crystal Palace, Sydenham. The brass band movement, started in the 1820s, was the most popular form of amateur instrumental music-making in the country. At one

[12]   10 June 1928.

time there were about twenty thousand bands in Great Britain, important for their social as well as their musical value. The competition festivals ensured that the standards were high, and, though some of the music was arranged and some was of doubtful quality, in 1928 the test piece was Holst's *Moorside Suite*, who described the players as 'musicians conducted by musicians'. Bliss composed his *Kenilworth Suite* in 1936 for the competition, and Birtwistle his *Grimethorpe Aria* in 1973.

Elgar dedicated his Suite Op. 87 to Bernard Shaw, who responded flamboyantly: 'it will secure my immortality when all my plays are dead and dammed and forgotten'.[13] Shaw was present at the famous lunch party when Elgar put the painter and critic Roger Fry in his place on the respective merits of music and the visual arts. Fry had remarked that 'all the arts are the same'. Elgar retorted 'Music is written on the skies ... and you compare that to a DAMNED imitation.'[14] Shaw's days as a music critic were long past, when he had shocked the establishment with his 'lively and unstable pen' but in whose writing Elgar found 'always a substratum of practical matter'. When Elgar's 'lumbago' (the early symptoms of his cancer) prevented his getting to the Crystal Palace for the *Severn Suite* on 27 September, Shaw reported: 'I heard the *Severn Suite* yesterday only eight times as extreme hunger and the need for catching the 5.10 train at King's Cross forced me to surrender before I had ceased finding new things in it.' Of the performers he said, 'All keen: no professional staleness.' Peter Warlock also attended, and praised playing that would 'astonish ears that have only heard brass bands at the street corner'. Among the four entrants Shaw missed were the winners, Foden's Motor Works Band conducted by Fred Mortimer, who then recorded an abridged version of the Suite (reissued in 1993). Shaw advised Elgar if there was a new edition of the score to 'drop the old Italian indications and use the language of the bandsmen. For instance – Remember that the Minuet is a dance and not a bloody hymn.'[15] Elgar did not take his advice.

[13]   25 May 1930.

[14]   L. Woolf, *Beginning Again* (London, 1964), p. 126.

[15]   28 September 1930.

Although the movements run without breaks, Elgar gave each a title with a local association. That year he wrote the Foreword to Hubert Leicester's *Forgotten Worcester*, so the city's history was in his mind. Not all of the *Severn Suite* was newly composed. The Cathedral Fugue began as a keyboard piece in 1923. The Minuet and the two Trios are based on music for the early wind quintets. Since Elgar was unfamiliar with instruments such as euphonium and flugelhorn, the work was submitted to Henry Geehl, an expert in the field. He found Elgar 'not an easy man to work with', but Elgar's scoring has since been shown to be acceptable. Geehl arranged the suite for military band. The orchestral score is Elgar's, and in his recording he takes full account of his direction 'pomposo' at the start, and brings out the occasional similarities to *Falstaff* (Gadshill at night, the scarecrow army, and so on). In the Cathedral Fugue there is a hint of 'Nimrod', and – perhaps? – Elgar's muchloved Schumann; Cologne on the Rhine and Worcester on the Severn are both celebrated in solemn, diatonic polyphony.

In 1930 a new idea came from W. L. Streeton of HMV who, hearing that Elgar had come across some of his early unpublished compositions, thought they might make a little suite. The recent birth of Princess Margaret Rose suggested a subject. By December Elgar had completed the *Nursery Suite*. It was recorded at Kingsway Hall on 23 May 1931 before its public performance. Herbert Hughes wrote[16] of W. H. Reed 'trying over, very gingerly', the cadenza in 'Envoy'. It is affecting to hear those old friends, Edward and Billy, together on the recording, one conducting, the other playing. To the second session came the Duke with the Duchess of York, who had accepted the dedication to herself and her two daughters.

The music has all the freshness of the early String Serenade with even more charm, and opens with the same lilt. In 'The Aubade' – 'memories of happy and peaceful awakenings'[17] – Elgar quotes, with more subtle harmony, his 1870s hymn-tune 'Drake's Broughton', the name of a village near Worcester. His

[16] *The Daily Telegraph*, 25 May 1931.
[17] J. Northrop Moore gives Elgar's programme notes in *Elgar on Record* (London, 1974), pp. 137–8.

hand has lost none of its cunning. The 'Aubade' is in G major. With a 'W. N.'–'Nimrod' one-note link he sets the hymn tune in E flat; modulates with throw-away sequences back to G, where he recapitulates the hymn grandly; starts off on his sequencing again but doubles back on himself; sinks for one retrospective bar into E flat, and ends in G. All as smooth as milk and honey. 'The Serious Doll' – 'a semi-serious solo' – was written for Gordon Walker, the finest flautist of the day. Elgar provided simpler arabesques as *ossias* for those less accomplished. 'Busyness' suggests 'tireless energy'. It has the glitter and tunefulness of 'Sun Dance' in the first *Wand of Youth* suite, and the long-familiar rat-tat-tat rhythm (see Ex. 1.2). Elgar described 'The Sad Doll' as a 'pathetic tired little puppet'. It is a ghostly waltz, an innocent wraithlike version of the more knowing waltzes in *Der Rosenkavalier*. In 'The Wagon (passes)' the waggoner's whistle is at first amusing, but as the volume of the *ostinato* increases to the 'jar and crash of the heavy horses and wheels' it becomes threatening and overwhelming. It is markedly like Mussorgsky's 'Bydlo', a sound-picture of a lumbering Polish ox-cart. Elgar's use of the word 'wheels' links his wagon to the 'wheels go over my head' passage in the Second Symphony, as in a terrifying nightmare (see p. 129). 'The Merry Doll' suggests the endearing postcards he used to send his daughter Carice when she was little. Elgar described 'Dreaming' as 'soft and tender childish slumbers'. But this piece is not childish. It is mature Elgar, and probes the source of his inspiration. As early as *King Olaf*, dreams found in him a deep and poetic response (see Ex. 1.8). A violin cadenza (with Billy impish in the recording between cues 63 and 64) reviews previous themes, and the Suite ends with 'Aubade', as insouciantly as it began.

❦

In July 1932 Elgar recorded his Violin Concerto with the sixteen-year-old Yehudi Menuhin. The following year they performed it in Paris. Elgar flew there, and visited Delius at Grez. Shaw had persuaded the BBC to commission a third symphony, which was announced at the last of three concerts to celebrate Elgar's seventy-fifth birthday. At the same time Elgar approached Barry Jackson with grand ideas for an opera.

Vocal Music, 1923–32

In the words Elgar chose for his late partsongs it is hard not to see a reflection of his own state – 'in a lonely place'. Though domestically he was cared for by good staff, he was without close companionship. In 1923 Robin Legge asked him for part-songs for the American male-voice group, the DeReske Singers, made up of pupils of Jean De Reske. Elgar had had experience in writing for male voices in setting the Greek Anthology poems. He found the anonymous poem 'The Wanderer' in the anthology *Wit and Drollery* of 1661, reprinted in Isaac d'Israeli's *Curiosities of Literature*, and wrote the first stanza himself – 'day's a-dying'. It is a modified strophic song, and Elgar breaks the form for an outburst at 'to the wilderness I wander' and for the final sad 'Methinks it is no journey'. He wrote the words of 'Zut! Zut! Zut!' himself, under the pseudonym Richard Mardon. The subtitle is 'Remembrance'. He wanted the word 'zut', used simply as 'accompaniment' to the 'old-time march-song', pronounced to rhyme with 'wood'.

In 1925 came 'The Herald', also for male voices, with words by the Glaswegian poet Alexander Smith (1829–67). It is through-composed, portraying a 'grim old king', victorious but wounded in battle, mourned by his lords and even more lovingly by his horse. He stabs himself and his soul goes shrieking out as Elgar's notes chase it frantically. In great block chords, way outside the basic E flat, his herald declaims 'My master comes!' It is a dramatic song with something about it of Greek tragedy. De la Mare's 'The Prince of Sleep' is an ambiguous figure, 'lovely in a lonely place', and Elgar's setting (1925) for mixed voices is beautiful and mysterious, a lyrical triple-time centre enclosed by abstruse and shadowy harmonies (Ex. 5.2).

In 1928 he found a carol by Ben Jonson, 'I sing the birth', and set it in austere unaccompanied solos for tenor, alto, and bass in turn, adding timeless modal 'alleluias' that recall the

Ex. 5.2

Litany in *Gerontius*. It is the nearest Elgar came to his great
contemporary Holst. Also in 1928 Walford Davies asked him
to mark the king's recovery from serious illness. Elgar chose
'Good Morrow' by George Gascoigne (1634–77), ending 'He
will our health restore'. He revised his early hymn tune 'Praise
ye the Lord', and called it 'a simple carol for His Majesty's
happy recovery'. In 1902 he had greeted Queen Alexandra
on her coronation as 'Daughter of Ancient Kings'. In 1932 he
set words by the poet laureate John Masefield, 'So many true
princesses who have gone', to be sung at the unveiling of a
memorial to the Queen in the garden of Marlborough House,
London: 'here, at this place, she often sat'. It was performed to
an audience of dignatories by the choirs of the Chapels Royals
and Westminster Abbey with the band of the Welsh Guards.
Elgar conducted, wearing his doctor's robes over Court Dress.
The young David Willcocks was at one end of the row of choristers and felt Elgar's eyes on him, but found that a boy at the
far end had felt exactly the same. 'Elgar had that all embracing
gaze ... great charisma.' In 2004 Anthony Payne scored the
Ode for full orchestra.

Elgar's unison songs of the period are less interesting. He
produced 'The Song of the Bull' for male voices for a May
week revue in 1924. In 1930, for Joan Elwes, a young soprano
whose voice he admired, he set a Scots poem 'It isnae me' by
Sally Holmes, about the power of song to stir memories. In
1932 Stephen Moore, a young local schoolmaster, asked for
songs for the Worcester City Schools Festival. Elgar would have
been well inclined to Moore, for he was the son of the vicar of
Claines, in which churchyard he used to find the solitude to

read scores as a boy. He consulted his daughter about words, then chose three poems from Charles Mackay (1814–89) for unison or two-part pieces. 'The Rapid Stream' and 'The Woodland Stream' have Schubertian accompaniments. Setting 'When Swallows fly', did he remember, after he left 'Plas Gwyn', going back during the next Hereford Festival to see if 'the swallows are still cared for?'

Instrumental Music, 1923–32

In 1923 came a request from a William Starmer, who had conducted Elgar's music in his home town of Tunbridge Wells and elsewhere. Starmer was advising on a new carillon as a war memorial for Loughborough, and wanted music. Elgar at once offered a few bars, asking for information as to the 'position' of chords. Starmer sent technical details and some specimens. Elgar composed quite a substantial piece in several sections. The carillon was opened by the Belgian Jef Denyn, the famous municipal carilloneur of Mechelen. So Elgar once more memorialized the war dead in a carillon. He began, but did not complete, a version for organ. Another 'chime' ended badly. Sir Albert Richardson, the expert on Georgian architecture and a member of Brooks's, Elgar's club, was restoring the church at Eaton Socon, Bedfordshire. He asked Elgar for a chime for the clock of eight bells. This Elgar provided, possibly basing it on an 1879 hymn-tune. He was thoroughly nettled when the church council held a competition, which was won by a local man. (In 1927 he made a carillon obbligato descant for 'Land of Hope and Glory' for Ottawa.)

In 1927, at Percy Hull's request, he composed a two-minute Civic Fanfare to accompany the mayor's procession into Hereford Cathedral for the opening service of the Festival. It was to precede the National Anthem, and, since the LSO would already be assembled, Elgar composed for large orchestra, with organ and percussion but curiously without violins. He designed the Fanfare practically, with the opening five bars to be repeated two or three times, should the procession straggle. 1927 was the year recording was first allowed at the Festival. Elgar approved of it, and had acted as intermediary, so the Fanfare was recorded live under his direction.

To Hull he dedicated a fifth *Pomp and Circumstance* march, as he had already favoured his fellow Three Choirs organists, Atkins (No. 3) and Sinclair (No. 4). While out for a drive through the countryside with his valet/chauffeur Dick Mountford, Elgar scribbled an idea on to the only paper they could find, an Ordnance Survey map. Sketches for a sixth march were completed by Anthony Payne in 2006.

In 1930 Elgar planned a suite for oboe and orchestra for Leon Goossens, whose playing he described as 'divine'. It got no further than one movement drafted for oboe and piano. Gordon Jacob later scored it and Goossens himself gave the first performance on BBC television in 1967. Called *Soliloquy*, it is a brief but intense piece, languorous, with exotic arabesques *ad lib.* for Goossens to display his celebrated *rubato*. The range between the *Soliloquy*, the abstruse harmonies of 'The Prince of Sleep', and the austerity of 'Good Morrow', show that Elgar, at least in small forms, was still reaching extremes and still exploring.

Two of his last pieces, all for piano and all from 1932, were tributes to his friendships. He dedicated the *Serenade* to John Austin, the Worcester violinist he had known since 1898, and who had devotedly checked proofs with him. The simple sad *Adieu*, which received no dedication, begins in B minor but ends on a chord of F sharp minor. Perhaps it was Elgar's own farewell. *Mina* he dedicated to Fred Gaisberg, whose enlightened encouragement of Elgar's recordings put musicians forever in his debt. Elgar scored it in 1933: the tune waltzes wraith-like through celeste and glockenspiel. Mina was a cairn terrier, with the spaniel Marco and Meg his constant companions in his old age.

Coda

Elgar died on 23 February 1934. He left sketches for the unfinished third oratorio, a piano concerto, the opera *The Spanish
Lady*, and a third symphony.

All his life Elgar loved music in the theatre. But nothing
came of his Rabelais ballet, nor yet of the 'Opera in 3 Acts'
heading in a 1909 sketchbook. Later he contemplated, though
never began, a Hardy opera, even a *Lear*. Among many other
librettos, he was offered and refused a *Pilgrim's Progress*. Then
Barry Jackson (1879–1961) of the Birmingham Repertory
founded a Drama Festival at Malvern; the first, in 1929, was
dedicated to Shaw. Elgar became stage-struck. He asked Shaw
for a libretto, but Shaw replied that 'the verbal music' of his
plays 'would make a very queer sort of counterpoint'[1] with
Elgar's music. Elgar then turned to Ben Jonson, his choice
falling on *The Devil is an Ass* (1616). In 1932 he asked Jackson
for help. Jackson at first considered the play moribund, then
– thinking he might deprive the world of Elgar's opera – delivered a rough libretto, working from the copious markings on
Elgar's own copy.

Elgar was determined his opera was to be no less grand
than Wagner or Strauss – he would 'out-Meistersinger the
Meistersinger'. He planned stage sets, and drew up cast lists,
the vocal ranges based on *Tosca*. He ransacked his sketchbooks
for musical ideas, and Jonson's other plays (and other poets)
for lyrics. He planned to use sketches from 1878 onwards,
and passages rejected from his earlier works, but some music
was newly composed. His libretto was never more than work
in progress, excitedly scribbled over: around the plot swarm

[1]   W. H. Reed, *Elgar as I Knew Him* (London, 1936) p. 89.

minor characters, and all the bustle of the streets and taverns of Jacobean London.[2]

Elgar once declared he wanted something 'heroic & noble' for a subject, but was offered only 'blood & lust'.[3] In Jonson, Satan sends his apprentice, Pug, to visit the earth to make mischief, but Pug finds London so sleazy and corrupt that he can do no worse. Jackson and Elgar, however, sweetened the play, romantically changing Frances (the heroine) from wife to ward, cutting Satan, and making Pug simply a manservant.

Elgar left about 180 sketches. Many were wordless, not all were fixed in their final positions in the libretto. Some were bare outlines, some extended, and only a few bars were fully scored. Elgar relished the idea of setting Jonson's dialogue as recitative; in the event, scarcely any pieces were connected or developed. A longish dialogue turns out to be discarded from The Kingdom. There is some ravishing, tender love music, a catchy song with male chorus, a striking if drunken 'Memento Mori', a rich sarabande, and a dashing bolero. Most of it is instantly recognizable Elgar.

The 'Spanish' dances (partly based on very early material) were nearly complete. Percy Young edited them (1956) and two songs (1955). He broadcast talks on the opera, arranged a concert performance at St John's, Smith Square, London, in 1986, and in 1991 published the sketches for the Elgar Complete Edition. He also 'edited, arranged, and orchestrated'

---

[2]   The plot in brief. Wittipol (tenor, Cavaradossi) loves Frances (soprano, Tosca), heiress and ward of Fitzdottrel (basso *cantabile*), who also loves her, but covets new clothes more. Meercraft (baritone, Scarpia) is a con-man, a bogus company promoter, who tricks Fitzdottrel into believing he can make him a duke. So Fitzdottrel wishes his ward to be taught noble manners, for which service he will pay a diamond ring. Wittipol dresses up as a Spanish Lady, just arrived in town with news of fashion and etiquette. In Act II, a reception at Lady Tailbush's, 'she' arrives, and Fitzdottrel, eager for 'her' to instruct his ward, leaves them together. Wittipol discards his disguise, and a priest is found to marry the young lovers – 'a true love-knot will hardly be untied'.

[3]   To Walford Davies, October 1919. See also Barry Jackson, BBC script for 'The Fifteenth Variation', recorded in May 1957, and Barry Jackson, 'Elgar's Spanish Lady', *Music & Letters* xxiv (1943), reprinted in C. Redwood (ed.), *An Elgar Companion* (Ashbourne, 1982), pp. 209–229.

the opera for the stage performance at Cambridge in 1994. His libretto is not quite Elgar's and Jackson's, but there is no knowing how they might have revised it. His main problem was how to stretch the music over the action; he needed to add from other Elgar sources. From all this he salvaged something between a ballad opera, with set numbers and spoken dialogue, and a masque with dances.

Perhaps *The Devil is an Ass* is not such a strange choice for the composer of *The Dream of Gerontius*. Jonson's play is satirical, mocking greed, vanity, dishonesty, lewd behaviour. Elgar, born a Catholic, kept a strong sense of sin. Two other strands in this late opera ran through his life. There are Spanish idioms in works spanning *The Black Knight* (1892) to the Piano Quintet (1918). The other strand is that of disguise – things are not always what they seem. In his note about 'Enigma', Elgar wrote: 'So the principal Theme never appears, even as in some late dramas … the chief character is never on the stage.' Both strands come together in the Spanish quotation on his Violin Concerto, which leaves a blank for the essential word. The 'Spanish Lady', who never existed, seems yet another example of his love of mystery and disguise.

Disaster struck the opera when the BBC commission came for a third symphony. Neither opera nor symphony was completed before Elgar's death: each killed the other.

The unfinished symphony posed a moral problem. Knowing he was too ill to complete it, Elgar had begged Billy Reed not to allow anyone to 'tinker' with it. Reed published an account of the work and some facsimiles in *The Listener* of 28 August 1935, then in his *Elgar as I Knew Him*.

During his last couple of years Elgar had worked hard at the symphony, enthusiastically playing sketches at the piano to friends such as Reed and Fred Gaisberg. Reed felt that the composer's vision of the whole work was forming, and Gaisberg summed up in his diary that the symphony was complete in structure and design. But that was in Elgar's mind. The existing sketches revealed little continuity beyond the opening of the first movement. It was normal for his way of composing, for his mosaic style meant that so long as all the ideas came 'from the same oven', as he told Sanford Terry, their assembling into a coherent whole came later. He was drawing heavily on earlier material, notably on the *Last Judgment*, 'Callicles', *Cockaigne* No. 2 (the *City of Dreadful Night*) and *Arthur*. Again, that need not have indicated flagging invention, for plundering earlier material had always been his custom.

Naturally the sketches aroused curiosity and were studied and written about.[4] The general conclusion was that nothing could be done with them, for no-one but Elgar could have drawn the fragments together. The stark pounding opening, of parallel fourths and fifths, sounds like late Elgar, even Sibelius, but belongs to his oratorio period. Elgar initialed the apparently new second subject 'V. H.', a tribute to his last love, Vera Hockman. The opening of the great Adagio, which Elgar described as opening 'some vast bronze doors onto something strangely familiar', belonged to the *City of Dreadful Night* and/ or the *Last Judgment*.

Critics, scholars, biographers looked, as it were, from the outside. But the composer Anthony Payne had been pondering the sketches for twenty-five years. At one point he admitted there were 'crucial gaps that will always prevent a convincing completion'. As a composer he was gradually drawn inside Elgar's creative imagination. Living closely with the music, he found signposts, serendipitous connections. He was 'in love with the fragments'. He forged links, composed some stretches. One major challenge he faced was the symphony's conclusion, which Elgar had never reached. Boldly, he drew on 'The Wagon passes', that 'dark and visionary piece', as he called it, allowing its menacing ostinato to fade into silence.

There remained the ethical problem, until the Elgar family courageously gave him permission to publish. One clinching argument is that whatever Payne made from the sketches, they remained intact. If a painting or a building is modified, the original is altered, if not destroyed. That is not so with

---

[4]   B. Maine, 'Elgar's sketches in relation to musicology', *Basil Maine on Music* (London, 1945), p. 31; H. Burton, 'Elgar and the BBC, with particular reference to the unfinished Third Symphony', *Journal of the Royal Society of the Arts*, cxxvii (1979), p. 224; C. Kent, 'Elgar's Third Symphony: the sketches reconsidered', *The Musical Times*, cxxiii (August 1982), p. 532.

musical sketches. Schubert's 'Unfinished' has had more than one completion; so has Mahler's Tenth. Payne's conclusions would not invalidate a subsequent attempt. He has scrupulously documented his procedures, and has never claimed that the symphony is Elgar's: unassumingly he calls it his 'elaboration of Elgar's sketches'.[5]

The packed audience at the Royal Festival Hall on 15 February 1998 experienced something of the thrill of an Elgar première during his great days. It was impossible not to recall Elgar's magnificent remark to his doctor, Arthur Thomson: 'If I can't complete the Third Symphony, somebody will complete it – or write a better one – in fifty or five hundred years. Viewed from the point where I am now, on the brink of eternity, that's a mere moment in time.'

❧

Coming to maturity at the apogee of British imperialism, Elgar was bound to share the age's optimism, and the surface of his music glows with colour and opulence. He lived in a royalist country with, in his time, a great empire, ceremonial, and pageantry. The glamorous side of military might was what was visible: the Boer war didn't kill people in London or Worcester; there was no television to bring the dead and wounded into Elgar's front room. The 1914–18 war began the changes, and he was well aware of them. He refused to write music to celebrate the peace, finding the time 'too full of complexities'. Had he been born in a small republic without overseas dominions, would he have composed the music he did?

Constant Lambert's comment in *Music Ho!* (1933) on Elgar's music as having an 'almost intolerable air of smugness, self-assurance and autocratic benevolence' has too often been cited without his qualifying 'through no fault of its own', and 'for the present generation'. Reaction against the period's excesses made for reaction against Elgar. But temperamentally Elgar was sensitive and melancholic, and knew struggles in his life. There is on occasion an overwrought or over-protesting note from which one may flinch. But the pull between outward certainty

[5]   A. Payne, *Elgar's Third Symphony: the Story of the Reconstruction* (London, 1998).

and inward despondency is what makes his mature music endlessly fascinating and rewarding. Often the conflicting feelings are found in the same work, within bars of each other, even fused in the same passages. His music can hold opposed feelings at once, creating strong tensions. Such tensions made his life well-nigh intolerable, but they fructified his music. Yeats spoke of Elgar's 'heroic melancholy'; under his grandest music runs the refrain 'Lest we forget – lest we forget!'.

It is significant how often he used the word 'hope' about his music. 'I hope little' ('Enigma'), 'a massive hope' (First Symphony), 'If hope failed not' (The Apostles). Are the conclusions of the First Symphony, the Introduction and Allegro, The Kingdom really positive, or founded on hope? But he had the courage of his idealism, while recognizing the frailty of its foundation. Any mention of 'dreaming', even in a slight song, brings a sudden depth and inwardness to his music. Always he sought to reconcile his dreams and reality.

Now perhaps the pendulum has swung too far, and the dark tormented side of the composer is over-stressed. Of course it is there. But it should not be exaggerated. Let not the life-affirming, positive, glowing, exuberant Elgar be underestimated. His huge capacity for boisterous enjoyment leaps out of his letters, side by side with his wish to 'curse the power that gave me gifts'. Both sides of him were true. He may have found the Spirit of Delight fugitive and capricious, but it existed, and he knew it. His achievement was tremendous. If his influence on those who followed was slight, his example was enduring. He was every inch a professional composer, acclaimed in Germany and the United States. The sheer quantity of first-class music he produced is amazing. He was such a late developer, had such a short composing life. His first big work, Froissart, came at the age of thirty-three, by which time Britten had already composed Peter Grimes and The Rape of Lucretia. His last great work, the Cello Concerto, came when he was sixty-two, at which age Vaughan Williams was composing the fourth of his nine symphonies. After that: rumours, as with Sibelius, but almost silence.

Perhaps the English-countryside aspect of Elgar's music has been over-emphasized. Could we now strip him of the accumulated meanings and symbols of 'Heritage', and listen to him as if for the first time, what shocks we might get! The pastoral, poetic element is there, and to be cherished. The bard of Empire is to be experienced, as part of history. But the complete Elgar was tougher than that. He was above all a maker of music – not a teacher, not a founder of a school, not a committee man – 'just' a composer. The Birmingham professorship was his only academic appointment, and his only attempt, apart from freelance teaching in his early days, and some conducting, to earn money other than by composing. He rose from humble obscurity to the highest honours, unlike, say, Parry or Vaughan Williams, who were born with material advantages. He was independent of all academic institutions, but, coming from nowhere, he crowned the English musical Renaissance.

He guarded his privacy but invited speculation. 'Enigma' is the first of his private puzzles, in which he publicly paraded a coded confidential message. The enigmatic inscription on the Violin Concerto is another, and some knowledge of his life and music is needed for full appreciation of the self-referential *Music Makers*. Another paradox is that this secretive man allowed his dutiful, devoted wife to hoard every sketch, letter, press-cutting, indeed scrap – unlike, say, Hardy (with whose career Elgar's has something in common), who destroyed all he could. He set himself up as an English gentleman but was plainly happiest in Bavaria and Italy. Sometimes it seems that the more is known about his life, the more enigmatic he becomes. The sources of his inspiration must interest anyone who loves his music, but ultimately they are his affair, and unimportant. Often they may be multiple, none of which need exclude the others. Elgar's first international success paid homage to the intimacies of friendship. That little group is now familiar to audiences worldwide through the Variations, but it is the quality of their music, the notes and invention, that makes them so. As he said, 'I prefer the listener to draw what he can from the sounds he hears.' In the end what matters is not just the private man's experience but the leap of the composer's imagination: and that, no-one can explain. His riverside, his orchards, his romantic aspirations, his regal *nobilmente*, his land of Cockayne, his spirit of England, his dream of 'strange refreshment' – all this was created by his imagination, and was ever threatened by his own vulnerability. But in his music he gave permanence to his visions.

For his thirty-sixth birthday he was given a full score of *Tristan und Isolde*. In it he wrote: 'This Book contains the Height, – the Depth, – the Breadth, – the Sweetness,- the Sorrow,- the Best and the whole of the Best of this World and the Next.' It is an astonishing comment to come from the man who was to compose *Gerontius*. Neither Elgar's life nor his music is simple. In both there are many layers, contradictions, and ambiguities. He and his music grew and changed. That is partly why each generation can make fresh observations about the music, perhaps turning previous ideas topsy-turvy, perhaps just sharpening previous perceptions.

It was his good fortune that with his complicated nature he was born at a time when harmonic resources enabled him to express such ambiguities. In Elgar the passionate extremes of emotion found a composer of utter professionalism: technique and genius were fully matched. The great achievement of his music is how he integrated the uncertainties within it.

List of Works

Elgar left some works unpublished and many incomplete. Only those that have been completed, published, or recorded since his death are listed below. Elgar did not give Opus numbers to lesser works, so they are inserted chronologically. For additional unpublished juvenilia and unfinished works, see C. Kent, *Edward Elgar: A Guide to Research* (1993) and D. McVeagh, 'Edward Elgar', in *The New Grove* (2001). Works published in the ongoing Elgar Collected Edition are given at the end of entries thus: E followed by the number of the volume.

Opus
– Humoreske 'a tune from Broadheath', c. 1867, unpubd

Music for St George's Church, Worcester
– Kyrie Eleison in A SATB, c. 1868
– Gloria [from Mozart: Violin Sonata, F, K547: Allegro], soloists chor, org 1872
– Credo [on themes from Beethoven: Syms. Nos. 5, 7, and 9], in A chor, org 1873
– Gloria SATB, org 1877
– Kyrie STB, 1877
– O salutaris hostia in G voice, org 1877
– Salve regina, soloists, chor, in D, org 1876; St George's, 6 June 1880?
– Tantum ergo, soloists, chor, in D, org 1876; St George's, 29 June 1879
– Credo in E minor, chor, org 1877
– Hymn tunes, 1878, 'Praise ye the Lord' [revised as 'Good morrow' in 1929], 'Now with the fast departing light' [both Leicester private collection]; and 'Hear Thy children' [pubd 1896 as Drake's Broughton, used in Nursery Suite]; in E flat, 1880; A flat, 1879 [?used for clock chimes in 1931]

- Domine salvam fac, motet, chor, org 1879; St George's, 21 June
    1879
- Benedictus in G, chor, org, strgs, 1882
- Chant for Stabat mater, 1886
- O salutaris hostia: F, chor, org 1880, pubd 1898; E flat, chor, org
    1880, pubd 1898; E flat, B solo, org 1882
- Four Litanies BVM, pubd 1882

Music for Wind Quintet
(2 flutes, oboe, clarinet, bassoon or cello). All pubd items ed. by R.
McNicol, 1976–77
- Peckham March, 1877, unpubd
- Harmony Music [known also as Shed] 1–4 [no. 3 inc], 1878; no.
    4 The Farm Yard (from string trio, 1978); E 38
- Promenades 1–6, 1878: 1 Moderato e molto maestoso, 2
    Moderato 'Madame Taussaud's' (sic), 3 Presto, 4 Andante
    'Somniferous', 5 Allegro molto [rev. for Minuet, Severn Suite,
    1930], 6 Allegro maestoso 'Hell and Tommy'
- Andante con variazioni 'Evesham Andante', 1878
- Adagio cantabile 'Mrs Winslow's Soothing Syrup', 1878
- Intermezzos 1–5, 1879: 1 Allegro moderato 'The Farmyard', 2
    Adagio [reused for Cantique] 3 Allegretto 'Nancy', 4 Andante
    con moto, 5 Allegretto
- Four Dances: Menuetto, 1878, Gavotte 'The Alphonsa', 1879,
    Sarabande (Largo), 1879 [recopied 1933 for The Spanish
    Lady], Gigue, 1879
- Harmony Music 5, 1879: 1 Allegro moderato 'The Mission', 2
    Menuetto [rev. for Minuet and Trio of Severn Suite], 3 Andante
    'Noah's Ark', 4 Finale (1977)
- Harmony Music 6, 1879: 1 Allegro molto [from 1878 Intona-
    tion no. 2], 2 Andante arioso [rev. for 1912 Cantique], Menuet
    and Trio, Finale, unpubd
- Harmony Music 7, 1 Allegro 2 Scherzo and Trio 1881, unpubd

Music for Powick
Dances for Worcester City and County Pauper Lunatic Asylum,
Powick:
- Five quadrilles: La Brunette, Die junge Kokette, L'Assom[m]oir
    [No. 5 reused for The Wild Bears in Wand of Youth Suite 2],
    1879

    Five quadrilles, Paris, 1880

Five lancers, The Valentine, 1880

Polkas: Maud, Nelly, La Blonde, Helcia, Blumine, 1880–4

First complete modern performance, Powick Hospital, Sept 1988, Rutland Sinfonia, cond. B. Collett

1a & b The Wand of Youth Suites nos. 1–2 [incl. rev. of Humoreske Broadheath and childhood play music]: 1a, 1907, 1 Overture 2 Serenade 3 Minuet 4 Sun Dance 5 Fairy Pipers 6 Slumber Scene 7 Fairies and Giants, cond. H. J. Wood, Queen's Hall, London, 14 Dec 1907; 1b, 1907–08, 1 March 2 The Little Bells 3 Moths and Butterflies 4 Fountain Dance 5 The Tame Bear 6 The Wild Bears [see Powick L'Assom[m]oir], cond. Elgar, Worcester Festival, 9 Sept 1908; E 25

- The Language of Flowers (J. G. Percival), song, 1872, unpubd
- Chantant, pf, 1872, unpubd
- The Self Banished (E Waller), song, c. 1875, unpubd
- Reminiscences, vn, pf, 1877; pubd 1997
- Romance, vn, pf, 1878; Worcester, 20 Oct 1885
- Menuetto (Scherzo), 1878, copied 1930
- Minuet in g, 1878
- Introductory Overture, inc, Worcester Music Hall, 12 June 1878; and song arrs. for the Christy Minstrels, 1878
- Symphony movt [after Mozart: Sym. No. 40], 1878, inc
- Study for Strengthening the Third Finger, vn, 1878, rev. 1920, in *The Daily Telegraph*, 24 Dec 1920
- Str Qt movts, B flat, 1878, inc; A minor, 1878, inc; D minor, 1878 inc [proposed for The Spanish Lady]; G, 1879 [used in Harmony Music 7]; D minor, 888 [used in Vesper Voluntaries] also fragments; all in E 38
- Str Trio, C, 1878, inc [used in Shed 4]; E 38
- Étude Caprice, solo vn, 1878; [ad lib. pf acc by W. H. Reed, 1940]
- Two Polonaises, D minor, F minor [Bolero in Spanish Lady; E 41], vn, pf, 1879, inc
- 2nd study for vn unacc, 1879; also studies in A minor, 1879, in D, 1881
- Hungarian (Melody), 1879, unpubd
- Pastourelle (Air de ballet), pf, orch, 1881, unpubd: cond. A. J. Caldicott, Worcester, 17 May 1881
- Pas redoublé no. 2, orch, 1881, cond. A. J. Caldicott, Guildhall, Worc, 20 Feb 1882 [see Suite in D, Spanish Lady]

- Fantasia on Irish Airs, vn, pf, 1881, inc
- Fugue, f sharp inc, 1881 [recopied for The Spanish Lady]
- Menuetto and Trio, G, vn, vc, pf, 1882, as Douce pensée, pf [see Rosemary, 1915]; E 38
- Suite in D: 1 Mazurka, 2 Intermezzo-Sérénade mauresque (1883), 3 Fantasia gavotte, 4 March – pas redoublé (1882) [rev. as Op. 10]; 23 Feb 1888, cond. W. C. Stockley, Birmingham
- Fugue, d, ob, vn, 1883
- The Lakes, ov., orch, 1883, fragments, unpubd
- Griffinesque, pf, 1884; pubd 1981
- Melody in E flat, unpubd
2   1 Ave verum [orig. Pie Jesu], 1886–87, rev. 1902 (1907, Jesu, word of God incarnate); 2 Ave Maria, c. 1887, rev. 1907 (1907, Jesu, Lord of Life and Glory); 3 Ave maris stella, c. 1887, rev. 1907 (1907, Jesu, meek and lowly); all chorus and organ
3   Cantique [rev. of Andante Arioso, 1879 Harmony Music No. 6], org, pf, small orch, 1912; Royal Albert Hall, London, cond. L. Ronald, 15 Dec 1912; E 36
4   1 Une Idyll, 1884; 2 Pastourelle, 1884; 3 Virelai, 1884; all vn, pf
5   A Soldier's Song (C. F. Hayward), unison male voices, pf, 1884; Worcester Glee Club, 17 March 1884; repubd 1903 as A War Song; Royal Albert Hall, 1 Oct 1903
- Gavotte, vn, pf, 1885
- Scottish Overture, orch, 1884–85, fragments, unpubd
- Allegretto on G-E-D-G-E, vn, pf, 1885; Malvern, 27 March 1885
7   Sevillana, orch, 1884, rev. 1889; cond. W. Done, Public Hall, Worcester, 1 May 1884
- A Phylactery (J Hay), song, c. 1885 (see The Spanish Lady; E 41)
- Is she not passing fair? (d'Orléans, trans. L. S. Costello), song, 1886
- Four Litanies for the Blessed Virgin Mary, unacc chor, 1886
- As I laye a-thynkynge ('Thomas Ingoldsby' [R. H. Barham]), song, 1887
- Queen Mary's Song (Tennyson), song, 1887, rev. 1889
8   String Quartet, 1887, destroyed
9   Violin Sonata, 1887, inc (?used in Sursum Corda, 1894)
- A Song of Autumn (A. L. Gordon), song, ?1887

– Three Pieces, str, 1 Spring Song – Allegro, 2 Elegy – Adagio, 3 Finale – Presto, unpubd, lost; ?rev. as Op. 20; cond. E. Vine Hall, Worcester, 7 May 1888

– String Quartet, 1888, inc; 3rd movt Intermezzo arr. for org as No. 3 of Vesper Voluntaries

10 Three Characteristic Pieces [rev. of orch Suite, D], 1899; 1 Mazurka (also vn and pf) 2 Sérénade mauresque 3 Contrasts: The Gavotte AD 1700 & 1900, cond. Elgar, New Brighton, 16 July 1899

– The Wind at Dawn (C. A. Roberts), song 1888; orchd 1912

– Violin Concerto, ?1890, inc [possible frag. of slow movt]

– March, D, 1887, unpubd

– Pf Trio, 1886, frag; E 38

– Enina Valse, pf, 1886, unpubd

– Laura Valse, pf, 1887, unpubd

– Duett, trbn, db, 1887; ed. R. Slatford (1970)

11 Sursum corda (Elévation), brass, org, str, timp, 1894 [includes 1887 vln sonata sketch, and from Offertoire (Andante religioso) vl, pf, 1893 under pseudonym Gustav Francke]; cond. H. Blair, Worcester Cathedral, 8 April 1894

12 Salut d'amour (Liebesgrüss), vn, pf, 1888; arr. for pf, for orch 1889; cond. A. Manns, London, Crystal Palace, 11 Nov 1889

– Sonatina, pf, 1889, rev. 1931

– Ecce sacerdos magnus, chorus, org, 1888; Worcester, St George's [with orch, 1893, unpubd], 9 Oct 1888

– Presto, pf, 1889

13 1 Mot d'amour (Liebesahnung), 2 Bizarrerie, vn, pf, 1889

14 Vesper Voluntaries, org, 1889: Introduction, 1 Andante, 2 Allegro, 3 Andantino [rev. from 1888 str qt in D] 4 Allegro piacevole, Intermezzo, 5 Poco lento, 6 Moderato, 7 Allegretto pensoso, 8 Poco allegro, Coda]; E 36

15 1 Chanson de nuit, vn, pf, 1897, orchd 1899; 2 Chanson de matin, vn, pf, 1899 [rev. of earlier sketch], 1901; cond. H. Wood, Queen's Hall, 14 Sept 1901

16 1 The Shepherd's Song (B. Pain), 1892, 2 Through the long days (J. Hay), song, 1885, C. Phillips, London, St James's Hall, 25 Feb 1897, 3 Rondel (Longfellow, from Froissart), song, 1894; St James's Hall, 1 Dec 1897

17 La Capricieuse, vn, pf, 1891

18 1 O happy eyes (C. A. Elgar), SATB, unacc, 1889, rev. 1893; 2
Love (A. Macquarie), SATB, unacc, 1907; 3 My love dwelt in
a northern land (A. Lang), SATB, unacc, 1889–90; 3 cond. J.
Hampton, Tenbury Musical Society, 13 Nov 1890

19 Froissart, orch, 1890, rev. 1901; cond. Elgar, Worcester Festival,
Public Hall, 10 Sept 1890

20 Serenade in E minor, str, 1892 [?rev. of 1888 str pieces]; cond.
Elgar, Worcester Ladies' Orchestral Class, 1892; Antwerp, 23
July 1896

21 Minuet, pf, small orch, 1897; cond. Elgar, New Brighton, 16 July
1899

–   Ophelia's Song (Shakespeare), ?1892, unpubd [subsumed into
The Light of Life]

22 Very Easy Melodious Exercises in the First Position, vn, pf,
1892

–   A Spear, a Sword; Loose, loose the sails (C. A. Elgar), 1892, lost;
Miss Simpson and Elgar, Malvern, Aug 1892

23 Spanish Serenade (Stars of the summer night) (Longfellow),
SATB, 2 vn, pf, 1892, orchd 1893; cond. Revd J. Hampton,
Hereford, 7 April 1893

24 Etudes caractéristiques, vn, 1878

–   Like to the damask rose (S. Wastell), song, ?1892; C. Phillips,
London, St James's Hall, 25 Feb 1897

–   The Poet's Life ('E. Burroughs' [S. Jewett]), song, 1892

–   The Mill-wheel Songs: 1 Winter [subsumed into King Olaf], 2
May (Rhapsody) lost (C. A. Elgar), 1892

25 The Black Knight (J. L. Uhland, trans. Longfellow), sym. for
chorus and orch, 1878–79, 1889, 1892–93; rev. 1898; cond.
Elgar, Worcester, Festival Choral Society, 18 April 1893

26 1 The Snow; 2 Fly, singing bird (C. A. Elgar), SSA, 2 vn, pf, 1894;
orchd 1903; London, Queen's Hall, 12 March 1904

27 Scenes from the Bavarian Highlands (C. A. Elgar, after Bavarian
trad.), chorus, pf, 1895: 1 The Dance, 2 False Love, 3 Lullaby
(also vn and pf), 4 Aspiration, 5 On the Alm, 6 The Marksman;
orchd 1896; cond. Elgar, Worcester, Festival Choral Society, 21
April 1896

–   Three Bavarian Dances, 1896 [arr. of Nos. 1, 3 and 6, also pf];
cond. A. Manns, London, Crystal Palace, 23 Oct 1897

28 Sonata in G, org, 1895; cond. H. Blair, Worcester Cathedral, 8 July
1895; E 36

29 The Light of Life (Lux Christi) (E. Capel Cure, after Bible, John,

ix), short oratorio, S, A, T, B, chorus, orch, 1896, rev. 1899;
A. Williams, J. King, E. Lloyd, W. Mills, cond. Elgar, Worcester
Festival, 8 Sept 1896; E 3

30 Scenes from the Saga of King Olaf (Longfellow, H. A. Acworth),
cantata, S, T, B, chorus, orch, 1894–96; M. Henson, E. Lloyd,
D. Ffrangcon-Davies, cond. Elgar, Hanley, Staffs, 30 Oct 1896

31 1 After (P. B. Marston), 1895; 2 A Song of Flight (C. Rossetti),
1895; H. Plunket Greene, L. Borwick, London, St James's Hall,
2 March 1900

32 Imperial March, 1897, orch also pf; cond. A. Manns, London,
Crystal Palace, 19 April 1897

33 The Banner of St George ('S. Wensley' [H. S. Bunce]) ballad,
chorus, orch, 1896–97; London, St Cuthbert's Hall Choral
Society, cond. C. Miller, 18 May 1897

– Sérénade lyrique, pf, small orch, 1899; London, St James's Hall,
Ivan Caryll's orchestra, 27 Nov 1900

34 Te Deum, Benedictus, chorus, org, or orch, 1897; cond. G. R.
Sinclair, Hereford Cathedral, 12 Sept 1897

– Grete Malverne on a Rocke (from Historic Worcestershire by W.
Salt Brassington). SATB unacc, private Christmas card, 1897

– Roundel (The little eyes that never knew light) (Swinburne),
1897, unpubd; G. Walker, Elgar, Worcester Musical Union, 26
April 1897

– Love alone will stay (Lute Song) (C. A. Elgar), 1897 (possibly
based on an 1889 song); rev. as No. 2 Sea Pictures

35 Caractacus (H. A. Acworth), cantata, S, T, Bar, B, chorus, orch,
1887, 1898; M. Henson, E. Lloyd, A. Black, J. Browning, C.
Knowles, cond. Elgar, Leeds Festival, 5 Oct 1898; E 5

– Dry those fair, those crystal eyes (H. King), song; London, Royal
Albert Hall, 21 June 1899 [pubd in Charing Cross Hospital
charity souvenir volume, 1899]

– The Pipes of Pan ('A. Ross' [A. R. Ropes]), pf, orch, 1899; L.
Blouvelt, London, Crystal Palace, 30 April 1900

– To her beneath whose stedfast star (F. W. H. Myers), SATB, unacc,
1899, orchd 1902; cond. Elgar, Windsor Castle, 24 May 1899

36 Variations on an Original Theme ('Enigma'), 1898–99; cond. H.
Richter, London, St James's Hall, 19 June 1899; with extended
finale, cond. Elgar, Worcester Festival, 13 Sept 1899; E 27

37 Sea Pictures, A, orch: 1 Sea Slumber Song (R. Noel), 2 In
Haven (Capri) (C. A. Elgar), 3 Sabbath Morning at Sea (E. B.
Browning), 4 Where corals lie (R. Garnett), 5 The Swimmer

(A. L. Gordon), 1899 [no. 2 is rev. of song with pf, Love alone
will stay, 1897]; C. Butt, cond. Elgar, Norwich, 5 Oct 1899

38 The Dream of Gerontius (J. H. Newman), Mez, T, B, semi-chorus,
chorus, orch, 1896, 1898, 1899–1900; M. Brema, E. Lloyd, H.
Plunket Greene, cond. H. Richter, Birmingham Festival, Town
Hall, 3 Oct 1900; E 6

−   May Song, vn, pf, orch, 1901; cond. Elgar, Worcester, 10 May
1902

−   Skizze, pf, 1901 (ed. J. N. Moore, 1976); Elgar, Ridgehurst, Herts,
17 Jan 1903

−   Always and Everywhere (N. A. Z. Krasiński, trans. F. Fortey),
song, 1901

−   Come, gentle night (C. Bingham), song, 1901; London, Royal
Albert Hall, 31 Oct 1901

−   ballet (after Rabelais), 1902–03, inc, sketches used elsewhere

39 Military Marches ('Pomp and Circumstance') Nos. 1–5: 1, in D,
1901 [see also Coronation Ode Op. 44 and Land of Hope and
Glory, song] and 2, in A minor, 1901, cond. A. E. Rodewald,
Liverpool, 19 Oct 1901; 3, in C minor, 1904, cond. Elgar, LSO,
London, Queen's Hall, 8 March 1905; 4, in G, 1907, cond.
H. Wood, Queen's Hall, 24 Aug 1907 [see also song The King's
Way, 1909]; 5, in C, 1929–30, cond. Elgar, London, Kingsway
Hall [HMV recording session], 18 Sept 1930; 6, inc ?1930,
completed A. Payne, 2007

40 Cockaigne (In London Town), 1900–01; cond. Elgar, London,
Queen's Hall, 20 June 1901 [sketches for projected Cockaigne
No. 2]

41 1 In the Dawn; 2 Speak, Music (A. C. Benson), 1902; London,
Queen's Hall, 26 Oct 1901

42 Grania and Diarmid (G. Moore) 1901: Incidental Music, Funeral
March, 'There are seven that pull the thread' [S, small orch,
song] (W. B. Yeats); Dublin, Gaiety Theatre, 21 Oct 1901;
Funeral March, H. Wood, London, Queen's Hall, 18 Jan 1902

−   Weary wind of the west (T. E. Brown), SATB, unacc, 1902; Morecambe Festival, 2 May 1903

−   Land of Hope and Glory (A. C. Benson), A, chorus, orch, 1902
[arr. from trio of Pomp and Circumstance No. 1 and, with
different words, Coronation Ode]; C. Butt, London, Royal
Albert Hall, 21 June 1902; carillon obbl. 1927

43 Dream Children, 2 pieces after C. Lamb, pf, small orch, 1902;
cond. A. W. Payne, London, Queen's Hall, 4 Sept 1902; E 25

44 Coronation Ode (A. C. Benson), S, A, T, B, chorus, orch, optional military band, 1902: 1 Crown the King, 2 Daughter of Ancient Kings [True Queen of British homes, substituted in 1911], 3 Britain, ask of thyself, 4 Hark, upon the hallowed air, 5 Only let the heart be pure, 6 Peace, gentle peace, 7 Land of Hope and Glory [using trio tune of Pomp and Circumstance No. 1]; A. Nicholls, M. Foster, J. Coates, D. Ffrangcon-Davies, cond. Elgar, Sheffield, 2 Oct 1902

45 Five Partsongs from the Greek Anthology, TTBB unacc, 1902: 1 Yea, cast me from the heights (anon., trans. A. Strettell), 2 Whether I find thee (anon., trans. A. Lang), 3 After many a dusty mile (anon., trans. E. Gosse), 4 It's oh! to be a wild wind (anon., trans. W. M. Hardinge), 5 Feasting I watch (Marcus Argentarius, trans. R. Garnett); London Choral Society, cond. A. Fagge, London, Royal Albert Hall, 25 April 1904

– O Mightiest of the Mighty (S. Childs Clarke), hymn, 1902, chorus, org; cond. F. Bridge, London, Westminster Abbey, coronation of Edward VII, 9 Aug 1902

– Speak, my heart! (A. C. Benson), song, 1903 [tune originally to words by 'A. Ross']

– Evening Scene (C. Patmore), SATB, unacc, 1905; Morecambe Festival, 12 May 1906

– In Smyrna, pf, 1905; (ed. J. N. Moore, 1976)

– Callicles (M. Arnold), 1905, 1913, inc [see The Spanish Lady]

– For Dot's Nuns, org, 1906; E 36

– How calmly the evening (T. Lynch), SATB, unacc, 1907

– Two single chants for the Venite, in D, in G, 1907

– Two double chants for Psalms lxviii and lxxv, in D, 1907 (2 further chants unpubd)

46 Concert Allegro, pf, 1901; F. Davies, London, St James's Hall, 2 Dec 1901; pubd 1982

47 Introduction and Allegro, str qt, str orch, 1901, 1905; cond. Elgar, A. W. Payne, W. H. Eaynes, A. Hobday, B. P. Parker, LSO, London, Queen's Hall, 8 March 1905

48 Pleading (A. L Salmon), song, 1908; 1v, pf or small orch, Lady Maud Warrender, Elgar, Hereford, Nov 1908

49 The Apostles (Elgar, compiled from Scriptures), oratorio, S, A, T, 3 B, semi-chorus, chorus, orch, 1896, 1901, 1902–03; E. Albani, M. Foster, J. Coates, R. Kennerly Rumford, A. Black, D. Ffrangcon-Davies, cond. Elgar, Birmingham Town Hall, 14 Oct 1903; E 8

50 In the South (Alassio), 1899, 1902, 1904, cond. Elgar, London, Royal Opera House, 16 March 1904; extract for small orch, cond. G. R. Sinclair, Hereford, 22 Nov 1904; In Moonlight (Shelley) [song arr. by Elgar of Canto popolare], 1904

51 The Kingdom (Elgar, compiled from Scriptures), oratorio, S, A, T, B; S and A semi-chorus, chorus, orch, 1901–03, 1905–06; A. Nicholls, M. Foster, J. Coates, W. Higley, cond. Elgar, Birmingham Festival, Town Hall, 3 Oct 1906; E 9

52 A Christmas Greeting (C. A. Elgar) carol, 2 S, male chorus ad lib., 2 vn, pf, 1907; cond. G. R. Sinclair, Hereford, Cathedral choristers, 1 Jan 1908

— Andantino, vn, mand, gui, 1907, inc; E 38

— Follow the Colours, Marching Song for Soldiers (W. de Courcy Stretton), unison voices, orch. 1907–08, London, Royal Albert Hall, 24 May 1908

53 Four Choral Songs, SSAATTBB, 1907–08: 1 There is sweet music (Tennyson), 2 Deep in my soul (Byron), 3 O wild west wind (Shelley), 4 Owls, an Epitaph (Elgar)

54 The Reveille (B. Harte), TTBB, unacc, 1907; Blackpool Festival, 17 Oct 1908

55 Symphony No. 1, A flat, 1904, 1907–08; Hallé Orch, cond. Richter, Free Trade Hall, Manchester, 3 Dec 1908; E 30 [see also E 38]

— Lo! Christ the Lord is born (S. Wensley), 1908 [after Grete Malverne on a Rocke, 1897]

56 Angelus (Tuscan, adapted Elgar), SATB, unacc, 1909; London, Royal Albert Hall, 8 Dec 1910

57 Go, song of mine (Cavalcanti, trans. D. G. Rossetti), SSAATTB, 1909; cond. Elgar, Hereford, 9 Sept 1909

58 Elegy, str, 1909; London, Mansion House, 13 July 1909

— They are at rest (J H Newman), SATB, unacc, 1909; Windsor, Frogmore [Royal Mausoleum], 22 Jan 1910

59 Song Cycle (G. Parker), Mez, orch, 1909–10: 3 Oh, soft was the song, 5 Was it some golden star?, 6 Twilight [1, 2, and 4 incomplete: Proem, The Waking, There is an Orchard]; M. Foster, cond. Elgar, London, Queen's Hall, 24 Jan 1910

60 1 The Torch, 2 The River (Pietro d'Alba [Elgar]), after East European trad., Mez, pf, orch, 1912; M. Foster, cond. G. R. Sinclair, Hereford Festival, 11 Sept 1912

— A Child Asleep (E. B. Browning) song, 1909

— The King's Way (C. A. Elgar), 1909 [adapted from trio of Pomp and Circumstance March No. 4; later alternative words by A. Noyes and A. P. Herbert]; C. Butt, London, Alexandra Palace, 15 Jan 1910

61 Violin Concerto, B minor, 1905, 1909–10; F. Kreisler, cond. Elgar, Philharmonic Society, London, Queen's Hall, 10 Nov 1910; E 32

62 Romance, bsn, orch, 1910; E. James, cond. Elgar, Hereford, 16 Feb 1911

63 Symphony No. 2, E flat, 1905, 1909–11; cond. Elgar, London, Queen's Hall, 24 May 1911; E 31

64 O hearken Thou (Intende voci orationis meae), (from Psalm 5) offertory, chorus, org or orch, 1911; coronation of George V, Westminster Abbey, London, 22 June 1911, cond. F. Bridge

65 Coronation March, 1911 [incorporating sketches from abandoned 1902 Rabelais ballet]; Westminster Abbey, cond. F. Bridge, 22 June 1911

66 The Crown of India (imperial masque, H. Hamilton), A, T, chorus, orch, 1912 [using part of In Smyrna and sketches from 1902 onwards]: 1a Introduction, 1b Sacred Measure, 2 Dance of Nautch Girls, 2a India greets her Cities, 3 Song: 'Hail, Immemorial Ind!', 3a Entrance of Calcutta, 3b Entrance of Delhi, 4a Introduction, 4b March of the Mogul Emperors, 5 Entrance of 'John Company', 5a Entrance of St George, 6 Song: 'The Rule of England', 7 Interlude, 8a Introduction, 8b Warriors' Dance, 9 The Cities of Ind, 10 March: The Crown of India, 10a The Homage of Ind, 11 The Crowning of Delhi, 12 'Ave Imperator!'; M. Beeley, H. Dearth, cond. Elgar, London, Coliseum, 11 March 1912; Suite from the Crown of India, Nos. 1a, 1b, 2, 5, 8b, 7, 4b; cond. Elgar, Hereford Festival, 11 Sept 1912; E 18

67 Great is the Lord, anthem (Psalm 48), SSAATB chorus, bass solo, org, 1910–12; with orch, 1913 cond. F. Bridge, Westminster Abbey, 16 July 1912

– Carissima, pf, vn and pf, small orch, 1913; cond. Elgar, Hayes, Middlesex [HMV recording session], 21 Jan 1914

68 Falstaff, symphonic study in C minor with two interludes, 1902–03, 1913; cond. Elgar, Leeds, Town Hall, 1 Oct 1913; E 33

69 The Music Makers (A. O'Shaughnessy), ode, A, chorus, orch, 1902, 1912 [quotations from earlier published works]; M. Foster, cond. Elgar, Birmingham Festival, 1 Oct 1912; E 10 (see also E 38)

—   Fear not O Land, (Joel, chap ii) harvest anthem, chor, org, 1914

70 Sospiri, str, harp, org; 1913–14; cond. H. Wood, London, Queen's Hall, 15 Aug 1915

71 1 The Shower, 2 The Fountain (H. Vaughan), SATB, unacc, 1914

72 Death on the hills (A. N. Maikov, trans. Newmarch), SATB, unacc, 1914

73 1 Love's Tempest (A. N. Maikov), 2 Serenade ('N. M. Minsky' [N. Vilenkin]), both trans. R. Newmarch, SATB, unacc, 1914

74 Give unto the Lord, anthem (Psalm 29), chorus, bass solo, org or orch, 1914; London, St Paul's Cathedral, 30 April 1914

—   The Merry-go-round (F. C. Fox), The Brook (E. Soule), The Windlass (W. Allingham), SATB, 1914, children's song

—   The Birthright (G. A. Stocks), 1914; unison boys, bugles, drums, or SATB (1914)

—   Arabian Serenade (M. Lawrence) song, 1914

—   The Chariots of the Lord (J. Brownlie), song with orch, 1914; C. Butt, London, Royal Albert Hall, 28 June 1914

—   Soldier's Song: the Roll Call (H. Begbie), 1914; C. Butt, London, 10 Oct 1914; unpubd, withdrawn

75 Carillon (E. Cammaerts), reciter, orch, 1914; T. Brand Cammaerts, cond. Elgar, London, Queen's Hall, 7 Dec 1914; new text by Binyon, 1942

—   Rosemary, 1915, orch [from 1882, 1886 sketches]

76 Polonia, sym. prelude; cond. Elgar, Queen's Hall, 6 July 1915; E 33

77 Une voix dans le désert (E. Cammaerts, trans. T. B. Cammaerts), S, reciter, orch, 1915, incl. song Quand nos bourgeons se rouvriront; C. Liten, O. Lynn, cond. Elgar, London, Shaftesbury Theatre, 29 Jan 1916

78 The Starlight Express (V. Pearn, after A. Blackwood: A Prisoner in Fairyland), incidental music, melodrama and songs, S, Bar, orch [incl. music from The Wand of Youth Suites, 1907, 1908], 1915, unpubd: Songs: 1 To the Children, 2 The Blue-eyes Fairy, 3 Curfew Song (Orion), 4 Laugh a little ev'ry day, 5 I'm everywhere, 6 Night Winds, 7 Oh stars shine brightly, 8 We shall meet the morning spiders, 9 My Old Tunes, 10 Dandelions, Daffodils, 11 They're all soft-shiny now, 12 Oh, think beauty, 13 Hearts must be soft-shiny dressed, duet; C. Hine, C. Mott, cond. J. Harrison, London, Kingsway Theatre, 29 Dec 1915 [broadcast 1965, cond. L. Salter, P. Barr, N. Howlett, D.

Dowling] [nos. 1, 2 and 9, voice, pf, arr. J Harrison, pubd 1916]

79 Le drapeau belge (E. Cammaerts, trans. Lord Curzon of Kedleston), reciter, orch, 1916; C. Liten, cond. H. Harty, London, Queen's Hall, 14 April 1917

− Fugue, G, 1869, inc; pubd in The Music Student (Aug 1916); E 36

80 The Spirit of England (L. Binyon), S/T, chorus, orch:

  1 The Fourth of August, 1915–17; R. Buckman, cond. A. Matthews, Birmingham, 4 Oct 1917

  2 To Women, 1915–16; J. Booth, cond. Elgar, Leeds Choral Union, 3 May 1916

  3 For the Fallen, 1915; A. Nicholls, cond. Elgar, Leeds Choral Union, 3 May 1916

  complete: R. Buckman, cond. A. Matthews, Birmingham, 4 Oct 1917; then A. Nicholls, cond. Elgar, Leeds, 31 Oct 1917; E 10

  With proud thanksgiving (Binyon), chorus, military or brass band or orch, 1920–21 [reworking of 80/3]; cond. Elgar, London, Royal Albert Hall, 7 May 1921; E 10

− Fight for Right (W. Morris), 1916; G. Elwes, Queen's Hall, March 1916

81 The Sanguine Fan (ballet), scenario by I. Lowther, based on a fan design by C. Conder, 1917, cond. Elgar, London, Chelsea Palace, 20 March 1917 [Echo's Dance arr. pf 1917] score ed. by D. Lloyd-Jones 2002

− The Fringes of the Fleet (R. Kipling): 1 The Lowestoft Boat, 2 Fate's Discourtesy, 3 Submarines, 4 The Sweepers, 4 Bar, orch, 1917; C. Mott, H. Barratt, F. Henry, F. Stewart, cond. Elgar, London, Coliseum, 11 June 1917

  Inside the Bar (G. Parker), 4 Bar unacc, added 25 June 1917 [piano score 1917]

− Ozymandias (Shelley), 1917, inc (2 versions)

− Liebesweh (D. Wilcox), 1918, song, unpubd (considered for use in The Spanish Lady)

82 Sonata, E minor, vn, pf, 1918; W. H. Reed, Landon Ronald, London, Aeolian Hall, 21 March 1919

83 String quartet, E minor, 1918; A. Sammons, W. H. Reed, R. Jeremy, F. Salmond, London, Wigmore Hall, 21 May 1919; E 38

84 Piano Quintet, A minor, 1918–19; A. Sammons, W. H. Reed, R.

Jeremy, F. Salmond, W. Murdoch, Wigmore Hall, 21 May 1919;
E 38

85 Cello Concerto, E minor, 1918, 1919; F. Salmond, cond. Elgar,
London, LSO, Queen's Hall, 27 Oct 1919; arr. as vla conc. by
L. Tertis, 1929; Tertis, cond. Elgar, Queen's Hall, 21 March
1930; E 32

− Big Steamers (Kipling), unison voices, pf, 1918
Smoking Cantata, 1919, unpubd

86 J. S. Bach: Fantasia and Fugue, BWV 537, 1922, 1921; Fugue,
cond. E. Goossens, London, Queen's Hall, 27 Oct 1921;
Fantasia, LSO, cond. Elgar, Gloucester, 7 Sept 1922

− G. F. Handel: Overture (from Chandos Anthem no. 2), 1923;
LSO, cond. Elgar, Worcester, 2 Sept 1923

− F. Chopin: Funeral March, Piano Sonata, Op 35: 1932; BBC SO,
cond. A. Boult, EMI studio, 30 May 1932

− Arthur (incidental music, L. Binyon), 1923, small orch, unpubd
[used in The Spanish Lady and Sym 3]: cond. Elgar, London,
Old Vic, 12 March 1923; Suite ed. A. Barlow, 1973

− Memorial Chime, 1923, unpubd; J. Denyn, Loughborough War
Memorial Carillon inauguration, 22 July 1923; arr. org; E 36

− The Wanderer (Elgar, after anon. in Wit and Drollery, 1661),
TTBB, unacc, 1923; De Reszke Singers, London, Wigmore Hall,
13 Nov 1923

− Zut! Zut! Zut! (Richard Mardon [Elgar]), TTBB, unacc, 1923; De
Reszke Singers, Wigmore Hall, 13 Nov 1923

− Fugue in C minor, 1923 [orig for pf, reworked for Severn Suite],
I. Atkins, 16 April 1925, Worcester Cathedral; E 36

− The Pageant of Empire (A. Noyes), 1v/chorus, orch. 1924: 1
Shakespeare's Kingdom, 2 The Islands, 3 The Blue Mountains,
4 The Heart of Canada, 5 Sailing Westward, 6 Merchant Adven-
turers, 7 The Immortal Legions, 8 A Song of Union; voice &
piano pubd 1924

− Empire March, 1924; cond. H. Jaxon, London, Wembley Stadium,
21 July 1924

− The Song of the Bull (F. Hamilton), 1924, male voices, pf, for
Cambridge Univ May Week

− The Herald (A. Smith), TTBB, unacc, 1925

− The Prince of Sleep (W. de la Mare), SATB, unacc, 1925

− Civic Fanfare, 1927, orch without violins, org; rev. 1933; cond.
Elgar, Hereford Festival, 4 Sept 1927, pubd 1991

- Beau Brummel (B. P. Matthews), incidental music orch, 1928, unpubd [used in The Spanish Lady and Sym 3]; cond. Elgar, Birmingham, Theatre Royal, 5 Nov 1928 Minuet pubd 1929
- I sing the birth (B. Jonson), carol, chor unacc 1928; cond. M. Sargent, London, Royal Albert Hall, 10 Dec 1928
- Goodmorrow (G. Gascoigne), carol, 1929, chor unacc [early hymn tune 'Praise ye the Lord'] cond. Walford Davies, St George's, Windsor, 9 Dec 1929
- Five 'Improvisations' for piano, recorded in 1929, realized and pubd by I. Farringdon, 2006

87 Severn Suite, brass band, 1930, incl. sketches also of 1903: 1 Introduction (Worcester Castle), 2 Toccata (Tournament), 3 Fugue (Cathedral) (after keyboard Fugue in C, 1923), 4 Minuet (Commandery) [after 1878 Promenade No. 5, and Harmony Music No. 5], 5 Coda; [H. Geehl's collaboration in scoring now debated]; test piece for National Brass Band Championship, Crystal Palace, 27 Sept 1930; scored for orch, 1930, cond. Elgar, London, Abbey Road [EMI recording session], 14 April 1932; orch pubd 1991

87a Sonata [arr. I. Atkins, from Severn Suite], 1932–33; E 36

- Nursery Suite, 1930: 1 Aubade [incl. hymn tune of 1878, Drake's Broughton], 2 The Serious Doll, 3 Busy-ness, 4 The Sad Doll, 5 The Wagon Passes, 6 The Merry Doll, 7 Dreaming-Envoy; cond. Elgar, London, Kingsway Hall [HMV recording session], 23 May 1931
- It isnae me (S. Holmes), 1930; J. Elwes, Dumfries, Oct 1930
- Soliloquy, oboe, orch, 1930–31, scored G. Jacob; L. Goossens, cond. Neils Gron, BBC tv 11 June 1967; pubd 1996
- Clock Chimes for Eaton Socon, 1931 [possibly based on 1879 hymn tune]

88 Symphony No. 3, 1932–33, inc unpubd [some sketches pubd in Reed, 1936, Anderson, 1990; incl. material from other inc works: The Last Judgment, Callicles, Arthur, and Piano Concerto]. Sketches elaborated by A. Payne as Elgar/Payne3, cond. A. Davis, RFH, London, 15 Feb 1998, score pubd 1998

89 The Spanish Lady, opera, 2 (Elgar, B. Jackson after Jonson: The Devil is an Ass), inc 1929–33 [using music from Beau Brummel, and sketches for other works from 1878 onwards]; reconstructed by P. Young for concert perf, singers of Guildhall School of Music, City University Symphony Orchestra, cond. Cem Mansur, St John's Smith Square, London, 15 May 1986;

staged by Cambridge University Opera Society, cond. Will Lacey, West Road Concert Hall, Cambridge, 24 Nov 1994

- Modest and Fair; Still to be neat (Jonson); (1955); suite for str orch (1956); vocal score, 1994, all ed. by P. M. Young; E 41
- When Swallows Fly, The Rapid Stream The Woodland Stream (C. Mackay), children's songs, 1932, Worcester Schools Festival, 18 May 1933
- Impromptu pf 1932 unpubd
- Serenade, pf, 1932
- Mina, pf, 1932, scored 1933; cond. J. Ainslie Murray, EMI recording studio, 8 Feb 1934
- Adieu, pf, 1932
- The Last Judgment [projected title], oratorio, 1906–, inc [used in Sym 3, piano concerto]
- **90** Piano Concerto, sketches 1913–33, inc, unpubd; used in The Spanish Lady. Poco andante completed and scored for pf, str, by P. M. Young (1950); sketches elaborated by R. Walker, pubd 2005
- Queen Alexandra Memorial Ode: So many true princesses who have gone (J. Masefield), chorus, military band, 1932; cond. Elgar, London, Marlborough House, 9 June 1932; scored for orch by A. Payne, 2004

Arrangements

R. Schumann: Scherzo from Overture, Scherzo and Finale, Op. 52 1883, unpubd

R. Wagner: Entry of the Minstrels, Tannhäuser, 1883, unpubd

R. Wagner: Good Friday Music, Parsifal, small orch or chamber?, 1894, unpubd, Worcs High School, 13 June 1894

Clapham Town End, folksong arr. 1v, pf, 1885, unpubd

G. F. Blackbourne [V. Beraud]: Berceuse, vn, pf, 1886, pubd 1907

The Holly and the Ivy, 1898, unpubd; chorus, orch, cond. Elgar, Worcs, 7 Jan 1899

J. S. Bach: St Matthew Passion: Two Chorales, O Mensch, O Haupt, brass, 1911, unpubd; Worcester, 14 Sept 1911

Orchestration of vocal works by other Composers

A. H. Brewer: Emmaus, 1901, Gloucester, 12 Sept 1901

God Save the King, S, chorus, military band/orch, 1902

I. Atkins: Abide with me, anthem 1908, 1928, Worcs, 2 Sept 1923

J. S. Bach: St Matthew Passion, performing edn 1911, collab. I. Atkins; Worcs, 14 Sept 1911

H. Parry: Jerusalem, 1922; cond. H. Allen, Leeds, 5 Oct 1922

J. Battishill: O Lord, Look down from Heaven, 1923; cond. I. Atkins, Worcs, 5 Sept 1923

S. S. Wesley: Let us Lift up our Hearts, 1923; cond. I. Atkins, 5 Sept 1923

H. Purcell: Jehova, quam multi sunt hostes mei, 1929; Worcs, 10 Sept 1929

Index of Music

Numbers in **bold** indicate a detailed discussion in the text

Index of Names

Numbers in **bold** indicate a detailed discussion in the text